LARGER THAN
LIFE

The Legacy of
Daniel Longwell and
Mary Fraser Longwell

A Memoir
by

Judith Haas Smith

authorHOUSE®

AuthorHouse™
1663 Liberty Drive
Bloomington, IN 47403
www.authorhouse.com
Phone: 1 (800) 839-8640

Published by AuthorHouse 07/09/2015

ISBN: 978-1-5049-2115-2 (sc)
ISBN: 978-1-5049-2116-9 (hc)

Dedication

To the memory of Mary Douglas Fraser Longwell
who saved eighty-nine boxes of ephemera

Contents

The Cover Design

The cover includes the timeless trademark of LIFE® magazine—its striking and bold graphic of the title which has been used with permission. The pen and ink drawing of Daniel Longwell by artist Tom Lea[1]* as well as the photograph of Mary Fraser Longwell by Alfred Eisenstadt** have also been used with permission. The cover design is by Joplin, MO designer Sandra Longman.

*Lea, Tom. [Daniel Longwell] 1945. Pen, watercolor and wash, 53cm x 44cm. **Art Collection**, Rare Book & Manuscript Library, Columbia University in the City of New York. Copyright James D. Lea. Used with permission.

Alfred Eisenstaedt/ The Life Picture Collection/Getty. Housed in Box 45, **Daniel Longwell Paper, Rare Book & Manuscript Library, Columbia University in the City of New York. Used with permission.

---

[1] This pen and ink drawing was done without sittings as a gift. It is inscribed, "To Dan Longwell from his friend, Tom Lea, 1945". Dan wrote to Tom after having it framed and said it scared him, but Mary and the girls (two Dachsunds) liked it which made Dan happy. Tom replied June 26, 1945: "I've intended to write ever since I sent the portrait and ever since you sent the telegram saying you liked it. … There is real joy in working on a head like Dan's. It has forms for an artist to get his hooks on—nothing small or vague or indecisive."

Foreword

Wander back among the stacks, and grab almost any file folder in the Time Inc. Archives' vast Subject Files, from the 1920s, 30s, 40s or 50s, and odds are exceedingly high that you will find the names Mary Fraser and Daniel Longwell peppered generously throughout. Next to Time Inc. co-founder, Henry R. Luce and longtime executive Roy E. Larsen, I know of no two people who played more important roles in the development of Time Inc. during its first four decades.

Was there any part and parcel of Luce's empire that they did not influence during their tenure? Was there a noteworthy writer, artist, photographer, or politician in the first half of the 20th century who they did not know (and, more often than not, befriend)? Judith Haas Smith's warm memoir of her friendship with the Longwells, sheds a welcome, long overdue light on this extraordinary couple.

Wed in December 1938, the marriage of Daniel Longwell and Mary Fraser was not a secret, but it certainly was discreet, within the halls of Time Inc. Looking through Mary's bio files in the Archives, never, *ever* is she referred to in any Time Inc. memos as Mary Longwell (and almost none of Mr. Longwell's official Time Inc. bios make any mention of his wife). She is always referred to as "Miss Mary Fraser." Only after she and Dan retired to Neosho, Missouri, in the mid-1950s, did she begin to sign correspondence as "Mary Longwell" or "Mary Fraser Longwell."

An interesting illustration of the circumspect nature of their relationship shows up in a series of memos from 1943, when Mary, while serving as Time Inc.'s Chief of Editorial Research, received a passionate seven page, handwritten letter from her friend, artist Georgia O'Keefe. O'Keefe was writing to Mary, hoping she would use her influence to convince LIFE magazine to do a story on a proposed dam in New Mexico that would flood several ancient Native American pueblos. Mary summarized O'Keefe's letter in a formal memo, stiffly addressed "To: Daniel Longwell," LIFE's Executive Editor, "From: M.F." Dan wrote back to "Miss Fraser," that he would send a reporter to look into the story, and signed with the initials "D.L." According to Richard B. Stolley (founding Managing Editor of PEOPLE, and a former Managing Editor of LIFE), "this gentle case of editorial nepotism produced a powerful picture story by staff photographer Peter Stackpole five months later," titled *DAM THREATENS PUEBLOS. New Mexico Indians, fighting to save their ancient villages, allowed LIFE to take these rare pictures* (LIFE, November 29, 1943). I like to think that LIFE's photo essay played a role in delaying the dam project for several decades (Alas, by the late 1950s, construction finally began on the Abiquiu Reservoir Dam, which was completed in 1963).

A few years before he retired, Daniel Longwell was asked by Roy Larsen to serve as Director of a Development

Department, "to subject promising staff-suggested Ideas for new Time Inc. publishing ventures to critical scrutiny." Larsen sent out a memo to the Time Inc. staff, soliciting suggestions. Robert Cowin, an ambitious young assistant circulation manager for TIME, sent Longwell a lengthy argument for a sports magazine as our next publishing venture. In March of 1951, when Longwell sent a summary of all the suggestions to members of the Development Department, Cowin's recommendation was at the very top of his list. And, several years later, SPORTS ILLUSTRATED was launched. It would be one of Longwell's final contributions, before he retired in 1954, and the last Time Inc. magazine title launched during Daniel Longwell's and Henry R. Luce's lifetime.

I cannot imagine a Time Inc. without the myriad contributions of Daniel and Mary Longwell. After reading LARGER THAN LIFE, I'm betting that you won't be able to either.

Bill Hooper, Time Inc. Archives,
New York City, May 2015

Preface

It is important to me that the reader know why this book has been written. It is to record the practice of publishing and journalism when the human element was attached to paper and ink well before the development of intelligence technology and social media. The framework of this era in this book is built around the lives of Daniel and Mary Fraser Longwell.

It is right and proper to place in the public memory the contributions of these giants in their fields. In the histories of corporate journalism they have each received only honorable mention. This book shows they deserve a higher recognition in the world of historic and professional journalism. Their passions and efforts to make journalism a respected profession full of accuracy and honesty has been somewhat obscured until now in the findings of this author, their unwitting protégé and young friend with memories of them back to 1954.

To the surprise of all their friends, Mr. and Mrs. Longwell retired from New York to a small town on the northwest edge of the Ozarks. No one-line sentence can describe the full impact the Longwells made on the community of Neosho, Missouri, population nearly 6,000. At the time, we did not fully appreciate who they were or what they had meant to the American scene. We just thought they loved Neosho. In fact, they did; and Neosho loved them, but history is never really seen when one is too close to it.

Fast forward to 2008. I had moved back to Neosho to my home down the street from where the Longwells had lived. My neighbor's son, Michael Shaver, was home from Sagamore Hill where he served as the Park Ranger at the Theodore Roosevelt estate. At dinner one evening, Mike mentioned that Mrs. Theodore Roosevelt, Jr. had written about Dan Longwell in her book, *Day Before Yesterday*. I read the book and pondered why Mrs. Roosevelt, Jr., did not bother to identify Dan Longwell to the reader. It was as though everyone knew who he was.

The winter of 2009, Shaver e-mailed me that there were Hemingway letters to Longwell at Columbia University. I phoned Columbia's Rare Books and Manuscript Library. Could they send me photocopies of the Longwell papers? I will never forget Tara Craig saying, "I'm afraid not. There are 89 Archival Boxes". I was on a plane to New York by January 2010 to see if I could work with what Columbia had.

I must admit having survived nine months of treatments for breast cancer at age 70, the opportunity to "spend time with the Longwells" became an obsession. I felt an obligation to raise both Longwells to their rightful place in the history of publishing. And while Dan is the chief subject of this book, Mary Douglas Fraser was no less important to Time Inc. She was the first woman in the executive suite and she really is the hero for this memoir. A stickler for accuracy in research and history, it was she who kept and filed their careers' worth of ephemera.

Writing this memoir has been a long process but it has been a total joy. A more deserving, enjoyable, and exemplary twosome would be hard to find. It has been my honor to describe their legacy and I hope the reader finds equal enjoyment from my exercise.

The Sources

It is easy to believe that the Longwells may have thought that one day their dedication to high publication standards and the reporting of American patriotic *joie de vivre* might need to be resurrected. Perhaps it was for this purpose that they kept all those pieces of paper that used to cross one's desk before the age of microwave communication without paper.

In a letter written October 26, 1976, early Time Inc. Archivist Lillian Owens wrote to Dan's widow, Mary, about the corporate histories in the works at Time Inc:

> I hope there will be others for we have enough LIFE material to fill volumes. The trouble is --- the best part of the story is in people's heads not in our papers.
>
> The real story of LIFE, which you know as well or better than anyone, is probably beyond telling. (Box 60, **Daniel Longwell Papers**, Rare Book & Manuscript Library, Columbia University in the City of New York)

Every new voice from the past clarifies history. The Daniel Longwell Papers housed at Columbia University reveal the Longwells' contributions to Doubleday Publishers as well as Time Inc. Due to the Longwells' knowledge of literature, art and historical trends, Time Inc. readers were enlightened about their world and country from the 1920's into the 1950's. Good times or bad, we had enjoyed being the Americans we were from Broadway to Hollywood, from wheat fields and corn fields to cotton fields and oil fields. We celebrated in the 'Happy Days' of the fifties but the American Big Time was soon to be overshadowed by the technical revolution in communication and the coming globalization of all life's aspects.

Perhaps Daniel and Mary Longwell sensed this and for that reason they created an archive of their own time and lives and housed it in the basement of their Neosho home until Mary sent it to Columbia University in 1977. The assessed value in 1968 of the archives now at Columbia was $27,180, and more material was added in 1977.

Both of the Longwells had given interviews to the newly assigned historians of Time Inc. after their retirements in 1954. At this writing, those files are only open to those with permission. In those archives are three parts to the Daniel Longwell interviews for the histories written in the 1950's. Mary Longwell wrote her own short offering. There are many letters, photos, and memos in these files. However, the bulk of the Longwell material is at Columbia University's Rare Books and Manuscript Library in the City of New York.

In their time Dan and Mary Longwell gave added strength to news journalism. The work they did benefitted the profession. The results of their work were widely respected. It would be an entertaining exercise to calculate the number of careers and lives helped along with the Longwell wit, wisdom, love and guts. Mine was one of those lives, but this book is their story.

Acknowledgements

Mr. Richard Stolley, whose name has been all over the masthead of LIFE and was the founding editor of PEOPLE, vouched for me as a legitimate researcher and former LIFE Reporter. With his approval, Bill Hooper, Director of the Time Inc. Archives gave me a desk next to the printer and a Time Inc Archives Copy stamp.

Bill Hooper agreed to write the Foreword and indeed he is the one who brought forward so much of the material that enhances this memoir. We have a working relationship that has grown into a friendship I will forever treasure. I early learned he was a great researcher and now we find he has the gift to write as well.

Daniel and Mary Fraser Longwell believed the best publications come from the best efforts of many and they called it Group Journalism. If there is any merit in this work it is due to the efforts of many. First on this list must be Sister Diane Langford who came late to the project, but organized its bits and pieces with care and and experience, knowledge, integrity laced with fascination and devotion. The title is her inspired composition. The last managing editor of the weekly LIFE inscribed his book, *The Life I*

Led, "To Judy Smith, Protector of the Longwell Legacy." and thus this memoir was set on its course.

The first encouragements came from Michael B. Shaver, former student of Neosho Junior High who became a Park Service Ranger at Sagamore Hill, the Roosevelt home and National Park Service site. He discovered our neighbor in Neosho had been a close friend of the Roosevelt family. It was Shaver's casting about on the internet that led me to the Columbia University Library Rare Books and Manuscript Library and its Longwell Collection. A phone call to the Director, Tara C. Craig, revealed there were 89 archival boxes of correspondence, papers, diaries, etc. She and all the staff at RBLM, especially Jennifer B. Lee and Jane R. Siegel were totally helpful and mindful for the five and a half years I visited there.

Realizing this was not to be a small project nor a short term one I must give great thanks to those who thought I could begin it and bring it to fruition. First would be Margaretta Barton Colt, former bookstore owner, author and friend of five decades and counting. Her guest room was a most welcome retreat during the many research trips to Columbia. At the end of each day's work, we would sift through the daily discoveries. Talking with Margaretta brings the cream to the top. Second would be Sally Scott Maran, former LIFE Reporter and later Managing Editor of *Smithsonian* magazine. When I first spoke with her about the project she said I had to do it.

Third would be my dear family. My husband appointed himself as the "Morale Officer". My daughters were supportive to the point of giving up their benefits from a life insurance policy in order that the money might be redirected to revitalizing the Longwell Museum at Crowder College which had been named for our Longwells and then rather forgotten.

The University of South Carolina's South Caroliana Library and Graham Duncan were most helpful to me and my friend, Patricia Goode, who helped me with researching John Shaw Billings' Diaries. His daily reports of working at TIME and LIFE with Longwell are uninhibited insights. Billings "never lost his pencil" and the continuity of his Diaries makes them a priceless resource.

It was Bill Hooper who put me in touch with Lillian Owens of the original Time Inc. archives which we called "the morgue." Her level headed assessments kept me from wandering out into the weeds. Not only had she hired and trained Bill, she was the Director of the Archives during the Robert Elson's writing of the corporate history. She in turn put me onto the Diaries of Dan Longwell's best friend at LIFE, John Shaw Billings.

I am also most grateful to Betty Morris who was Daniel Longwell's last secretary but also his and Mary's friend who helped them with the visits of Longwell protégés to New York City after the Longwells had moved to Neosho. MO. It has been a true joy to know and love her.

A more recent moral support came from Adair Margo, founder and head of the Tom Lea Institute in El Paso, TX. Tom Lea was the first War Artist hired by Longwell for LIFE and Margo is of the opinion that I am the only person now living who knew of the development of Lea's friendship with Longwell which also included which also included Holland McCombs and the Dallas Museum of Fine Arts.

I cannot end these acknowledgements without thanking our landlords and friends in East Corinth and East Barnard, Vermont, names John and Sue Foster, then Glenn and Joani Yankee who moved her sewing room and quilts aside for my 6 file boxes and laptop so that summers among the muses in the Green Mountains of Vermont might be usefully spent. I must not forget the women and girls who run the Columbia University Butler Library snack shop. I thank them for all the almond croissants they sold me with the milk steamed just the way I like it.

Many citizens and friends of Neosho have allowed me to interview them and while this book could be encyclopedic with their reports, I truly thank them for the rich flavor they added to the retirement years of Dan and Mary and therefore also to this book.

I am appreciative of people who answer their phones and emails. To speak to the grandson of Christopher Morley, John Christopher Woodruff, executor of the Morley Estate, was a banner day. The Hemingway Foundation people were most helpful though they and the Hemingway family hold all the rights. I could not bring myself to paraphrase Hemingway.

Had it not been for Daniel and Mary Fraser Longwell, keeping all these living pieces of paper and keeping them organized for some half a century, this book would not be the work that it is. They get the most credit and all my gratitude.

Judith Haas Smith

CHAPTER ONE

BEGINNINGS

"There's something called the big time...
but you may have already missed it."

--Daniel Longwell to Judy Haas, 1958

Daniel Longwell, formerly of New York, retired editor of LIFE Magazine was just climbing out of my brand new black, highly polished, 1957 Ford Thunderbird, complete with Continental Kit. Dan Longwell sensed that college bound, Judy Haas from three doors down the hill had no idea what was the 'Big Time'. How could she? This was Neosho, Missouri, barely more than a village in the foothills of the Ozarks.

Now at seventy instead of seventeen, I know what Dan Longwell was saying. He was thinking that the world in which he and his wife, Mary Douglas Fraser Longwell, had worked was probably gone. It must have been a sad epiphany because the Longwells had lived an historical life among historical people. In fact, their lives had the advantage of being at the top of America's literary, art and journalism worlds. The Longwells' friends were people whose books line our libraries and whose paintings hang in our museums. During Dan's fifteen years at Doubleday publishing headquarters in Garden City, New York, he brought forth the classic American historical fictions writers of the early part of the twentieth century including Edna Ferber, Stephen Vincent Benet, and Sinclair Lewis. His best friends were the likes of Nelson Doubleday, Sr., Theodore Roosevelt, Jr., and Ogden Nash.

He was mentored by Christopher Morley about all things bookshop and he credited Frank Nelson Doubleday and Alfred Knopf for teaching him about the publishing of books. By the time Longwell left Doubleday for Time Inc., he had fifteen full years of experience in publishing, promotion, and a corps of literary writers and book illustrators who had become his personal friends. In the world of publishing in the 1930's, his knowledge was encyclopedic.

Daniel and Mary Longwell were part of the reporting, producing, and promoting of some of America's finest hours and deepest sorrows.

Childhood First—Always Remember Where You Come From

The bouncing baby boy born at 1508 N. 17th Street in Omaha, Nebraska, near the Metz Brewery but away from the railroad yards, stock yards and packing houses of South Omaha was Daniel Longwell. He was not the first Daniel Longwell. That would be his grandfather who had been born in 1824, in Steuben County, New York. That Daniel was one of nine children of Ira and Zillah Carver Longwell who moved their large family from Elmira, New York to Posey Township, Fayette County, Indiana. Ira became clerk of the Baptist community in 1839. He was the church's clerk for twenty-three years until June 13, 1863, less than a month before he died.

The first Daniel Longwell married Hannah Pattison in 1850. They also had nine children. Following in his father's footsteps, Ira's son, the second Daniel Longwell, became chief clerk of the Baptist church from 1872 to 1879, which disbanded in 1888, according to a last entry. It was noted that both Ira and Daniel wrote a beautiful script. However, Ira spelled Longwill with an "i" while Daniel spelled it with an "e".

Daniel and Hannah Longwell named one of their sons Alfred Marshall. Alfred Marshall had been born in Posey County, Indiana in 1854. Though the family was a farming family, Alfred chose to attend a new small secular college in Valparaiso, Indiana with the imposing name Northern Indiana Normal School and Business Institute, now Valparaiso University. Alfred studied bookkeeping.

At some time, Alfred met Alice Charlotte Haynes who had been born in St. Louis, Missouri in 1864. Her family later moved to Springfield, Missouri. There Alice attended school at what was then known as Drury Academy, now Drury University. Alice was twenty and Alfred was thirty when they married in 1884. They tried a bit of homesteading and after living in Indiana for a time; they tried South Dakota and York, Nebraska where Alfred's parents had finally settled.

Alfred and Alice had four children. Alfred Emerson Longwell was born in 1887. Neosho H. Longwell, a girl, was born in 1889. Neosho died during her third year in 1892. Five years later, James Carver Longwell was born in 1897. Daniel Longwell, our subject here, was born on July 11, 1899, at his parents' home with Dr. C.W. Hayes as attending physician. He was christened without a middle name.

Dan was photographed at age two (c. 1901) with long curly hair in a dress trimmed with lace and in black high button boots. (John Shaw Billings Collection, Courtesy of South Caroliniana Library, University of South Carolina, Columbia, SC)

With his hands on hips and a determined stare, there is no doubting the confident nature of this little boy. He may well have been the darling of the family.

The family left Omaha and tried homesteading again in South Dakota. One family photo shows Dan with another little boy sitting in a wooden wash tub with paddles as if the prairie were at least a pond, and, no doubt, wishing that the vast dry prairie was water instead of dirt. Mary Fraser Longwell later labeled the photo, "At seven he

(Box 47, Daniel Longwell Papers, Rare Book & Manuscript Library, Columbia University in the City of New York)

rowed across the Prairies of Pennington County, South Dakota" (c. 1905).

Dan learned to play baseball and pitch hay. As his family moved around the northern Midwest during his elementary years, he attended schools in Omaha, Nebraska and Pennington County, South Dakota.

His older brother, Alfred, wanted to try farming but needed land.

Sailing Across the Prairie (John Shaw Billings Collection, Courtesy of South Caroliniana Library, University of South Carolina, Columbia, SC)

Their father found and bought a two hundred acre farm eight miles southwest of Neosho, MO, a rural Missouri railhead community, about 400 miles south of Omaha. He spent his eighth grade year at Ragan School in Newton County, Missouri, most of which has blown away since he lived there.

(The little sister who had died had not been named after this Neosho town but after her mother's cousin, Neosho River Hobart.)

The town of Neosho was near his mother's sister who lived in Springfield, Missouri,

"Ragan Community School" by Mary Fraser Longwell (Author's Personal Collection)

5

some seventy miles to the northeast. Dan later wrote, "…there were a number of relatives in Springfield, but none of them were prominent."

In 1913, Dan was sent to Neosho to live with his brother on the farm. The Ragan area was and is a romantic, Hollywood movie set sort of place. It was bucolic beauty with woods and streams, dirt roads, crawdads and arrow heads. Dan spent a fair amount of time down near the Arkansas border at a place called Tigris, Missouri. It was just a store then and is now only known by the road that went to it. Dan roamed these hills as a hunter and young explorer as only country kids can do. In 1937, he wrote an office bio sketch for the Time, Inc. Promotion Department: "Tigris is a pretty obscure place…I doubt if many copies of LIFE get that deeply into the Ozarks except to be used as wallpaper." (Time Inc. Archives)

In the Time, Inc. promotion memo written as LIFE magazine was being launched, Dan wrote, "On the whole, the Longwell background is pretty poor ground for publicity seeds." But by 1934 Dan's circle of friends alone made his life fertile ground for publicity though he eschewed such.

High School Years

A year of hauling hay convinced Alfred Longwell that he did not like farming all that much so the brothers returned to Omaha from Missouri. Alfred joined the Army and left for Boston. He became an engineer, married, had two sons, and moved to Swarthmore, Pennsylvania. Daniel entered Central High School in Omaha, and was a student of distinction from 1914 until his graduation in 1918. Adjusting to Central High in Omaha with over two hundred in his graduating class would be somewhat daunting to an adolescent who had spent a year in a country school with fewer than fifty pupils.

Education was important to the Longwell family and there is a history of educators. It was not until after his retirement that Dan learned just how involved in teaching one family member had been. In a 1955 letter written to Joseph Kastner[2], LIFE's quintessential copy editor, Dan wrote: (Box 68, **Daniel Longwell Papers**, Rare Book & Manuscript Library, Columbia University in the City of New York.)

> I went up to the nearby Drury College the other evening, made a little talk about authors to their Writers Conference. I must have worked a little extra hard on the talk because my Mother attended Drury when it was still an academy and not a college. So I was feeling sentimental. I only talked fifteen minutes but to my astonishment, I got an ovation. ...and the next morning the papers said I was thrilling.
>
> But the astonishing news is this, the president of the college asked me if I was any kin to O.H. Longwell who founded Highland Park College in Des Moines. I said he was my father's first

---

[2] It is always fun to see how life strings these pearls of information together for us. Joe Kastner as a teenager had been hired into Time, Inc. as a CBOB – "college boy office boy" – by Mary Fraser who later became Mrs. Daniel Longwell.

cousin, and I remembered him from boyhood, always wore a silk hat and a great black Gladstone coat when he came to visit us. My host told me his mother and father had attended Highland Park and later became teachers and they always used Longwell's GRAMMAR. He said O.H. Longwell's GRAMMAR was a widely used book and he had been taught grammar from it when he was in school.

Meanwhile in Omaha in 1914, Dan's father took a position as a bookkeeper for the United States Automobile Supply Company. Brother James was a junior and Dan was a freshman. When basketball season came around, Dan went out for the sport as did 50% of the boys at the high school. He was elected captain of the freshman team.

Dan must have been a gregarious and fun loving kid with an uncommon sense of what it meant to be a leader with responsibility. His Christian heritage held a Presbyterian background which provided a connection to Henry Luce's personal history. Luce's father was a Presbyterian missionary in China, where Luce spent his childhood.[3]

Perhaps this strong Christian tradition was imbedded in Longwell's DNA or perhaps he discovered it through

---

[3] It was Longwell's opinion that Luce felt he missed something in his early life by not having an American hometown or early learning of American History. Luce loved America but, unlike Longwell, he did not have the depth of knowledge about the USA that Longwell had and Luce had none of the Midwestern small town or emerging metropolis experience which Longwell had in abundance. (Box 60, **Daniel Longwell Papers**, Rare Book & Manuscript Library, Columbia University in the City of New York.)

joining the Y.M.C.A. as a young teenager. He joined the Young Men's Christian Association in 1915 as a freshman. First he passed the official test for boys in First Aid to the Injured. Then he took classes in Bible Study offered by the Omaha Y.M.C.A. As a sophomore, he scored 91% in the course "Jesus the Leader", and as a junior he scored 85% on the exam of the "Life and Works of Jesus." At age sixteen, he had joined the High School Student Christian Movement of the Y.M.C.A. The motto of this group was "Deus Vult", Latin meaning "God's will." As a requirement, Dan took a vow, a portion of which is here quoted:

> I realize that this involves doing God's will in my life from this date in definite service for others whether I am in school, in college, or engaged in a business, professional or other vocation….I purpose from this time to give at least one hour a week in definite service to help make it easier for some boy in school or some other person in my community to be better, happier, or more active in extending the Master's Kingdom. (Box 72, **Daniel Longwell Papers**, Rare Book & Manuscript Library, Columbia University in the City of New York)

This early training in honor and fair play was exhibited when Dan took up umpiring a championship series of playground ballgames between the teams of seven supervised recreational centers. Dan and another young man named Paul Nicholson were awarded medals for umpiring "without one instance of rowdyism happening."

The newspaper report carried portrait photos of the two boys along with an explanation of their tasks as umpires. The section below on how the scoring was done at the ball game is a reflection of the times which were the background of Longwell's adolescence.

> In scoring these games, language and conduct of the players were considerations. Points were taken off for swearing, calling names, losing temper or for other forms of rowdyism. These umpires imposed no penalties for slang expressions, although they did not approve of slang. Saying "Dern the luck" during these games was not regarded as an egregious offense. The remark, "Oh, you boob," was overlooked by the umpires, Longwell and Nicholson. "These .... young umpires did much to improve the *esprit d' corps* at the recreation centers. They served as examples as well as umpires and Mr. English expects to retain them for next season. Superintendent English has presented Masters Longwell and Nicholson medals for their efficient services as official umpires during the inter-park series. (*Omaha World-Herald,* Issue unknown)

Such attention to biblical scholarship and devotion to moral duty is not all that common among teenage boys. The conflagration in Europe was drawing attention to patriotic duty and the attendant advantages of military training for a young man. Dan Longwell joined the Central High School S.A.T.C., The Student Army Training Corps. He attained their highest rank, Cadet Lieutenant Colonel, and graduated with an appointment to West Point from Nebraska Senator Gilbert Hitchcock. (Box 72, **Daniel Longwell Papers**, Rare Book & Manuscript Library, Columbia University in the City of New York)

A further testimony of the exorbitant energy and popularity of young Longwell, was reported in a special dispatch to the *Omaha World-Herald* when he was elected President of the Y.M.C.A. Boys Conference of some 300 'older boys' held in Fremont, Nebraska. In his capacity as President of the Hi-Y Clubs of the state of Nebraska, he conducted statewide anti-smoking campaigns. The campaigning taught him a lot about promoting, but it did not keep smoking from becoming fashionable.[4]

Cadet Lieutenant Colonel Daniel Longwell, Omaha, NE, c.1917 (John Shaw Billings Collection, Courtesy of South Caroliniana Library, University of South Carolina, Columbia, SC)

High school years are salad days when everything is fresh and easy. In his junior year, he edited the school magazine, "The Register," during the one month when juniors were permitted that honor. There was an editorial staff of twenty-four and a business department of seven.

---

[4] Unfortunately, Dad did smoke as an adult and during a bout with pneumonia, he lost the lower lobe of his left lung. (Box 72, **Daniel Longwell Papers**, Rare Book & Manuscript Library, Columbia University in the City of New York.)

On August 9, 1955, Dan recounted this experience in a letter to Mr. William Benton, Publisher of the <u>Encyclopedia Britannica</u>.

> After our reminiscences the other day, I recalled that as a junior in Omaha High School, editing the one issue of the high school magazine the juniors were allowed to edit, I called back Jimmy Williamson, who had graduated the year before and was waiting around to get into Yale and had him do a four-page illustrated insert. This was my first experience in pictorial journalism. The next year I dropped journalism and became Cadet Colonel of the High School Regiment—a position Mac Baldridge (yours and Harry's[5] great football friend at Yale) had held when I was a freshman. (Box 72, **Daniel Longwell Papers,** Rare Book & Manuscript Library, Columbia University in the City of New York.)

Danny Boy Heads East

Just how does an eighteen year old boy from Omaha, Nebraska, begin the rest of his life in a strange city like the metropolis of New York City in the fall of 1918? We know the background of the boy, but what was the backdrop of Omaha? It was not cornfields, prairie, and houses out of sod. These short summaries of the first three chapters sum

---

[5] That person called Harry was Henry Luce, president of Time Inc.

up the face of Omaha. (*Omaha World- Herald, June 13, 2004, Special Magazine*)

- CHAPTER 1 1854-1879: The Beginning. The terminus of the transcontinental railroad puts Omaha on the national map.
- CHAPTER 2 1879-1904: Boomtown. The livestock industry leads a stampede of growth as "the smell of money" wafts from South Omaha.
- CHAPTER 3 1904-1929: Unrest. The city is scarred by racial and ethnic hatred, labor strife, corrupt politics and wide open vice.

Daniel Longwell lived most of his years in Omaha during the episodes recalled in "Chapter Three" of the commemorative magazine. No wonder the family sent him to Missouri for the eighth grade in 1913. Perhaps they had been caught in the 1913 Easter Sunday tornado that leveled four and a half miles of neighborhoods, destroyed 2,000 homes and killed 150 people.

It can be assumed that young Dan'l did not arrive as a "barefoot boy with cheek"[6] to be swallowed up in the big city. Omaha had an eleven-story skyscraper—The New York Life Building renamed the Omaha Building in 1909. The public library had been completed in Renaissance style in 1893. Omaha had hosted a world's fair in 1898, the Trans-Mississippi and International Exposition and

---

[6] Reference to Max Shulman's (1919-1988) 1943 book, *Barefoot Boy with Cheek*, a satire on the 1930's college life of a boy from Minnesota. en.wikipedia.org/wiki/**Max_Shulman**

Indian Congress, which had forty states and ten countries participating. Acres of corn stubble had given way to bricked courtyards, lavish landscaping and ornate buildings.

Electrical lights, however, would prove to be the biggest marvel. The fair was opened on June 1, 1898, by President McKinley who gave the cue to turn on the fair's lights in a telegraphed message from the White House. Up to that point, only street lights, streetcars and mansions had electricity. That same year, 1898, the Spanish-American War Armistice was signed in October and President McKinley celebrated in Omaha. It is not surprising that the Longwell family decided to give up homesteading in South Dakota to settle down in Omaha.

This is the city that Longwell left when he arrived in New York by train, probably at Pennsylvania Station at 34th Street and went right up Broadway by bus or street car to Columbia University at 114th. He immediately joined the S.A.T.C. (Student Army Training Corps) of Columbia with the thought of going on to West Point. America had become engaged in World War I in April of 1917, with President Woodrow Wilson's insistence that this was a "war to make the world safe for democracy." After unbelievable bloodshed and collapsing governments, an armistice was signed November 11, 1918. (Box 81, **Daniel Longwell Papers**, Rare Book & Manuscript Library, Columbia University in the City of New York)

Longwell had actually packed his bag and started up the Hudson River by ferry. As he approached the great gray bastion, he admitted to himself he would rather be a college student in New York City. He was demobilized from the

S.A.T.C. in January of 1919, with the rank of private and admitted into Columbia University. His course schedule included the usual English courses, algebra, geometry, physics, Latin and French, World Issues, Contemporary Civics, history, topography and physical education. Over a period of six years, he did very well in Latin, English, history and the social sciences, but he could not master the required French and hence never graduated though he took courses for six years. Columbia still regards him as having been in the class of 1922.

CHAPTER TWO

DAN'S LIFE AT DOUBLEDAY

"Literature was on the march. The whole vitality of American literature was vibrant in the book shop ...."

--Dan Longwell, 1970 (cited below)

Beginnings at Doubleday

The college life of Daniel Longwell and the publishing life of Daniel Longwell dovetailed when he went to work at the Doubleday Page and Company Book Shop inside Penn Station as their night clerk. He never forgot those early days of working his way through school, notwithstanding the $250 from Uncle Arthur…whom he never met. Mary wisely wrote down their evening conversation in her Diary for June 1968 just six months before he died. (Box 8d, **Daniel Longwell Papers**, Rare Book & Manuscript Library, Columbia University in the City of New York.)

> A rainy, dismal day. DL tired, tired of being in the house. Wants to get out and try walking but it is raining. After dinner (by ourselves) reminisces

a bit. "I wonder what would have happened to me if I had stayed in Omaha." Mary then urges him forward with, "And you just sort of happened into publishing?"

"Yes, I was looking for a job and the Columbia placement bureau said they needed a night clerk at the Doubleday shop in Penn Terminal. I went down and they offered me $5.00 a week. I figured I could almost live on it. Pretty soon they thought I was a bright boy and offered me $12, and finally to $25. Then they asked me to go to Garden City at $35 a week. I figured I could do it and keep going to college at night. My father had died and I had to support my mother.

But after a year I got sick and they said, 'Too bad, he could go to the top if he had good health.' So they shipped me off to Grace Richmond's in Fredonia, New York. I was rooming with Ted Richmond, her son, and I took long walks and there was snow and it was clean and I went to bed early.

When I came back, my boss in the advertising department thought he was an actor and quit and I got his job at $40. Then came SO BIG and SHOWBOAT, (Edna Ferber) and Ellen Glasgow and they kept raising me. I got $80 a week and thought I was rich—it was more money than my father ever made. I gave my mother $45 a week to live on.

Before that the boys at TIME had heard about me and offered me a job at $25 a week, but I couldn't afford it.

Finally I was up to $12,000 a year and with bonuses I made about $25,000. That's when I went to Time, Inc. I went at $8,000 but Harry raised me to $12,000 the first year.

Picture if you will a young man of the 1920's, also in his 20's, clerking in a book store which was sheltered by the vaulted Beaux Arts 150-foot ceilings at the center of the Pennsylvania Railroad. He loves this opportunity to create displays and observe customers. He generally feels he is at the center of commerce and politics. He is fashion conscious and wears a dapper tweed suit with a Norfolk jacket which had made its stylish appearance out of the hunting forests of England onto the daytime streets of New York. Dressed in his only suit, the young man has riveting blue eyes. He does not wear glasses. The word "nerd" is not in his extensive vocabulary nor was it applicable to him (July 12, 1955 Letter to Thomas Burns, Box 57, **Daniel Longwell Papers**, Rare Book & Manuscript Library, Columbia University in the City of New York.)

Dan Longwell, "Publisher's Young Man" (John Shaw Billings Collection, Courtesy of South Caroliniana Library, University of South Carolina, Columbia, SC)

The boy became a man and thirty years later, in 1951, Stanley Marcus of Neiman-Marcus invited him to address the Texas Institute of Letters' annual meeting in Dallas. On November 16, 1951, Lon Tinkle, President of the Texas Institute of Letters, invited him back to Dallas. This time he was to speak to a group of Texas authors.

In the good fun of the Saturday breakfast, the authors presented Longwell with a plaque of appreciation based on the history of author, Cabeza de Vaca, an early Spanish explorer who was shipwrecked and wandered among the Texas natives and later wrote an account of his travels. The Society recognizes de Vaca as author of the first literature about Texas ever produced by a foreigner. Mr. Longwell, native of Nebraska, New York and Missouri, and also being a "foreign writer" was seen as equally impressed with Texas.

The above digression is only to set the scene of the talk Longwell gave at the Friday night dinner. His are the best words about the Doubleday Bookshop and the first author he met. (Box 71, Speeches Folder, **Daniel Longwell Papers**, Rare Book & Manuscript Library, Columbia University in the City of New York.)

> As to the relationship between publishers and authors, I can only tell it from the publisher's side and from my own experience. To tell it properly I must go back 30 odd years to the first time I ever met an author. I was the night book clerk in the oldest of Doubleday's bookshops, the one tucked in the Pennsylvania Terminal's main arcade. As I remember it, it was a Spring evening, and the great terminal, built as a copy of some famous

Roman baths, with high pillars, light streaming in from tall windows, was quiet and rather lovely. A little Catholic church around the corner had just chimed out its angelus at sundown. On that romantic mood, I saw my first author. He was dressed in tweeds, he was smoking a pipe. He deliberately "browsed" around the shop. I knew his books—*Shandygaff, The Haunted Bookshop, Parnassus on Wheels.* They were bibles to young booksellers in those days. We all modeled ourselves on Roger Mifflin, the bookseller hero of those novels and essays. I was myself wearing a Norfolk jacket with a belt—an old tweed suit cut down from one of my uncle's cast-offs. I was also smoking a pipe. Of course I recognized Christopher Morley "browsing"…a word he had done much to popularize. … I was too shy to speak to him, and I now know he wanted me to do just that. I was resolved not to ask him for his autograph, although he was rather famous for giving them. I wouldn't be forward with an author. Morley finally broke the ice. He spoke to me, bought a book, and, turning tables on me, asked me to autograph it for him. He says he still has it—one of the rare Longwell autographs.

Morely became a great friend—he had been a predecessor of mine at Doubleday's as a Publisher's Young Man. A few years after this first meeting, when I had finished college and moved to the main offices of Doubleday in Garden City, Morley paid me a great compliment of writing a little essay called, "Grub Street Runners" which he said was written about me. It was really about all the publishers' young men Morley had known, including himself, and in it he used that wonderful word, "Gruntling," which he had invented. Morley contended that the natural state of an author is to be disgruntled. Therefore, the thing for the publisher to do is to gruntle their authors. The publishers hired young men to gruntle their authors. Of the publisher's young men, Morley says,

"He must be a scholar among scholars and a rake among rakes. In the authors he has to gruntle, he must draw no line of race, color, age, or previous condition of pulchritude. Connoisseur of honest writing, he must not himself be tainted by any hankering to write. That is fatal.

And Dan continued:

Later, Morley and Frank Henry, now Vice President of Greystone Press, and I went into a little publishing venture of our own. Each Christmas, we needed money, so we founded the firm of Henry, Longwell and Another and brought out small autographed books in very limited editions.[7] Collectors were avid buyers of such nonsense in the late 1920's. Our first one—if I remember rightly—was a little 16-page affair, an essay called *The Brown Owl* by

---

[7] These small books were listed as "Briefcase Breviaries".

21

H. M. Tomlinson. We had Tomlinson autograph it, and then because autographs were popular, as publishers, we generously autographed the books too. The "Another" in the firm was, of course, Christopher Morley.

In March of 1970, Mary Longwell typed a five-page memoir Dan had dictated in 1961 or 1962 before his 1965 stroke. She included it in the Columbia collection.

It is my opinion that Mary wished Dan would write his own "Memoir" because she more than anyone knew the fullness of his busy life as well as his ability to put it on paper. I know it may not be good editing to report the same situation twice in a researched memoir, however, I beg to break tradition in this case because it gives an evidence that Dan Longwell's wonderful memory lasted over the years and his good wife had the sense to preserve that treasure. Equally important, the reader can enjoy the effusive at-home recollections which are always edited down for speeches. The reader can see Dan Longwell never had to create a "bucket list" and probably would have rejected the phrase.

In this source Dan is dictating or writing in the first person. The reader may not recognize the names of authors who were commonly known in those days which is just another item on the list of what we have forgotten. But the reader cannot miss the internalized joy he had of clerking in a book shop and recalling it years later.

Twenty eight years ago I was hired as the night clerk at the Pennsylvania Terminal Book

Shop of Doubleday, Page and Company. ...
Through the shop I met many people. I remember
Walter Hines Page, old and ill, returning from
his ambassadorial post in London. ...I think the
record would show that I am one of the oldest and
largest book buyers of the Doubleday Shops, but
books, some of them a quarter of a century old,
still stand in my library in their original jackets.
... I can remember F. N. Doubleday (Effendi) as
a sweet caller, always interested in the business
of the shop, always interested in the display of
his great authors, Kipling, Conrad and O Henry.

It is foolish to think that a book shop can
play something in National affairs, but I rather
think that the Penn Terminal Book Shop in my
time played a part in the defeat of the League
of Nations. Harcourt Brace was then a young
company. They had got an extraordinary book
called *The Economic Consequences of the Peace*
by John Maynard Keynes. Each night their
sales manager would bring me 25 to 50 copies
of the book. I would sell them between 5 and
10:30. I remember selling copies to ex-President
Taft, Senator McCormick and many others. The
book by an extraneous passage dealing with
Clemenceau's grey gloves, and not through its
economic thought, so influenced Congress that
the League of Nations was defeated.

Literature was on the march. The whole
vitality of American literature was vibrant in the
book shop .... (Box 72, **Daniel Longwell Papers**,

Rare Book & Manuscript Library, Columbia University in the City of New York).

"Literature vibrant in a bookshop" gives off a sense of internal holy glowing that only book lovers can realize. Reading a book is one joy, but paper and ink to publication and payment is making dirt from compost. It must be like sharing creation with God.

This writing is for those of us who love to browse in a book shop, to find a treasure to take home to our own shelves, to feel the warm glow of a reading lamp above our left shoulder as we sit in our favorite chair and turn the pages some poetical person has created for our enjoyment or enlightenment. We are grateful for the gifts of authors, and we understand the pride and joy a young man remembers of being a clerk in a book shop. The subject of this memoir cut his teeth on publishing in a book shop, but his other natural gifts allowed him to be so in tune with the authors of Doubleday that he was singularly able to shape the publishing world of his time.

His abilities did not go unnoticed at Doubleday headquarters. Daniel Longwell was recruited to come to work in the headquarters that had been built in 1910 in Garden City, Long Island. Today, Doubleday Publishing no longer stands in buildings or on paper. But when it did occupy real estate its buildings were magnificent and so was its authors' list. To simply say it was an office building and a factory with presses is architectural heresy. If the descriptions written by Terry Considine Williams in "Once Doubleday was a King, Now House Gets a New Look," for the *New York Times*, and published on October 6, 1996, are to be believed, it was an edifice for the ages.

To be invited there was considered honor enough. To be recruited to work there must have been very heady. For a young man in his idealistic years who obviously psychologically internalized his surroundings, working at Doubleday in Garden City, Long Island, must have filled Longwell to near choking. In fact we are fortunate to have Longwell's 1951 letter to his good friend and former co-managing editor and cohort executive at Time Inc., John Shaw Billings. They were both pretty bored on the executive floor of Time Inc. A good bit of their friendship was based on American history. To his friend Billings, Longwell wrote "Just a few notes on publishing in the country" on January 31, 1951.

> I suppose the real leader in this notion was my old boss, F.N. Doubleday. "Effendi" was forty five or thereabouts when he founded his own firm. He had been general manager of Scribners, had had brilliant Sam McClure as a partner, when he later teamed up with Walter Page (who quit his editorship of the *Atlantic Monthly* to join him); J.P. Morgan & Co. asked the new partners to take over almost century-old Harpers and rehabilitate that company. After a brief experience with Harpers, Effendi, …moved his business to Garden City. This was about 1907. Teddy Roosevelt laid the cornerstone for the Country Life Press and there were great news stories about decentralization. Garden was a lovely little cathedral town…

Effendi's greatest publishing successes came after he moved the entire firm to Garden City. This, however, was not due to Garden City. It was due to the publishing energy that Walter Page and Effendi had stored up before they made the move.

Fourteen or fifteen years later when I went to Garden City, the place was prosperous, big, and the publishing firm had huge hidden assets in its list of authors, but publishing-wise, dead rot had set in. The printing presses were already dictating to the publishing. The entire later cheapening of publishing objectives at Doubledays—the Literary Guild, the Book Clubs etc.—was due to the maw[8] of the printing presses.

You must remember that many young men had gone to Garden City to instill youth into the structure—Alfred Knopf, Christopher Morley, Sam Saxon, a host of others. They had all left their mark but been somewhat defeated and retreated.

I was the first young man to take hold there after WW I. Garden City was a lovely place to work. I lived nearby and because I was still attending college afternoons, I had to work most evenings. I used to love it—the gardens were pretty and cool, nine o'clock at night the night shift of the presses would start rolling and I'd work until 10 or 11 to the low rumble of their music. ...

---

[8] Maw: the throat, jaws, or oral cavity of some voracious animal (Webster's New World Dictionary, Cleveland, NY, 1957)

There is no denying that the printing plant in Garden City was a success as a personnel operation. A great copper plate stood over the composing room door reading, "This is an open shop, first, last and always." It's true to this day. We had two and three generations of people who worked at the plant at Garden City. Our secretaries were generally the daughters of old compositors or pressmen. Nothing could be more perfect for working conditions. My final office there was huge. It was next in size to Nelson Doubleday's and right next to his. Ivy climbed around my windows and I looked out on a fountain. (Box 27, **Daniel Longwell Papers,** Rare Book & Manuscript Library, Columbia University in the City of New York.)

In his article, Terry Considine Williams describes the physical structure and landscaping of what was then Doubleday Page & Co. We will start at ground and go up.

Theodore Roosevelt laid the cornerstone for Doubleday's Country Life Press on August 19, 1910. That building was erected in ninety-four days. The genius behind this "factory" was Frank Nelson Doubleday himself. He would reign here until his death in 1934, the year that Dan Longwell made his move to Time Inc.

But by the time Dan made the move, he had internalized the ways and means of the Doubleday house like a tonic. His own energy and that tonic made him a strong force in the new world of magazine publishing just as he had learned to be a force in his former world of book publishing.

Just what did the Doubleday plant look like? Some say it looked like Hampton Court of Henry VIII. The building was a basic "U" shape built of red brick at front and the long west wing. The east wing was called the tin building and it housed the Country Life Presses where the books were printed and bound. Paper came off the freight rail cars at the north end and books came out at the south end to be picked up by train for distribution.

Each wing was 490 feet long and 200 feet wide. Inside this "U" was a court yard with two pools, each at 300 feet in diameter with elevated fountains.

Men in the composition factory were given five clean uniforms a week and milk was brought to them on the job. A doctor and dentist were on call and a registered nurse was on duty all the time. Vitamins were available at the drinking fountains. Cleanliness was stressed and there were vacuum cleaner outlets every 75 feet. Not only did supplies arrive by train, but employees and authors did as well.

The front redbrick entrance had above its door the Doubleday trademark of an anchor and dolphin (see footnote below). Originally this was the mark of an early Italian printer, Aldus, who invented italic type. Inside there was a pink marble staircase rising above a dolphin fountain. Christopher Morley used F.N.D's exclamation about the motors under the hood of a car sounding like "dynamite and wildcats," when he gave tribute to Doubleday. "There are dynamite and wildcats, too, in the prenatal life of a book. It was never less than fairy tale to think of the adventures of words in that long brick building." And this was the subject of the stained glass windows which traced the journey of a book from writer to reader.

The building was designed so that each of the 600 employees was never more than 40 feet from a window, most of which looked out onto the courtyard, fountains, gardens, and the two miles of trails through plant gardens and orchards. One "kitchen garden" grew vegetables for the company's Japanese chef.

At the end of one path leading from a reflecting pool, there was the famous "Printers Sundial," surrounded by tall cedars. It represented the beginnings of printing starting with Gutenberg in 1455. Gutenberg had no printer's mark but he was represented with a Bible opened to the 19th chapter of Job, verse 23: *"Oh that my words were now written! Oh that they were printed in a book!"* (Williams, *New York Times*, October 6, 1996).

This sundial was built of brass and bronze and engraved by the engraving department of Country Life Press. There were twelve hour spaces with the marks of twelve early printers including Aldus.[9]

The building and grounds were wonder enough, but the minds that functioned inside and the authors who came and went are a syllabus of American literature of the first half of our Twentieth Century. Others of the trade laughed

---

[9] **Aldus Pius Manutius** (1449 – 1515), Italian, became a printer and publisher when he founded the Aldine Press at Venice. He invented various punctuation methods that have lasted to this day including the semi-colon and the modern presentation of the comma. He also invented italic type. He used an emblem from a Roman coin of a dolphin around an anchor. This emblem was adapted by Doubleday for their own press emblem. (Williams, *New York Times*, Oct. 6, 1996; and en.wikipedia.org/wiki/**Aldus_Manutius**)

at Frank Nelson Doubleday for building his plant and total operation some twenty-two miles from Manhattan. As he later is quoted, "I never could figure out why an attractive factory would not make more money than an unattractive one."

It is notable, too, that Rudyard Kipling was the man who penned the nickname of F.N.D. as "Effendi" which is Turkish for "Chief." Kipling was Doubleday's first best-selling author and they were close personal friends throughout their lives.

A Kipling biographer, Harry Ricketts, in his book *The Unforgiving Minute: A Life of Rudyard Kipling* (page 257) discusses a lung ailment that struck Kipling in 1899, and the care given him by Mr. Doubleday.

> Of the many friends who rallied round, the most indefatigable was Frank Doubleday, who had become Kipling's American publisher. Doubleday now turned into a close family friend, and Kipling took to calling him 'Effendi' a pun on his initials FND. It was Effendi who on 17 April moved the whole Kipling entourage by private railcar to Lakewood, a New Jersey resort, where Kipling took gentle exercise and put on some much-needed weight. On 9 May, the invalid party proceeded, again by private railcar, to Morristown for a month with other American friends.....Then there followed a week at Effendi's house on Long Island, before 13 June found them back in New York.

Doubleday[10] said however, "Kipling himself never called me anything but Frank all his life."

Effendi also had a feeling of friendship for Dan Longwell as is evidenced by a Christmas thank you note typed and signed on personal note paper with the heading, "F.N.D., Oyster Bay, N.Y." which reads (typographical errors included),

> Dear Dan;
>
> I think we are in debt to you for z very charming copy of Morley's "Bermuda". We have been reading it to night and I am looking forward to reading more of it as soon as I have finished writing polite lies about my Christmas gifts.
>
> Yours for health and happiness
>
> s/ Effendi
>
> December twenty-seventh 1931
> (Box 31, **Daniel Longwell Papers**, Rare Book & Manuscript Library, Columbia University in the City of New York.)

Returning to the speech Longwell gave at the annual meeting of the Texas Institute of Letters, in Dallas, November 16, 1951, Longwell described his relationship with various authors while he worked at Doubleday. Beneath

---

[10] *The Memoirs of a Publisher* by F. N. Doubleday. Doubleday & Co. Inc. 1972. Chapter 9, "My Lifelong Intimacy with Rudyard Kipling", p. 69, speaks of the pneumonia time, but without mention of the rail journeys by private rail car. However, at a New York Hotel, Doubleday did himself keep watch over the patient, "slept on the floor just outside the sick room", and brought in doctors and nurses as well as food for everyone as all the family, excepting Mrs. Kipling, had come down with pneumonia and the oldest child, Josephine, died.

these few words are the unspoken comments on what he did at Doubleday as a book agent for authors. He does not speak of the hard work of promoting books, working with authors to develop attractive and enticing book jackets, and anticipating the book's success all the while convincing others that success is imminent.

But I must get back to my point of what authors should know. I have a final warning for you as authors. If you find a publisher you like and admire, and who likes and admires you, bind him to you with hoops of steel! It's a delicate relationship—but it can be an enduring and a rewarding one. If you find the right publisher, stick with him. Remember he is the frustrated writer working for your success and your and his financial gain ... Sometimes, he may seem to be paying more attention to some new enthusiasm—but that new enthusiasm may be very important to you, too, for the success of the house.

I think I can confess now that, as a younger man, one of my dilemmas was that I once published FOUR GREAT BEST SELLERS by four different women in one year—and managed to come out friends of all four. Fortunately, however, two of the ladies were in England—MARGARET KENNEDY who wrote "The Constant Nymph", and ELIZABETH, COUNTESS RUSSELL, who wrote "The Enchanted April". The two in the U.S. were EDNA FERBER, who had written "So Big", and ELLEN GLASGOW, whose book that year was "Barren Ground", --two wonderful writers and rewarding friends. A few years after this episode, I remember two letters arriving at my office on the same day. Ellen Glasgow's letter from Richmond was dignified, quiet and sweet, but there was a little note in there asking how her novel "The Romantic Comedians", was selling and a small addenda about city girls that referred to the advertising we were giving Edna Ferber's "Show Boat." The other note that day was from Edna Ferber—and she had something to say about—"It sure does take these Southern girls to raise hell."

My boss of those days, F. N. Doubleday, once asked me if I had ever kissed Ellen Glasgow—and I said I had not. He smiles and said he had. The occasion was that she had left Doubleday to go to Macmillan—and after they published one book, she came back to F. N. Doubleday and scolded him for letting her do it. He said he couldn't explain—he just up and kissed her!

I repeat my point—publishing is a very close relationship. Authors and publishers form enduring friendships. (Box 71, **Daniel Longwell Papers**, Rare Book & Manuscript Library, Columbia University in the City of New York)

One of those enduring relationships was with Edna Ferber, author of *So Big*, *Cimarron*, and *Showboat* and it was Edna Ferber who nailed the reality of Dan Longwell at Doubleday in 1923, when he was twenty-four years old. She had just submitted to Russell Doubleday her manuscript of *So Big!* She doubted that it should even be a book and that anyone would read it. She asked him to discuss it with "other members of the firm". It was well-received to her surprise and she writes in her autobiography, *A Peculiar Treasure,* (Doubleday, Doran & Company, Inc., 1939, p. 281) the following:

> There was on the Doubleday staff a chap named Dan Longwell. I knew him as a shy quiet-spoken young fellow who seemed to have an unusual understanding of books and writing and writers. Unlike most publishers and publisher's young men, he knew books not only as merchandise but as a form of creative art. He was sympathetic, intuitive and shrewd—a rare combination. He mapped out a campaign for the selling of *So Big.* Like most of the firm, he believed in the book, but everyone thought his faith in it went much too far. He actually made a substantial bet that the book would sell fifty thousand copies....
>
> That June I went to Europe. The first day out and everyday of the voyage thereafter, the decks, port and starboard, showed an unbroken line of orange color which was the blazing dust jacket of *So Big.* I knew then, astonishingly enough, that I had a best seller on my hands.
>
> *So Big* sold three hundred and twenty-three thousand copies. This was before the day of book clubs and book guilds, to whose members books are sold at reduced prices. Automatically this skyrockets a book's sales figures. ... It received

the Pulitzer Prize for the American Novel in 1924. It was published in Germany, England, Holland, Finland, Sweden, Norway, Poland, Russia, Denmark.

Edna Ferber's relationship with Dan Longwell lasted until her death in 1968. Upon her death, Dan remembered his experience of publishing *So Big!* It is the old story of being in the right place at the right time, but also being prepared when the chances come. Mary put his rememberings on paper.

At Doubleday a (manuscript) came in to Russell Doubleday (younger brother of Effendi) from Edna of a new novel—he didn't know what to do with it, had no promotion feeling about a book. He asked me to read it—they couldn't decide whether to call it "So Big" or "Cabbage Is Beautiful." I read it and was very enthusiastic—said it would sell 100,000 copies and win the Pulitzer Prize. So he sent me to see Edna. (DL was just out of Columbia, still taking night courses there). Edna let me see a little medallion or silhouette of her that C. Leroy Baldridge had done—I took it back to the office and used it as a silhouette on the back cover of the book. She liked that. She had me to dinner. She liked being promoted as a novelist in the class with Ellen Glasgow, Edith Wharton, and she lived up to it. I met her friends. That's where I met Morrie Ernst and George Kaufman and that whole crowd. She was very good to me—she shared her friends. When I heard a rumor the book was to get the Pulitzer, I called her. She was thrilled when she got it and thought I was a very bright boy. I got to be a sort of extra man for her—....

Then *Show Boat* came along and I handled that. The book had gone to press but still had no jacket. Very bad. I went into town and talked to Ed Wilson. He suggested I see Rene Clark, who was just back from Paris with a new impressionistic style. I talked to him and he was willing to try. I had only a couple of hundred dollars to offer him for it..... He came up with a sketch of people walking up a gangplank and made a little dummy with end papers. I went to Edna—She had an apartment on 57ᵗʰ street with a fireplace. I took the dummy out of my pocket and put it on the mantel piece and asked her how she liked it. She loved it. (Box 72, **Daniel Longwell Papers**, Rare Book & Manuscript Library, Columbia University in the City of New York.)

Not in agreement with Dan Longwell, a New York newspaper book reviewer had written that though *So Big!* was selling exceptionally well, he predicted that in a year it would be as forgotten as his review. Instead it became required reading in the literature courses of American public schools and colleges.

There are copies of letters in the files from many famous people heaping praise on Dan Longwell, but what Edna Ferber wrote to Dan after his stroke in 1965 is nothing short of grateful worship. Dan had a debilitating stroke, April 15, 1965. The left arm and leg were weakened but his mind and personality were intact. With Mary to take dictation and then to have letters typed at their Neosho office, Dan could remain in touch with his friends.

June 12, 1965, he dictated a memo to Edna Ferber. Found in Box 72, **Daniel Longwell Papers**, Rare Book & Manuscript Library, Columbia University in the City of New York, in Mary's hand, it reads, "Edna, Now get to work. Stop staring at that blank wall." He knew her working habits. He recalls that once in a while in her past "she came very close to that illusive thing, the American story." He then proceeds to suggest a book be written about "Commerce on the Prairies". He waxes poetic about Jewish peddlers who became department store developers and that in many ways, department stores educated the public and led the public in style and taste. Longwell thought Ferber could develop this theme into a novel.

That letter would have been typed and mailed that week. Probably Mary inserted a note that told Edna of Dan's CVA (cardiovascular accident), which was what the Neosho doctors were calling his stroke.

On June 25, 1965, a letter from 730 Park Avenue, New York, carried Edna's immediate response to Dan:

> Dan dear,
> All writers spend a great deal of time staring at a blank wall. I wouldn't give you a cent for one who didn't.

I loved your letter—but then, any letter from you is an event for me. I am sending you a copy of a book of which you may have heard almost four decades ago. It is called CIMMARON. I have not opened its covers for many, many years, but after I had read and deeply enjoyed your letter I began to thumb through that old novel in order to reassure myself that I had't completely lost my mind.

There is in this book a character named Sol Levy. He was a pack peddler, Jewish, who became a merchant of affluence and of considerable standing even in the narrow society of that Oklahoma community. ... In an old notebook which I haven't seen in years, I remember having scrawled sometime after the publication of CIMARRON, "How about a novel of the Jewish peddler of the mid-century in the United States."...

I am sending you a copy of CIMARRON with markers stuck in a few of the pages on which Sol Levy still wanders to this day.....

My fondest love to you and dear Mary,
s/ Edna.

(Box 72, **Daniel Longwell Papers**, Rare Book & Manuscript Library, Columbia University in the City of New York)

At the Texas Institute of Letters (1951), Longwell proceeded to discuss other authors who became friends and it all seems magical.

STEPHEN VINCENT BENET was such a friend of mine. Another close associate in publishing in those days was the poet, OGDEN NASH. When the manuscript of Benét's *John Brown's Body* came in to the Doubleday office, Ogden and I took it away from everyone else and published it. We were not supposed to handle the manuscript. It should have gone to Steve's old friend, JOHN FARRAR. John was a nice guy, and Ogden and I liked him—but he has since admitted that Ogden and I, fearing anyone else touching the book, published and advertised it single handed. Our admiration was so great that we distrusted anyone but ourselves. It was, of course, the most successful poem published in our time.

STEVE BENÉT was a wonderfully rewarding friend. He and I had a habit of exchanging American place names. In going through a mail order list I happened to come across three towns near one another in Oklahoma named, Okay, Slick and Slim, I would pass them on to Steve. He would come back with more beautiful ones, PRETTY PRAIRIE, MOUNTAIN HOME, AND ROCKY COMFORT, and finally he rewarded me, after Farrar had left the firm, by staying with me to publish his "Ballads and Poems." Never was I so proud of publishing anything!—not even "John Brown's Body"—As BENÉT'S BALLAD AND POEMS, led off by his poem, "American Names….."

I have fallen in love with American names
The sharp names that never get fat,
The snakeskin-titles of mining claims
The plumed war-bonnet of Medicine Hat
Tucson and Deadwood and Lost Mule Flat.

OGDEN NASH and I had wonderful times at Doubleday! With great glee we published the books of P.G. WODEHOUSE, BOOTH TARKINGTON, THORNE SMITH, CLEMENCE DANE, KENNETH ROBERTS, ALDOUS HUXLEY and a host of others. We had a free hand. We had the best list of books in the world. And—we were young and full of enthusiasm. Of course, I didn't think OGDEN NASH was a poet. You never quite see the genius in a friend who has worked with you in some other capacity. But I was bright enough to advise Ogden to send his first poem to the New Yorker. This came about in this way. My office was in Garden City, and I transferred Ogden to an office in New York. We had just installed a teletype between the two offices. One spring day, a single line of teletype was put on my desk.

It read, 'HERE I SIT AT 244 MADISON AVENUE.' An hour passed. Another teletype came in. The second one read, 'AND SAY TO MYSELF, YOU HAVE A RESPONSIBLE JOB, HAVEN'T YOU?

All afternoon the poem came in, line by line,--and when it was finished, I called up Nash and said to send it to The New Yorker. They accepted it, and it was his first paid-for published poem. A few poems later and I lost my assistant. Nash was hired by The New Yorker.... I don't know what the moral is except you never really realize how good your friends are. (Box 71, **Daniel Longwell Papers**, Rare Book & Manuscript Library, Columbia University in the City of New York)

Considering the importance of Ogden Nash in the literary history of this story and America's story, it only seems right to here relate all of that afternoon's lines published in *The New Yorker*, May 3, 1930, under the title, "Spring Comes to Murray Hill."

Here I sit at 244 Madison Avenue,
And say to myself You have a responsible job,
    havenue?
Why then do you fritter away your time on
    this doggerel?
If you have a sore throat you can cure it by
    using a good goggeral,
If you have a sore foot you can get it fixed up by
    a chiropodist,
And you can get your original sin removed by
    St. John the Bopodist.
Why then should this flocculent lassitude be
    incurable?
Kansas City, Kansas, proves that even Kansas
    City needn't be always Missourible.
Up up my soul! This inaction is abominable.
Perhaps it is the result of disturbances
    abdominable.

The pilgrims settled Massachusetts
    in 1620 when they landed on a stone
    hummock.
Maybe if they were here now they
    would settle my stomach.
Oh if I only had the wings of a bird
Instead of being confined on
    Madison Avenue I could soar in a jiffy to
    Second or Third.[11]

One gets a sense of the fun these men had with one another and being in separate offices was no doubt something of a work place adjustment. This is further apparent in the Nash biography which reports that he once compared *The New Yorker* office environment to the aura at Doubleday. He went there on an assignment from Doubleday in his capacity as an editor for the *The New Yorker Album* which Doubleday published. In his words, "I went over to *The New Yorker* for a session on a new collection of their stuff. It's the dullest office in New York. I'm sure there's much more frolicsome wit in 90% of our freight yards."

No wonder Mary Longwell asked Ogden Nash to speak to the Friends of the Columbia Libraries, on "Reminiscences of Dan Longwell."[12] He tells what fun it was to work with

---

[11] Nash, Ogden, Many Years Ago, Little, Brown, and Company, Boston: 1931, pp. 249. Copyright © 1931 by Ogden Nash, renewed. Reprinted by permission of Curtis Brown, Ltd. Copyright © 1945 by Ogden Nash, renewed.
Reprinted by permission of Curtis Brown, Ltd.

[12] Nash, Ogden, "Reminiscences of Dan Longwell," *Columbia Library Columns*, Vol. XIX, May 1970, University of Columbia, New York

his friend at Doubleday and in the telling, one wishes one could have been there with them.

The "Reminiscences of Dan Longwell" by Ogden Nash date to March of 1925. He said that Dan rescued him "from the decaying empire of Baron G. Collier, the king of street car advertising," where he had worked for two years but was "not having much fun." He said he met Dan through Doubleday's publishing a children's book that Nash and a friend had written. Nash described his first work with Longwell at Doubleday.

> At the moment he was advertising manager and he had just lost his assistant.... His departure left a vacancy in the assistant's chair which Dan offered to me. He was able to offer me only $90 a month, and, in addition to taking the loss in salary, I had to buy a commutation ticket, because I was living in New York and Doubleday's was in Garden City.
>
> He had the faculty of inspiring people with great excitement. It was fun to work with him. He taught me how to write a letter.... He taught me to write as if I were talking, not in a smarmy way, to the person I was writing to; to be clear and to the point, and to say what I wanted to say. ...
>
> Aside from the hard work there was also, I am happy to say, a certain amount of play. Some of our most relaxed moments were spent at the Columbia University Club on 43rd Street, even though I was a Harvard dropout, ... Dan would occasionally take me and another friend from

Doubleday's in there, and there was an expert bartender. This was during Prohibition but they made an old fashion there. In fact, I think for the first ten years of my drinking life I did not think you could make an old fashion with anything except scotch. It was very good…. Dan was a hardboiled bachelor in those days. He had his work. There were no girls in his life whatever, and the joke among our friends in Garden City, was that Dan's entire love life consisted of the kiss he blew to Edna Ferber every year when she embarked on her annual voyage to Europe.

He was an earnest golfer… The one thing that emerged from our golf days together was that one afternoon, a Saturday …, we had been asked to play golf at Piping Rock by Mr. Russell Doubleday, one of the older members of the establishment. It was in the late 20's, on the day after Admiral Byrd had accomplished some peculiar feat in the Antarctic. While we were relaxing at the 19th hole, I scrawled a bit of doggerel on the back of what was, I guess, a scorecard. Dan retrieved it and disappeared, presumably to deposit it in an appropriate place. I thought no more about it until the next morning when I picked up "The Conning Tower" in the *New York World*….In "The Conning Tower" which was the goal of every aspiring writer, I read what I had written on the score card, stimulated by Mr. Russell Doubleday and a tom collins.

Huzza, Huzza for Admiral Byrd
About whom many fine things I have
heard.

Huzza Huzza for the gallant crew
About whom many fine things have I
heard too.
Huzza Huzza for their spirit of
adventure,
So very different from senile dementia.
And another Huzza for the USA
Who produces so many heroes like
they.[13]

Dan in his temporary absence had written out
a telegram and sent it to FPA (Frank P. Adams,
syndicated New York columnist who wrote witty
poems in his columns), and in so doing had set my
foot on the first rung of the literary ladder.

In return for that I wrote him a little verse for
himself alone.

L is for the leader of this grand old firm,
O is for his eyes of blue,
N for his ideals and his spirit of cooperation,
G for his influence on me and you.
W for his ability to collect and coordinate
    facts,
E double L for the labor saving card index
    system he put through.
Put them all together, they spell LONGWELL,
And what the hell did you expect them to do?

---

[13] First published in "The Conning Tower", *New York World*. Date unknown;
year, 1929. **Reprinted by permission of Curtis Brown, Ltd.**
Copyright © 1931 by Ogden Nash, renewed. Copyright © 1945 by Ogden
Nash, renewed. Reprinted by permission of Curtis Brown, Ltd.

...So he kept me going at my own work in addition to working at top speed for him and for Doubleday....[14]

(Columbia Library Columns Magazine, cited in footnote 12, Box 47, **Daniel Longwell Papers**, Rare Book & Manuscript Library, Columbia University in the City of New York)

Now at Doubleday both Nash and Longwell were established and working at top speed. An actor named Roland Young brought them a children's book under the title, *"Not for Children."* It was about animals and all in verse. Some of them were good and memorable. For example,

> Here we behold the jolly flea
> We cannot tell the he from she.
> But he can tell and so can she.

Some of the other verses were not as winsome and Nash proceeded to edit in some of his own suggestions which Young rejected. However Longwell thought that Nash had hit upon something and he suggested Nash try a similar book on his own. One of the Nash examples that Mr. Young turned down was one which became quite famous for Nash and it was the basis of his first book: "The Turtle."

But Nash did not just write verse for publication, he also wrote such when teasing Longwell about duck hunting

---

[14] Grammar and punctuation, or lack thereof, in this excerpt is as it is in the original.

at the Doubleday plantation in South Carolina. Upon Dan's return to the office, Nash thought he was telling of accomplishments in duck hunting that, in "hunter fashion" were a little exaggerated. Hence the following verse from "The Hunter".[15]

> This grownup man, with talk and luck
> Is hoping to outwit a duck.
> (Box 47, **Daniel Longwell Papers**, Rare Book
> & Manuscript Library, Columbia University in
> the City of New York)

The Crime Club

In 1927, Daniel Longwell's life at Doubleday began to double up and even though it is a poor pun, it is the truth. The publishing company sent him to England. His passport, number 439512, issued July 16th, 1927, (Box 47, **Daniel Longwell Papers**, Rare Book & Manuscript Library, Columbia University in the City of New York), describes him as 5 foot 10 inches; hair: black; eyes: blue; born: Omaha, Nebraska, July 11, 1899; occupation: Publisher. The Bearer's foreign address is c/o William Heineman, 20-22 Bedford Street, London, W.C.I. In case of death or accident the person to notify was Lawrence McNaughton, Doubleday Page & Co., Garden City, N.Y. He left New York July 27, 1927, and entered the UK through Glasgow, Scotland, August 1, 1927.

---

[15] Location of publication unknown.

The photo of this twenty-eight year old shows a slender, young man with a long face and neck, fair amount of hair, business suit with sloping shoulders over a white shirt and tie. The crossing of the Atlantic was by ship followed by a train to London from Glasgow. Surely he was intrigued with the agricultural villages and landscape with its small fields and stone walls in contrast to the large fields and barbed-wire he knew in the Missouri/Nebraska/South Dakota, Iowa landscape.

Doubleday had purchased the Heinemann firm and they sent Dan to England to learn about publishing techniques and to become acquainted with the likes of Lord Beaverbrook. From that meeting Longwell met Randolph Churchill and from THAT meeting he met Winston Spencer Churchill. All this would be the foundation and cornerstone of one of Longwell's next adventures.

Being in the right place at the right time is often the basis of career success. Apparently Dan's career was paralleling the Doubleday publishing company. His own recollections and words are the best record. We have the "D.L. Notes on Book Publishing" which seem to be in keeping with other such notes from 1962 to 1963 (Box 72, **Daniel Longwell Papers**, Rare Book & Manuscript Library, Columbia University in the City of New York).

Building up the Windmill Press of the Heinemann firm gave Longwell an exposure to English and European publishing motifs that became the foundation for contacts and practices that would be used within the Doubleday structures after he returned to the United States. One of these imported ideas took the form of the "Crime Club" which became the baby of Nash and Longwell.

First is Longwell's story on the subject.

My first recollection of the Crime Club was being called into John Farrar's office shortly after the merger of Doubleday, Page and Company and the George H. Doran Company and discussing detective stories published by both companies with him. The Doran Company had a small list of detective stories [and I] remember that the author of BULLDOG DRUMMOND was the most prominent. Russell Doubleday, Vice President of Doubleday, Page and Company was a detective story ham and he had recently secured Edgar Wallace for the Doubleday list. ….

John Farrar wanted some scheme to sell detective stories as a distinctively Doubleday-Doran list. I worked out a scheme for publishing three or four detective stories a month under a distinctive trademark and submitted it to Farrar. John Farrar received this somewhat impatiently and said no, he wanted something like Book-of-the-Month Club. Doubleday was a great mail order house and we knew that only books that offered self-improvement or a great value could be sold successfully by mail. The detective story was strictly an entertainment book and was largely popular through circulating libraries at that time.

The average detective story sold between 2500 and 3500 and that was about the market. ...

George Stevens was then one of my assistants and a very brilliant fellow, so I took my memo to him and explained Farrar's wishes. Stevens wrote a memorandum suggesting a simulated book club which would not depend on straight mail orders but would work through the book stores securing members through booksellers.

I had just returned from a summer in England working at William Heinemann for Doubleday. Doubleday then owned William Heinemann and were building the Windmill Press for them. C.S. "Charles" Evans was editorial director of Heinemann and he took me on a week-end visit to F. Tennyson Jesse's home at Cut-Mill near Chester, England.

At that time, criminology was a great fad in England. There was a group called "Crimes Club." These were amateur criminologists who centered around William Roughhead who was then in the process of writing his famous series of Scottish trials....

Marie Bellok Lownes who was in the middle of writing her murder story, THE STORY OF IVY, was one of the company. She and F. Tennyson Jesse and Charley Evans were part of a group who called themselves "The Crimes Club Jr." They had prepared notes and papers and diagrams and after dinner they had a lengthy discussion on <u>The Mass Murders of Dusseldorf</u>.

It was a learned but lurid evening and I did not sleep too well in the top bedroom in the tower of the old Cut-Mill—what with owls hooting and water dripping over the mill wheel outside my window. I protested to my host next morning at breakfast that the house was haunted.

But it turned out that the rustling and clanking I heard during the night was Mrs. Marie Bellok Lownes fixing herself a cup of tea for her insomnia. It seemed she carried her own tea making outfit with her and the rustlings I had heard during the night and the clankings were her dressing gown brushing the floor and the rattle of the tea things. With the noises of the night fresh in my mind it was easy to suggest that George Stephens' scheme be called "The Crime Club." The name was immediately suggested and Alan Rhinehart was put in charge of coordinating the publication of the detective stories from the combined Doubleday-Doran lists. I believe this was in the summer of 1928.

…It was never a mail order effort like Book-of-the-Month Club: it was all to be done through book stores. To give it an entity, I also took steps through the lawyers to incorporate it in the State of New York, so it became Crime Club, Inc. (Box 72, **Daniel Longwell Papers**, Rare Book & Manuscript Library, Columbia University in the City of New York).

Ogden Nash had a part in the Crime Club, too, and he reports about it in his eulogy of Longwell. One interesting point is that Nash credits Longwell with putting Edgar Wallace on the Doubleday list, but Longwell, as you read above, credits Russell Doubleday with having signed him up. Nevertheless, this is Ogden Nash's recollection from his eulogy for Longwell.

Nash recalled:

> [Dan] moved over to England where he picked up the idea of the Crime Club. There was at that time an association of detective story writers who gathered together to discuss their work; rather a closed corporation, with only the crème de la crème of the mystery story writers allowed into it. Dan came back and persuaded the Doubleday top brass to form a subsidiary called the Crime Club, of which I was one of the editors. Nobody in America had thought of picking up the works of Edgar Wallace, but Dan brought back with him God knows how many Edgar Wallace books, and had the idea of publishing one a month for twelve months—which we did with enormous success. We absolutely swamped the public with copies of books by Edgar Wallace, and they are still to be found in reprint today. (Box 6, **Daniel Longwell Papers**, Rare Book & Manuscript Library, Columbia University in the City of New York; and Columbia Library Columns, Butler Library, Columbia University, New York, New York)

Twenty-five years later there in a newspaper or magazine column with the title "On the Books" dated 1953, with a subtitle, "Twenty-five Years of Murder" Longwell mentioned many of the founders and named places of employment at the time, such as John Farrar of Farrar, Straus & Young; Dan Longwell of LIFE magazine; and the first Crime Club editor, Ogden Nash. It reported that Nash helped publicize the new outfit by buying two human skulls from a medical school and lending them to bookstores for window displays. It also reported that the biggest producer in the early days was Edgar Wallace whose books brought in $250,000 in the first four years of the Crime Club. These lucrative years marked the first years of the Great Depression, beginning with the Stock Market Crash of 1929 and lasting well into the 1930's.[16] (Box 24, **Daniel Longwell Papers**, Rare Book & Manuscript Library, Columbia University in the City of New York).

---

[16] Later (1959-60) when I would spend my college "Junior Year Abroad" at the University of Glasgow, Mr. and Mrs. Longwell were good neighbors and took an interest in my own journey, doing what they could to show me the world outside of Neosho. I was only twenty at the time, and, as we Midwesterners were totally insulated, they arranged for me to meet an English Professor of Radcliffe, Dr. Dean Mace on board the *Liberté*. I met with Dr. Mace with some trepidation. That was a silly fear because he was kind and assured me that the Southern girls he had in his classes came in with sweet polite voices but then would knock the top off the class curve. This was confidence building because not only was I under the double quagmire of a Midwestern public high school and a southern girls' college, I was also only a sophomore "masquerading" as a junior. I think Mr. Longwell understood the importance of a confident ego over Midwestern reticence when one journeys out of one's comfort zone. In this instant, I borrowed some of Mr. Longwell's confidence. It has been a special gift for me to share the syncronicities of research and to relish the embryonal in the lives in the Longwells' careers. It was also enlightening and encouraging to learn that Dean Mace's hometown was Neosho, MO.

CHAPTER THREE

TRANSITIONING FROM DOUBLEDAY TO TIME INC.

"He was a man of strong ideas, a kind of powerful and benevolent natural force. His voice was not as loud as the thunder, but his illumination lasted longer than the lightning."

—Ogden Nash, Columbia Library Columns, Butler Library, Columbia University, New York, New York, p. 13

On January 26th of 1934, Longwell wrote to his good friend, Stephen Vincent Benét (Box 11, **Daniel Longwell Papers**, Rare Book & Manuscript Library, Columbia University in the City of New York) that he had come into a document of his family history which was clear Americana. It was the record book from the Posey Township Baptist Church of Christ, Posey Township, Indiana. He states that the records note the death of his Great-grandfather of a "century ago" with this "epitaph":

Brother Longwell has gone to his rest
Our meetings now are sad and drear
We look at the chair where so often he sat
But alas: Brother Longwell's not there.

He continues the letter saying they must get together to do an American Anthology "sometime." A group of letters that Longwell wrote in early 1934 give one a sense that his life is about to take a new turn.

January 30, 1934, Frank Nelson Doubleday, the master, Effendi, died. His tall son, Nelson, would now lead the company. Nelson was Daniel Longwell's best friend, but he had not been able to get Dan onto his Board of Directors. In February Longwell wrote to Edna Ferber about her letter of sympathy to Nelson being just the right things said and appreciated. He also reported that Nelson and his wife Ellen were soon off to Europe.

On April 13, 1934, Longwell mailed a hand-written six-page letter to childhood friends in Neosho who had married one another, apologizing for not having visited them at the time of his mother's death two years before. Jean Wood Lowder had been his eighth grade teacher at Ragan School and her husband, Knox Lowder, had been Daniel's best friend in the one-room school. Dan writes to them of his brothers and their families, Alfred in Philadelphia and Jim in New Brunswick, Georgia. He also summarized his own history as he saw it at that date.

Dear Jean,

I have been meaning to write you for I do not know how long. The last time I was in Missouri was two years ago at the time of Mother's death, and I reached for the phone twice that time meaning to call you and ask if I couldn't come down to Neosho for a day. Do write and tell me how you and Knox (Lowder) are and how many children you and Jennie have. And do give my best to Bob and Waltine and anyone who is there and remembers me.

…Alfred is in Philadelphia and has two fine boys. Jim is the manager of one of the W. T. Grant stores in Brunswick, Georgia, married to a very nice girl from Baton Rouge, and they expect their first child this summer.

Me. I turned out to be the ne'er do well of the family. I came East to university for five or six years, started in publishing books, and have stayed with the same company for all this time. I have the theory that I have a quiet life—but I seem to have got all over Europe and the United States without getting back to Neosho—which more or less remains home to me.

But I've had a lot of fun, lived comfortably and have had enough money for my needs—which I suppose is lucky.

… do you suppose I could drop off in Neosho sometime when I am going west and come down and see you both?

I hope this letter finds you – and finds you both well and happy.

With love,

Dan Longwell

P.S. Mother used to tell me she used to write to you. I suppose she told you I never married—so have no family—and small prospects of ever taking such a great step now that I am a middle aged bachelor, set in his ways. (Author's Personal Collection, Courtesy of the Lowder-Wolfe Family, Neosho, MO)

One can almost see Dan hunched over his desk at Doubleday writing his friends as he takes leave of his book publishing life. His office was lovely and comfortable and next to his friend, Nelson Doubleday. His heavy eyebrows pinched over clear but tired blue eyes, he listened to the presses and tried to assess his situation with pen and ink. Like the common man he was, with thoughts of ambition and life roiling in his mind, he practiced his thoughts by writing people far from the scene.

But like the uncommon man he was, the May 1934 decision demanded he write those close by and he began that task in June. He wrote each person an individual letter, some were journalists and some were book authors.

Among the journalists was Charles Merz who was an associate editor of the *New York Times* and who would become the editor-in-chief in 1938. Merz was also a transplant from the Midwest: Sandusky, Ohio; and the Ivy League, Yale. Longwell wrote June 7, 1934:

Dear` Charlie,

Before someone else tells you, I am leaving Garden City to go with Harry Luce on TIME and FORTUNE. I don't know just what I am going to do there as yet, but I am depending on having your blessings and good wishes, and an awful lot of help as I try to learn the job of being a journalist.

It has been a wretched thing leaving here. I knew but had no real realization of my deep affection and pride in the place. I am sorry I couldn't see you and talk about this. As you know, the question has been up for two or three years and finally I simply had to realize that my ambitions lie along that line and not in book publishing.

I hope I see you and Evelyn very soon.

Sincerely, Daniel Longwell

(Box 17, **Daniel Longwell Papers**, Rare Book & Manuscript Library, Columbia University in the City of New York.)

He wrote to MacKinlay Kantor in Westfield, New Jersey, on June 7, 1934 and gives additional information and encloses a news clip.

Dear Kantor:

I would like to read "The Hound-Tuner of Calloway". I've heard of that many, many times. Do send it to me….I shall be in Garden City until June 15th – and after that with TIME-FORTUNE in the Chrysler Building in New York. I am moving to town, and I hope I shall have more of a chance to see both you and Mrs. Kantor.

I am enclosing a different sort of hound dog story from the Missouri hills, thinking it may interest you.

Sincerely, Daniel Longwell
(Box 18, **Daniel Longwell Papers**, Rare Book & Manuscript Library, Columbia University in the City of New York)

I believe that particular "hound dog story" became *The Voice of Bugle Ann* by MacKinlay Kantor (Doubleday, 1935).

June 8, 1934, Longwell wrote to Sinclair Lewis, who with his wife, Dorothy Thompson, was living in South Pomfret, Vermont, at their estate, Twin Farms, just east of Barnard, VT.

Dear Lewis:

As you will probably hear in due time, I am leaving Garden City to go with TIME and FORTUNE magazines. Though it is no doubt sudden news to some people, it is not a sudden thing. I have been more or less contemplating going with those fellows for several years. I almost started in business with them before the first issue of TIME was put out so it is a long association. I don't know just what I am going to do yet, and I don't suppose they do, but I am to be more or less as I understand it, editorial assistant to Harry Luce who is president of the company and editor of TIME and FORTUNE. I almost went last year, and practically did go with them two years ago. I am writing you so there won't be any misunderstanding in your mind. I am scared to death because I have never tried anything like this before and as a matter of fact, I have never quit a job before. Nelson and Harry and Hessian and all the fellows here have been simply swell about it. They aren't only the best fellows in the world, but they are, I think, the best publishers too. They will not need any help from me but should they ever with any of your books, I will drop everything I am doing and help them because the publishing of ANN VICKERS and WORK OF ART, and knowing you, has given me as much pleasure and pride as anything I have done in publishing.[17]

Sincerely yours, Daniel Longwell.

P.S. Of course you know it has always been my private ambition to be Secretary of War someday and this step I hope will eventually lead to that. And by the way, if I do get to be Secretary of War, I will get out a general order that you get flourishes and ruffles at any Army Post you visit. (Box 17, **Daniel Longwell Papers**, Rare Book & Manuscript Library, Columbia University in the City of New York)

---

[17] Mark Schorer's *Sinclair Lewis—An American* describes Lewis's winning and accepting the Nobel Prize for Literature in 1931. Lewis who had turned down the Pulitzer Prize in 1926 for his novel, *Arrowsmith*, accepted the Nobel because it is for an author's body of work. In Lewis's opinion the Pulitzer recognition had limited merit.

Longwell's experience of luring Lewis to Doubleday is characteristic of his determination and creativity. Lewis had been awarded the Nobel Prize for Literature in 1931, but had not been happy with his publisher and he began to cast about for a new publishing house. It should be noted again that there was a lot of literature that was crossing the Atlantic especially between London and New York, and writers and editors were crossing with it. Doubleday, Doran & Co. owned William Heinemann, Ltd. And Heinemann editor, A. S. Frere, knew Longwell and fortuitously was an old friend of Sinclair Lewis. Naturally he was promoting the Doubleday, Doran house to get Lewis on their list. It is rather interesting that Schorer's book was able to create a scene of Longwell making a presentation to Lewis in 1931. Schorer wrote,

> …Doubleday, Doran & Company was an early contender [for Lewis' books]. An energetic young promotions man in the firm, Daniel Longwell, was determined to get at least his section of Doubleday out of the red, and he persuaded Nelson Doubleday to invite Lewis to lunch at Garden City, Long Island, where the firm's offices then were. Lewis accepted and Longwell prepared a full "presentation" as Madison Avenue now calls the layout of a promotion program: this is what they would do for the still nonexistent next novel. What they would do for Lewis more specifically was to give him a $25,000 advance against unearned royalties, a contract with a $25,000 advertising guarantee, and royalty rates

beginning at 15 per cent. Longwell planned to print 60,000 copies of whatever book came in from Lewis, and if they sold them, they would more than break even. On the drive back to Manhattan from Garden City with Frere, Lewis decided that he would go with Doubleday, and he had the car stopped and telephoned back to say so and to ask that the proposed contract be drawn up. "I like you," [Lewis] is reported to have said, "You're so God-damned *commercial!*" (Schorer, p.567)

Longwell was now the "Publisher's Young Man" and "Grub Street Runner" for Sinclair Lewis. With Lewis as his charge, everything Morley had written was writ large indeed. Longwell's promotional skills were in high gear and so were Lewis's. Having completed *Ann Vickers* and seeing it serialized in *Redbook*, seemed to vindicate Lewis' approach to getting "editorial" approval which was to have a party and thrust pages on his guests to read and respond (Schorer, p 575).

Longwell also had created plans for a new sort of promotion for *Ann Vickers* (1933). He was going to print a very limited first edition, only 2,350 copies. And he would only send one first edition with each order of twenty five copies of the regular printing. This caused a bit of a stir in the publishing community but it also caused great prepublication interest. Longwell's stock in the trade was creating prepublication interest which usually created word-of-mouth advertising which in his opinion was the best advertising for a book. He anticipated selling 100,000 copies of *Ann Vickers* in the first year. According to Schorer (p. 583), the novel finally went to 133,849 copies counting all editions. "Daniel Longwell's section of Doubleday was out of the red." Nelson Doubleday was with his new author in London and the two of them phoned Longwell. This was Longwell's first transatlantic call. Sinclair Lewis wanted to tell him "how delighted he was with the sale of *Ann Vickers* and with everything that Longwell had done for that book."

It should amuse the reader to note that the second novel referred to in this letter was the less successful *Work of Art* (1934) which only sold about 50,000 copies. Longwell had advertising money left over, but sales had stopped. He suggested they call in Lewis and explain how things were which they did. After explaining everything they had done from prepublication up to that day, they asked Lewis what he would do. Longwell, through Schorer, reports that Lewis immediately replied, "I'd stop advertising" (Schorer p. 598). This meant that Doubleday would retain the advertising dollars left over so no wonder they all "went out for a drink."

A little later, Lewis went to Austria. On January 15, 1933, he wrote, not typed, this letter to Longwell (Box 5, **Daniel Longwell Papers**, Rare Book & Manuscript Library, Columbia University in the City of New York).

Dear Dan:

Ten days now!

I have your letters of Dec. 17, & Jan 4, with vast envelopes of posters, cards, bulletins. I have never seen such a promotion campaign. Has there even been one?—that is, of course, ignoring such boob-bumping tripe=telling as the Book Supply Co. used to do for Harold Bell Wright in all the country stories. I don't believe there has been too much circusing, because the whole book=business has been so drab this past year that it needed a little color & noise.

I am working steadily on the plan for the new novel. I imagine it will be two & a half or three months before I start the actual MS, but by then half the real <u>work</u> will be done. Writing a novel is easy. You just learn all about some aspect of human life & then you think-up some elegant names for characters & one joke about sex & then you sit down & put all three of them together.[18]

Ever, (signed) S Lewis

Surely Christopher Morley was top of the list. Longwell's letter of June 8, 1934, is a man to man letter even though it reads more like son to father. Remember, the two first met when Dan was a clerk at the bookstore at Penn station.

Dear Chris:

I suppose you have heard that I am leaving Garden City to go with TIME and FORTUNE. It has been a wretched experience. I am so fond of all these fellows and so much of my pride and ambition lies in this place that only my greater

---

[18] The equal signs in this note are in the original, hand-written material, taking the place of the customary dashes.

ambition in wanting to be sometime a journalist or at least a periodical publisher, and the realization that I was getting along in years and if I were going to do something in journalism I had better be getting at it, that finally prompted me to take this step.

I cannot leave, Chris, without telling you that you and your books not only taught me what I know about this trade, but have given me more fun and pride than almost anything else.

(Box 18, **Daniel Longwell Papers**, Rare Book & Manuscript Library, Columbia University in the City of New York)

Immediately on his letterhead stationary of *The Saturday Review of Literature,* listing himself as Contributing Editor, Christopher Morley replies on June 11, 1934. (Box 6, **Daniel Longwell Papers**, Rare Book & Manuscript Library, Columbia University in the City of New York)

Dear Dan,

It was kind of you old son to write me that nice note and I hasten to congratulate. I know it is a wrench leaving Garden City but at the same time I do realize what great possibilities there will be in the magazine field. When you have time let's eat lunch together and chew the whole thing over. ….

With every affectionate greeting,

Yours always,

(signed) Chris

Another letter was sent to H.L. Mencken who was then living in Baltimore, Maryland.

> 704 Cathedral Street
> June 11, 1934
> Dear Mencken:
>
> I read in the papers the other day that you advised all managing editors to stop at thirty-five and do something else. In spite of your advice, I am, at almost thirty-five going to go into journalism. I'm leaving Doubleday's, with great regret and reluctance, and going to TIME and FORTUNE. I am going to be some sort of personal editorial assistant to Harry Luce the editor of the magazines—I don't know quite what yet. He's an old friend and we've been debating this change for several years.
>
> I hope I have your and Mrs. Mencken's good wishes. Meeting you both has been one of the nicest experiences I've had in book publishing.
>
> Sincerely yours,
Daniel Longwell

(Box 5, **Daniel Longwell Papers**, Rare Book & Manuscript Library, Columbia University in the City of New York)

This brought forth an immediate response dated June 14, 1934.

Dear Longwell:

The best of luck to you! The post looks interesting indeed, and I am certain that you'll bring a lot of valuable skill and experience to it. My pastor is instructed to pray for you.

My wife and I still hope that we'll see you soon in Baltimore.

Sincerely yours,
(Signed) HL Mencken

(Box 5, **Daniel Longwell Papers**, Rare Book & Manuscript Library, Columbia University in the City of New York)

Longwell's two most successful female writers, Edna Ferber and Ellen Glasgow reacted differently to his announced departure. Doubleday, Doran and Company was somewhat concerned that these two authors might bolt to another publishing house.

Ellen Glasgow was a well-established writer living at One West Main Street, Richmond, VA. The Doubleday house had published her books since 1900. In April, 1968, Longwell related the following to Mary and she typed his recollections:

At one point her contract was ready to be renegotiated and it was feared she might be going with Knopf publishing. Longwell suggested they offer her $5,000 in advance, [and] $5,000 for advertising but she would have to take a 5% cut in royalties from 20% to 15%. Russell

Doubleday went to see her and presented the idea of Doubleday's "bright young man." It was a gamble, but Ellen was a gambler so Doubleday sent Daniel Longwell to Richmond; [he] went to the hotel, called on her and it was instant friendship. He moved to her house and worked with her on plans for the book—BARREN GROUND. (Box 72, **Daniel Longwell Papers**, Rare Book & Manuscript Library, Columbia University in the City of New York)

According to a compilation of her letters, *Letters of Ellen Glasgow* (Rouse, 1958) Daniel Longwell was involved with designing a book jacket for *The Battle-Ground*, which was to be reprinted from the 1902 edition. She seems to have been pleased with Longwell's suggestions and he became the Doubleday "Publisher's Young Man" to her. Because Longwell had also become close with the Doubleday family, he was often invited to spend time at their plantation, Bonny Hall, at Yamassee, South Carolina. Stopping at Miss Glasgow's home in Richmond, Virginia, was not out of the way for this "Publisher's Young Man."

Glasgow wrote Longwell on February 6, 1934, (Box 72, original letter, **Daniel Longwell Papers**, Rare Book & Manuscript Library, Columbia University in the City of New York). She thanks him for sending her an essay with which she agrees and then closes with "We are expecting you soon, either this week-end or the next. There are things I wish to talk over. As usual, I am not satisfied with the way of the publishing world."

Years later, in a letter of January 5, 1957, (Box 83, **Daniel Longwell Papers**, Rare Book & Manuscript Library, Columbia University in the City of New York) Longwell recalls recommending a southern gentleman, George Gibson, as a non-resident member of New York's Century Club. Longwell refers to his former visits to Richmond and Miss Glasgow.

> George used to be such a delightful Sunday night supper visitor at Miss Ellen Glasgow's when I was taking care of her literary affairs. Miss Glasgow was well aware of the fact that I visited a little more than was needful, but she was also well aware of the fact that the Gibson house was up on Monument Avenue and I was drawn there too. (Box 83, **Daniel Longwell Papers**, Rare Book & Manuscript Library, Columbia University in the City of New York).

In the *The Letters of Ellen Glasgow* (Rouse, 1958, p. 156), Rouse references her writing to her friend and agent Irita Van Doren on June 9, 1934, that Dan has left Doubleday, Doran. Glasgow instructed Van Doren, to begin discussions with other publishing houses such as Harcourt or Houghton, Mifflin.

By July 5, 1934, Longwell had moved to the Luce offices but wrote to Nelson Doubleday that "there are loads of rumors around about Glasgow…but I think she will not make any decision until the first of next year…." And in that same letter Longwell told Doubleday he "had a note from Ferber in which she seems to be somewhat disgusted about your not calling her up."

It seems that the "gruntling" of disgruntled authors had departed with Longwell. He was called back in to try and "gruntle" Glasgow back into the fold. In an August 12, 1934, letter to Irita Van Doren, Glasgow related that Nelson Doubleday had been really lovely and appealing but she had made her decision to go with Mr. Harcourt of Harcourt, Brace. She wrote that Longwell had come down the night before and stayed two hours trying to persuade her not to leave Doubleday's. Ellen Glasgow died in 1945, at the age of 72, without ever returning to Doubleday publishing.

Edna Ferber had a different reaction. First of all she sent Dan a Western Union telegram from Westport, Connecticut, June 18, 1934. It read,

> DEAR DAN TIME AND FORTUNE LOVE
> AND LUCK FERBER.

> (Box 9, **Daniel Longwell Papers**, Rare Book
> & Manuscript Library, Columbia University in
> the City of New York)

In August she typed a two-page letter instructing him that he should be writing as a chief occupation. She had great respect for his sensitivity and his way with words. She did not leave her publisher, but she did keep writing to Dan and he continued to promote her, just from a different venue. Their friendship lasted a lifetime, but on August 11, 1934, she wrote him,

> …Now listen to Ferber. You write as you've
> written me—you write a piece about Washington
> and Baltimore—and put it in TIME. Or in
> FORTUNE. Or in something. Let them have a real
> piece of writing for once in their meager columns.
> (Box 9, **Daniel Longwell Papers**, Rare Book &
> Manuscript Library, Columbia University in the
> City of New York)

Little did she know that Daniel Longwell did not have
"meager columns" in mind. He was moving toward large
pages with large photographs and literature writ large

In 1939, Ferber published her first autobiography, and of
course sent Longwell a copy. His letter to her February 5,
tells a little of their mutual admiration.

> My dear Edna,
> Your book is very good. It is personal, lively,
> and has a great tug of the country in it. I think
> you underrate your short stories and yourself. …
> I was very touched by your generous mention
> of me and even more touched when I realized that
> the reason you missed the openings of *Show Boat*
> and *Dinner at Eight* was because you gave me
> your tickets. (Box 15, **Daniel Longwell Papers**,
> Rare Book & Manuscript Library, Columbia
> University in the City of New York)

In 1952, the Doubleday house asked Longwell if he
would write a biography of Ferber. In that year he had
serious issues with his lungs so it was decided they would

look for someone else to prepare it. As it turned out, in 1963 Ferber continued her own story in a second autobiography.

Booth Tarkington was thirty years Longwell's senior but Longwell wrote him on June 15, 1934.

> Dear Mr. Tarkington:
>
> Mr. Russell Doubleday may have told you that I am leaving Garden City to TIME and FORTUNE magazines....
>
> I am to be some sort of special assistant to Henry R. Luce, the President of TIME INC.. One doesn't, however, leave such good friends as these, nor the best publishing house in the country without being very greatly affected. After all, Effendi, Russell and the rest of them here in Garden City have more or less brought me up and have been very good to me. Nelson Doubleday has been my closest friend.
>
> I merely wanted you to know all this. Added to this, one of my greatest pleasures has been knowing you and working with your books, and knowing Kenneth Roberts whom you sent to us, and working with his books. I shall miss all of that enormously. I may no longer be able to play a part in the publishing of your books but certainly neither of you can ever lose me as a reader. (Box 21, **Daniel Longwell Papers**, Rare Book & Manuscript Library, Columbia University in the City of New York)

Tarkington wrote back and Longwell addressed him a second letter on July 14, 1934. As always, Longwell includes a little more amusing history, and, no doubt Tarkington was delighted to learn about this insider's shenanigan.

Dear Booth Tarkington:

How very nice of you to write me as you did. I would rather have your best wishes than almost anyone's –I'm doubly grateful in that they just so happened to have been written on my birthday.

When I was playing such a part as I did in the publishing of your books, I did not dare tell you how very much I like and admired them. I've been slowly collecting them for ten years—have most of them.

Ogden Nash and I agreed the other day that of all the good times we had when we were together in Garden City, the one we enjoyed the most was publishing THE PLUTOCRAT and the success of that book. We went so far in our enthusiasm that Upton Sinclair, in his book about advertising, used some of our efforts as alarming examples of the way advertising corrupted the public mind. He hadn't read the book—but he said we were making a hero of a businessman in our advertising. Nash and I were so delighted that we both bought copies of Sinclair's book and sent them to him asking for autographs. Not knowing who we were he wrote us very nice inscriptions and we were very proud of the books.

You have always had me as a devoted reader and you always shall. (Box 21, **Daniel Longwell**

Papers, Rare Book & Manuscript Library, Columbia University in the City of New York)

And since I have mentioned and quoted Tarkington, it is only right that I also mention and quote Kenneth Roberts. Roberts was fourteen years older than Tarkington. Tarkington had taken Roberts in hand and mentored him about writing, even did quite a bit of editing for him and then advised him to use Doubleday as his publisher. Longwell wrote Roberts a six-paragraph letter on June 8, 1934, and I quote in part:

> Dear Ken:
>
> I have some startling news for you and that is the fact that I am leaving Doubleday the middle of this month. One of my chief regrets in going is that I shall not be able to work with your books though my ambition for them will remain constant. You cannot lose me as a reader of these books and a rooter of their very great importance. One of the reasons why I am staying on here until the middle of the month is to arrange anything I can for your books so there won't be any hold up in this company with activities for them….
>
> Frankly, this is so well organized a place with such capable people that I am able to step out without any great change in operations…I hope I don't lose complete touch with you…I do think, Ken, you have tremendous things ahead of you. I know you are discouraged, but don't let anything keep you from finishing those books. (Box 20, **Daniel Longwell Papers**, Rare Book &

Manuscript Library, Columbia University in the City of New York.)

Roberts wrote back to Longwell on September 15, 1934, from his home in Kennebunk Beach, Maine. Roberts was a witty fellow, full of vigor and righteous indignation about conservation, contracts and correspondence. He reports to Longwell that other publishers are after him. You can hear the country in his letter.

> Dear Dan:
>
> It seems a hell of a long time since I had your letter…
>
> I don't quite know what started so many publishers baying at my heels all of a sudden; but they certainly started, and some of them are still baying. All very complimentary, of course, but I can't do anything about it as long as Doubleday continues to put the old push behind the books— and as long as my contract isn't broken. I have at last got in the clauses for which I started fighting a couple of years ago, and they have taken a load off my mind. The only thing on which we hung up was the cheap edition clause. You remember we discussed that. When I told Russell what you'd agreed to, he let out an anguished howl, and allowed as how it couldn't be done. Knowing that it could, I didn't feel that I could give in, so the upshot was that the cheap edition clause was removed from the contract;…. But what the hell do you care about book contracts? They're as far removed from you as Addis Ababa, I take it.

How do you like your new job? And what do you hear if anything?

If you come sometime in this direction, stop off and I'll load you up with Felton Rum ….You got any ideas for pushing CAPTAIN CAUTION? If you have, shoot 'em along. It's a damned good book though I do say it…; and for the sake of the whole property I am extremely eager to see it make the grade.

Best wishes,
(signed) Ken Roberts.
(Box 7, **Daniel Longwell Papers**, Rare Book & Manuscript Library, Columbia University in the City of New York.)

Longwell answered at once, September 18, 1934.

Dear Ken:

How nice to hear from you. I am delighted you worked out negotiations with Russell. I didn't want to interfere in any way. I told you frankly that I thought you ought to stay there for your own good because I think the property ought to be kept together. ….

Better news is the fact that you have started another book. I do want to come up to Kennebunk, and see you sometime either for some golf, a talk, a drink, duck shooting, or whatever you have to offer. (Box 20, **Daniel Longwell Papers**, Rare Book & Manuscript Library, Columbia University in the City of New York)

Roberts' *Captain Caution* came out in 1933. But in 1934, the epic best seller, *Northwest Passage* came out. This book is quintessential American history. Roberts was a stickler for historical accuracy. His descriptions of the daunting terrain and challenging adventures make this book hugely important for truly comprehending what our forebears were up against. Roberts sent Longwell an autographed copy, and Longwell was grateful. He was sincerely fond of the men and women he had worked with on the outside of the company, but his closest friends were those he had worked with inside those hallowed halls.

Christopher Morley and Ogden Nash had earlier taken their leave of Doubleday Publishing. Nelson Doubleday and Nash's wife Ellen continued to think of Longwell as nearly a member of the family.

Another close friend in the office was Theodore Roosevelt, Jr. and his wife and children. When it is written that Longwell was a "friend of the family," I mean he also kept an eye on the dogs and children as they grew into adults.

By his thirty-fifth birthday, July 11, 1934, it can be said that Daniel Longwell was well-established professionally and socially. He was not encumbered with any family responsibilities beyond distant relatives needing emotional support and occasional loans. Depression was the national economic buzzword explaining hard times, but Daniel Longwell was nowhere near depressed.

CHAPTER FOUR

BEGINNING AT TIME INC

"It is not what you know, but whom you know."

Daniel Longwell's intellectual prowess and his personable devotion to working authors had established him as Doubleday Publishers' "Young Man." After fifteen strong years with Doubleday, in 1934, he resigned from the world of book publishing to join Henry Robinson Luce at Time Inc and to try his hand at the new profession, "journalism" publishing.

In a deposition (1942, Corcoran Case[19]), Longwell focused on his

Daniel Longwell of Time Inc., New York City (John Shaw Billings Collection, Courtesy of South Caroliniana Library, University of South Carolina, Columbia, SC)

---

[19] The Corcoran Case: State of New York Supreme Court, Bronx County, 1942; transcript of Court Report by J. Stuart Duane, Court Reporter. All materials found in Box 17, **Daniel Longwell Papers**, Rare Book & Manuscript Library, Columbia University in the City of New York). The case was a lawsuit to determine who owned the "idea" of a picture magazine.

personal contribution to book publishing as he related his professional background prior to coming to Time Inc.

    May I explain myself in terms of my own working experience? My background before coming to the organization was much concerned with graphic arts. I've been actively and continuously in publishing in New York City for more than half my life—22 ½ years. From 1919 until 1934, I worked for Doubleday, Doran & Co. I was successively a book clerk, window dresser, copy writer, advertising and publicity manager and later publishing manager in full charge of publishing their authors. I should guess that Doubleday, Doran and other contemporary book publishers would admit that [the] …memory that I might have left with the book trade was more a graphic, than say, a literary one. I did not originate the well-designed modern commercial book in modern U.S.A. publishing. I should think that Mr. Alfred A. Knopf did that. Nor did I originate the modern method of rather graphic book advertising—I should think that Mr. Alfred A. Knopf also pioneered that notion. Mr. Knopf was a pupil of the late Mr. William Heinemann of London and so was I, to a much less personal extent. But I think I did, with larger resources than Mr. Knopf, play a part in popularizing the graphic intent of books and their presentation through their looks (i.e. their jackets, bindings and illustrations.) and the advertising of them. Mr. Knopf and Mr. Simon of Simon & Schuster would have to judge that. They were my contemporaries. I think I did much to influence book jacket designs and a good deal of the conception of publishers' advertising—by using illustrations, etc. I used pictures in books and in advertising as much as possible. (Corcorcan Case, Box 17, **Daniel Longwell Papers**, Rare Book & Manuscript Library, Columbia University in the City of New York)

As is often stated, "It is not what you know, but whom you know." Henry Luce, reigning chief of Time Inc. with TIME and FORTUNE magazines, had been trying to recruit Daniel Longwell away from Doubleday for a number of years. Luce was a magazine magnate and Longwell was a books man. Luce was not interested in books, but he wanted Longwell's brains which at this point after Longwell's return from England had a certain cache. In Longwell's case the "what" and the "who" came hand in hand. The questions before him became: Do you want to be in the book business or the magazine business? Do you want to advance literature or journalism? Longwell knew a lot about books. But he was dreaming about journalism. And, in fact, he finally merged the two.

Thus it was this Midwesterner from Omaha, Nebraska, took his chair and whip into the lion's cage of Time Inc. journalism![20]

---

[20] In a conversation with Bradie Metheny, Metheny asked Longwell: What are your duties as Chairman of the Board of Editors? Longwell replied, "I take a whip and chair into my office and try to tame the boys." (Bradie Metheny Interview, 2010)

It has been easy to overlook and not much time has been spent writing about a man who was a good person, loved his wife, had no lovers, kept no skeletons in his closet and just worked hard to do what he saw needed to be done and could be done. That kind of genius can make for very dull reading.

Dull—until one realizes he was intimately acquainted with all the other geniuses of his day and was willing to work at full capacity to display, explain, and explore their contributions to anyone with ten cents for a LIFE magazine.

However, there was an embryonic lag time between Longwell's going to work for Luce and Luce agreeing to publish a picture magazine. Longwell went to work at Time Inc. in mid-July of 1934. There was no contract or any clear cut statement between the two men on just what Longwell's job would be. The following piece introduces us to Longwell's beginnings in magazine publishing. In this June 17, 1966, dictation to his wife Longwell recalled his first assignment at Time Inc.

> Luce's first assignment to me, when I joined Time Inc., was to study what was going on at Archy Forum (*Architectural Forum*) and make a report. It didn't take me long. By spending a long time with…their advertising department, lunching with a bunch of account executives from the agencies, going to Washington and seeing the federal people involved, I found that it was wishful thinking to chart a course for a trade

publication in an industry that was not going to revive itself automatically.

The trouble with Archy Forum was that, born in a architectural world, it aimed itself at architects. Now there were no more so-called architects in the old sense. Houses were being built and sold to the public by builders. And the builders were an unruly lot of fellows who were only interested in a cut of the pie.

I liked the people at Archy Forum and thought they were doing a good job under the circumstances. There was one fatal fact about it—by being part of Time Inc. they had a sort of keeping up with the Joneses attitude toward the sales and edit departments of the two magazines. That meant lunching and entertaining well and fairly lavish expense accounts and the pay check always disappearing each month in the high cost of suburban living. (Box 81, **Daniel Longwell Papers**, Rare Book & Manuscript Library, Columbia University in the City of New York)

All of that was probably a very good introduction to being a Time Inc. man. After Longwell made that report, Charles Stillman (a Vice President) organized a lunch with C.D. Jackson (a Vice President), Bill Commons (Treasurer), Perry Prentice (Circulation), and John Billings (TIME co-managing editor). Discussion turned to a possible push to develop a woman's magazine which, it was thought, could reach a million circulation. Longwell, relying on his experience at Doubleday when they had launched *American*

Home and its accumulated headaches including a monthly deficit, discouraged starting a magazine geared just for women.

Fortuitously however, this lunch seems to have become the beginning of an epic friendship between Daniel Longwell and John Shaw Billings. Billings asked Longwell to come be his assistant on TIME. "He wanted a million circulation too. I tried to console him," Longwell said, and added, "Wait, wait, when the good Lord ordains it we'll have a million circulation" (Time Inc. Archives).

After Longwell finished the "Archy Forum Assignment," he was assigned to help with the promotion of the new monthly newsreels, *March of Time*. In fact in the same deposition of May 14, 1941, Longwell describes this other experience of his first coming to work at Time Inc.

> When I reported for work, I thought I would try to get in…the experimental department, but I found it had been abandoned in favor of starting the *March of Time* in movies. I was immediately assigned to the *March of Time* to do promotion work. I worked very closely with that organization and it was there I first learned about journalistic use of pictures.
>
> In the Spring of 1935, after M.O.T. was launched, I told Luce, "I've got to get out of the *March of Time*. We have got to get out a picture magazine." Luce said, "Yes, we must."
>
> In the summer of 1935, I went to England to help launch the *March of Time* in that country. I took extra time to go pretty thoroughly

through the English and French picture press. I spent considerable time with *Paris Soir* which was doing a remarkable job with pictures as a newspaper, and with Lord Beaverbrook and his colleagues who were also doing a remarkable picture improvement in the *Daily Express.* Lord Southwood of Odhams Press had a little picture magazine called *Weekly Illustrated* that with no effort at all was selling very well indeed. Dunbar who was editor of all of Southwood's publications gave me free rein to study the entire financial set-up of that magazine. I made tentative informal deals with several British publishers to secure their pictures when we got around to starting a picture magazine. I had no direct authority from Luce to do any of this.

When I returned to this country I resumed my picture experiments on TIME. I had arranged and made the second big picture spread that TIME ever had in the Oct. 18, 1934 issue and had been experimenting with TIME all through the spring of 1935. That Fall I really started to work experimenting in earnest. I hired photographer Tom McAvoy in Nov. 1935 and Peter Stackpole in January 1936. (Corcoran Case, Box 17, **Daniel Longwell Papers**, Rare Book & Manuscript Library, Columbia University in the City of New York)

Meanwhile Longwell was having to bring his well-honed "gruntling" talents to new and greater heights to find his niche in the executive labyrinth of Time Inc. The ever-maneuvering Ralph McAllister Ingersoll[21], General Manager of Time Inc., exercised more influence when Luce was absent—as he was at the end of 1935. Ingersoll began hovering over the experimental department.

The research of Loudon Wainwright in 1975, author of *The Great American Magazine, The Inside History of LIFE*, brought him to appreciate "how very central Mr. Longwell was to the making of LIFE", and that his influence on its tone, content and operations lasted for many years (Letter to Mary Longwell, Box 83, **Daniel Longwell Papers**, Rare Book & Manuscript Library, Columbia University in the City of New York)

It was Wainwright who eventually described Longwell as the anticipated picture magazine's "guiding genius," but a "skittery" one, fidgety and anxious. Wainwright saw Longwell as a complement to Billings whom he described as self-disciplined, with energy and stability (Wainwright, p. 13-14).

Rather than go more deeply into the types men who were managing the creation of LIFE, I will introduce one of the few women on the "front lines" of the beginnings of

---

[21] Ralph McAllister Ingersoll, known as Mac, joined TIME INC as the Associate Editor of *Fortune* in late 1930 and by September 1931, he had moved up to Editor. On August 12, 1935, Ingersoll was appointed "General Manager of Time Inc. and all subsidiaries". On March 19, 1936, he became Vice-President of Time Inc., and was named Publisher of TIME on March 25, 1937. In May 1938, Ingersoll relinquished title of General Manager of Time Inc.
On April 3, 1939, Henry Luce sent out a memo announcing to staff that Ingersoll was leaving Time Inc. on April 10th. At that point, Ingersoll was working on plans for a new daily newspaper. Of note: the first issue of LIFE was dated, November 23, 1936 (Time Inc. Archives).

that iconic magazine: Mary Fraser, chief of research at Time Inc.

Born August 14, 1902, in Perth Amboy, New Jersey, Mary Fraser was the daughter of a school-teaching mother, Margaret Huff Fraser, and a real estate broker father, Caleb Douglas Fraser. He had been born in Nova Scotia, but had moved to Perth Amboy in 1906, he helped organize the Fraser Brothers real estate firm of which he was a partner. He was an elder in the Presbyterian Church in

Mary Douglas Fraser, Chief of Research, Time Inc. (Getty Images, Used with Permission)

Perth Amboy and the stained-glass window of St. John is dedicated to his memory. He died in 1939 at age 69, two years after LIFE was born and one year after his daughter married one of its founders. Mary was the oldest of three siblings: one sister, Margaret who became a nurse and one brother, Douglas, who was a railroad engineer.

Mary was a 1923 graduate of Wellesley College where she had won the John Masefield Award in English Composition. Nicknamed "Polly" at Wellesley, at the Time Inc. offices she was known as "Fra"—with a long "a". On March 4, 1957, Mary typed her own brief biography in which she told about meeting Daniel Longwell. There is nothing new in these two paragraphs as far as information goes, but one does get a sense of what it was about Mr. Longwell that Miss Fraser had noticed.

> In 1934 a young man named Daniel Longwell came to work as assistant to Henry R. Luce, to work out experiments for a picture magazine. Mr. Longwell, a native of Omaha, Nebraska, attended Columbia College and started work for Doubleday Doran while still at Columbia [and] was their advertising manager at the age of 23. When he left Doubleday for TIME, he was publishing manager of the company, handling such authors as Edna Ferber, Ellen Glasgow, Stephen Vincent Benet, Kenneth Roberts, etc.
>
> The first issue of LIFE appeared in November 1936. By that time we had become acquainted (never were introduced) and were married in December 1938. (Couldn't get married until Daniel was sure LIFE was a success. It was.) (Box 62, **Daniel Longwell Papers**, Rare Book & Manuscript Library, Columbia University in the City of New York)

Mary Longwell, was a journalistic heroine in her own right as Chief of Research for all Time Inc. publications until their joint retirement in 1954. When Dan went to Time Inc., Mary had been there seven years and had early on served as the secretary to Briton Hadden, the creator of TIME, the weekly news-magazine, before his unexpected death in 1929. She had also been Director of Personnel and had hired many of Time Inc.'s key career staff.

Admittedly, some of the career staff were recruited, which is how Dan Longwell arrived at Time Inc., but Mary Fraser herself worked at getting hired. An intelligent woman who had lived through the suffrage movement and seen the adoption of the Nineteenth Amendment while she was in college, Fraser's words on being hired at Time Inc. are better than mine. Again, I am quoting her March 4, 1957, biography which may have been written for the Wellesley alumni office, found in Box 62, **Daniel Longwell Papers**, Rare Book & Manuscript Library, Columbia University in the City of New York.

> The year before I graduated from Wellesley, some young men from Yale had started a small weekly named TIME. Since Harry Luce had two sisters at Wellesley, girls from Wellesley with literary leanings tried to get on the staff. I had a friend there and applied for a job. I had had three weeks of secretarial training and could type after a fashion. I was hired by Roy Larsen, then circulation manager, as a typist in the circulation department. In the course of the year I managed to get myself the job of secretary to Briton Hadden, the editor.

The wild and crazy creative bunch that put TIME magazine to press every Monday night by everyone taking their copy and reference books on the subway to the printing shop convinced Mary that there was no future for her in this exercise. She cast about in the New York newspaper world for a while, but she could not land a job. She went home to

New Jersey and did columns for the *Daily Home News* of New Brunswick, NJ.

During her three years with that paper, she and her parents took "the grand tour" to Europe and she sent back travel columns which the New Brunswick paper printed. She said this success made her think she was ready for the big time, *The New York Times*. Their decision not to hire her was no worse than her leaving Time Inc. in the first place. While Mary Fraser was not working at Time Inc., Henry Luce moved the TIME operation to Cleveland, OH, as a cost cutting move while Hadden was "out of town." After coming "back to town" in 1927, Hadden returned the compliment and TIME was back in New York.

Mary Douglas Fraser went back to TIME and reminded Hadden she was the only secretary he had not fired. So she was hired this time as assistant to the Copy Chief, who later, after resigning from TIME, became Mrs. Alger Hiss[22]. Mary was moved into her position and as the little company's editorial department grew, she took on other responsibilities. In fact, she organized a reference library for fact- checking, a "morgue" file of clippings on notables kept over the years in order to be used for future articles or obituaries. This file was the embryo of the Time Inc. Archives.

She set up the first Research staff for FORTUNE and later one for LIFE. The case may be made that she

---

[22] Alger Hiss (1904-1996) was an attorney, lecturer, author and governmental official who was accused of being a Soviet spy in 1949. He was tried for espionage and found guilty, serving three and a half years of a ten year sentence. Hiss maintained his innocence until his death (http://en.wikipedia.org/wiki/Alger_Hiss).

single-handedly created a whole new profession for educated women: Researcher. She also created the TIME Correspondents Bureau and headed it for years.

From Mary's biography for Wellesley, one gets the flavor of how it was in the 1920's and 1930's at Time Inc., but there is more to the story. I share it as Dan Longwell told it to me. (Longwell, Mary, 1957, Autobiography, Box 62, **Daniel Longwell Papers**, Rare Book & Manuscript Library, Columbia University in the City of New York).

The same weekend that Dan took me to dinner at the St. Regis Hotel on his visit to New York in 1962 when I was a new employee of Time Inc. assigned to LIFE, Dan told me how important Mary had been to Time Inc. He bragged on her personal insights about people. According to Dan, Mary's insights into the position of Researcher had made two significant contributions to how things were done. She thought that the position of Researcher was best held by women. Dan said that in Mary's opinion, the natural conflict between the sexes created the best argumentative atmosphere of getting the most accurate copy written. At that time, writers were men. Mary made a point of hiring strong-willed women who would stand up to the male writers who were more prone to artistic license than accuracy.

Dan also credited her with the development of a system of checking for accuracy, a system still in use when I was a Researcher/Reporter at LIFE in 1962-1964.

When a writer had completed his/her story it went to the copy room and was typed onto pages that declared its fitting into margins. It was then sent to the Researcher who would check it for accuracy and the responsibility fell completely on the Researcher. Her decision could be overridden or nullified by an editor but not without a strong discussion if disagreement was in the air.

The checking was so simple that it is a wonder all publications did not use it. This is how it worked: all words had to have a dot over them which indicated the Researcher person had read it for sense, grammar, spelling and fact. Normal words had a lead pencil dot. Proper names had a red pencil dot. The upshot of this was that researchers became not only checkers of fact, but apprentice copy editors. Furthermore a standard of expected accuracy was set and there was company-wide pride in having a trustworthy text.

Today if one visits with former Time Inc. Researchers they will be moaning about the poor attention to these details in current publications.

Mary and Dan both thought the value of women in the work place was greatly underestimated. In fact, I will always believe that this mutual respect of the genders was one of the strengths of their marriage. They started out on an equal footing of mutual admiration and respect…and it could also be equality of power though Mary never claimed to have had much power or influence.

I do not know if the "rule" was written or unwritten, but the tradition at Time Inc. was that the writer's (a man) text had to conform to the researcher's (a woman) findings and verification. The stories of female researchers and male writers/editors arguing are probably legion throughout the company, but my favorite was told me in the LIFE copy room one closing night. I was told about the researcher (a woman) who refused to let LIFE [or TIME] go to press the night of the Truman-Dewey election in 1948. The editors thought Tom Dewey was a shoe-in. The polls said so.[23] A possible flaw did not occur to the editors at the *Chicago Tribune.* Their bold-type headline "DEWEY WINS" is an iconic journalistic example of what can happen when the facts are not checked. (1963, Conversation in "Copy Room" at LIFE with Jenny Sadler)

Mary Fraser's support of the women at Time Inc. surely had an effect on their becoming even stronger personalities. In fact, in an age when girls were brought up to think they would best be teachers, nurses or secretaries, Mary Fraser's new profession, the Researcher came with a certain amount of glamour. I am proud to say I was a Researcher for LIFE in the 1960's for LIFE and then for *National Geographic.* However Researchers at the *Geographic* had nowhere near the clout that a Time Inc. Researcher had. My experience was that even an embassy public affairs officer could and did override a Researcher at *Geographic.* The LIFE masthead had begun listing Researchers as Reporters…but I have always clung to "Researcher."

Mary's other significant contribution to Time Inc. dated back to her early days as secretary to Briton Hadden. Time Inc. was a small group of journalists working in very tight quarters in 1929, and Mary was then Chief of Research and a Jill-of-all-trades, including hiring personnel. She hired John Shaw Billings who became TIME's National Affairs

---

[23] I learned in political science class at Yale that these polls were flawed in 1948 because voter opinions were based on telephone interviews and there were more phones connected to the upper class than to the middle and lower class.

Editor, then TIME's Co-Managing Editor and in 1936 was called up to begin LIFE as Co-Managing editor with Dan Longwell and Henry Luce. But my favorite hiring story was told me by Mrs. Longwell herself.

TIME needed another CBOB (College Boy Office Boy) and they ran an ad for summer help. Mary said the outer office was crammed with all these young college kids and there was no time to go through any interviewing process. So Hadden quickly made up a quiz on baseball scores, mimeographed it and handed it out. While the applicants filled out the quiz, Mary observed them through the glass in the door. She chose Joe Kastner, a skinny fellow with glowing red hair. He went on to have a sterling career at Time Inc. and was Copy Editor at LIFE when I was there. That was a very powerful and respected position. (Author's 1962 Conversation with Mary Longwell)

From 1962-1964, my work arena at the new TIME-LIFE building was known as the "clip desk" on the 29th floor. My "desk" was a counter that stretched the whole length along the central north-south corridor. The AP Wire was at the south end of this hallway across from Marian MacPhail's office. She was Chief of Research and my boss. This training position centered on reading about eight newspapers from across the country and clipping out anything related to any stories being worked on and send them to the appropriate departments. The task was as old as Time Inc. itself and had evolved into a training position; I was the "clip girl" for LIFE.

One day, Joe Kastner, the Copy Editor was striding through and stopped to speak to me. I told him the story

Mary had told me about his being hired. He said he'd never heard that version of his hiring and said with surprise, "Oh, I thought it was because I got all the ball scores right!"

Mary had an uncanny knack about people and while she said she made some mistakes, I think all the fun stories about working at Time Inc. can often be traced to a lively smart human resources person, but of course it was called Personnel back then. Mary was head of Personnel until August of 1947 when she was elevated to Director of Research. For a long time she was the only woman on the "Executive Floor." (*FYI*, Time Inc., Archives)

The Climate at Time Inc.

There have been a number of books written about life at LIFE. And while this memoir is not meant to embellish all the stories about the fun and games, there does need to be presented a bit more about the levity in the work environment. One of my favorite stories comes from Mr. Longwell's last secretary, Betty Morris. Betty was a graduate of Mount Holyoke College. Her father was a highly respected prominent surgeon in New York City with privileges in eight hospitals including Bellevue.

After her graduation, Betty wanted to work but knew she would need typing. Therefore she enrolled in the prestigious Katherine Gibbs School. "Katie Gibbs," as it was affectionately called, was almost a finishing school for future executive secretaries. Dress code was hat and gloves, conservative cosmetics, hose and sensible heels, and proper decorum. Required typing speed was 55 words per minute on the old manual typewriters. Typing errors were not allowed. Grades were "perfect," "mailable," or "unmailable". After four months of typist training, Betty was given interviews for secretarial positions in different companies. None of them appealed to her. She wanted to work at Time Inc. and asked to be sent there. The Katherine Gibbs' response was "NO! They are drinkers over there." Betty promised she could handle that and insisted they get her an interview. She was hired by Time Inc. in 1944 and assigned to the LIFE Picture Bureau first. In 1950 she became secretary to Daniel Longwell until his retirement four years later.

Betty said there was drinking but it was self-controlled because at LIFE perfection was demanded. It was a most unusual work place in that everyone from the mail boys to the writers and editors had college educations and everyone was not only well educated but they were witty and fun and the place was fueled by mutual respect. She said, "They all deserved each other." (Morris Interviews, 2010-2015)

These same atmospheric conditions were described by one of the CGOGs. That acronym stood for College Girl Office Girl. The gender counterpart to the CBOB, College Boy Office Boy. Mary Longwell had told me about the CBOBs but I was not familiar with the term CGOG until I had the delightful experience of meeting Shirley Sprague McClintock.

Shirley had been accepted by Cornell University but there was no place to accommodate women on the campus as all the men home from W W II on the G.I. Bill were taking up all the housing. At age nineteen Shirley was accepted as a CGOG. This was when the Time Life Building was at 9

Rockefeller Plaza and the mail room was on the 26th floor. Her work began at 8:45 a.m. when mail was sorted to be delivered by 9:30. (As an aside, I have to say that my hours in 1962 were 10:00 a.m. to 6:00 p.m. which seemed very civilized.) Shirley said all the leg work was done by the college kids; writers never left their desks and secretaries would order their office supplies. The college boys and girls were never given anything to do that was demeaning. They were all called by their first names and the editorial staff was protective of them by nature. These college students were hired for their potential as future writers, researchers, copy editors etc. Basically, it was a training program. From the 17th to the 33rd floors at the Time-Life Building, there were thirty-nine CBOBs and CGOGs. Shirley started at $27 a week and in 6 months she was making $54 a week. Each week she was assigned a different floor to work.

Cornell University finally had room for Shirley when she was twenty-one years old. She majored in labor relations and to this day maintains that Time Inc. was a wonderful work experience. She claims that her short time at Time Inc. was a significant factor in her being hired by General Motors. General Motors had been looking for someone with a Master's degree. Cornell inquired how she got the GM job without having a Master's degree and she told them it was because of her Time Inc. experience. Shirley Sprague McClintock is a past President of the Cornell Club in Greater Buffalo, NY.

Since Shirley had an academic interest in labor relations anyway, I have decided to include what she wrote about how Mr. Luce and Time Inc. treated their employees as she observed it. She was very impressed with Mr. Luce's loyalty to his staff. This quote is from a letter Shirley sent me January 15, 2011.

- Henry Luce was as the devoted father, and his management was known as "paternal". The early days in our country, business owners often supplied the resources to protect their employees in time of need. Industry called them "Paternal Organizations."
- Work week was 37.5 hours. Overtime was paid for all hours over the 37.5.
- Vacation policy was generous: two weeks' vacation after six months service, longer service meant longer vacations.
- Benefit plans included health insurance, life insurance, pension plan and profit sharing.
- There was an in-house medical department on the 26th floor of the former TIME-LIFE building. A full-time doctor and full-time nurses were available for routine treatment: sore throat, colds, nothing requiring a medical exam. Air conditioned, dark rooms with beds for short naps were available. Since the building was not air conditioned offices could be close if temperatures rose above 90 degrees.
- Personnel (today's Human Resources) provided counseling for anyone with a problem. No one was ever fired for a personal problem such as drinking.

- Anyone in need of a loan did not have to go to a bank. A supervisor could approve a loan and the employee could take the approval to the accounting department, and it would be repaid at five dollars a week from the paycheck.
- A free copy of TIME and LIFE for each employee was available every week. This was a great status symbol in those days.
- The personnel policy made it possible for new employees from out-of-town to commence their jobs with as much assistance as needed. New hires were paid the first payday after their employment. No "two-week time lag" prevented hardships.
- A Christmas Party for all staff and top management was held at first class hotels, e.g., the Waldorf-Astoria, with every public room for banquet and dancing.
- TIME Out was a full day summer outing at the Westchester County Country Club: golf, tennis, swimming. Open bar and lunch at pool, open bar at 5:00, dinner at 6:00 and leave by 10:00. Management and staff lingered with ease. These were the days when drinking was the norm in publishing and advertising. Long lunch hours were common but time was made up at the end of the day.
- Henry Luce rarely fired anyone from Time Inc. An employee was given counseling for any problems but if no solution was available,

the employee was given a private office with a desk and phone to conduct a job search. Time Inc. never said an employee had been fired and supervisors could complain but had no authority to fire them.

- Luce considered temperamental people were part of a creative environment.
- When advertising revenues decreased, Luce would work in that department and assist with sales. He never fired the salesmen, some of the most dynamic people, and turnover was rare.
- To remember the time that you worked for Time Inc., is to yearn for those days again. Every job in Time Inc. made you a "somebody." (McClintock, Interviews and Correspondence, 2011-2015)

Betty Morris and Shirley Sprague McClintock would agree that the Personnel Department did a bang up job of putting together a fascinating bunch of people. Time Inc. was about people and the corporation assembled a dedicated and talented group of employees. Time Inc. is one of the few companies whose people formed an alumni society. Betty Morris and Shirley Sprague and I have maintained our membership in the Time Life Alumni Society (TLAS).

When Shirley read in the alumni new brochure, *TLAS 2010 Summer* edition that I was writing a memoir of Daniel Longwell, she wrote to me. Her letter included an anecdote from her days as a CGOG in 1947 when she had volunteered to work on a Saturday.

Mr. Luce called for a letter to be carried to Dan Longwell. Luce gave her the letter and told her she was to stay while Longwell read it and asked Shirley to report back to him Dan's reaction. She peeked and read the letter herself and she reports to me it was a letter Luce had composed to Winston Churchill which read, "I have spoken severely to my editor about whom you have complained."

Supposedly Luce was disciplining Longwell for his having shifted some blame for a late press run to Churchill's request for last minute changes. To date, Bill Hooper and I have not been able to find that letter, but Shirley reports that Longwell just laughed and said, "Go ahead and send it."

Shirley still feels that Henry Luce was very "paternal" toward his organization, but like many heads of households he was always interested in but never sure he had his finger on the pulse of his "family." This was exemplified when Mary Longwell had been elevated to the executive floor as Chief of Research for all the Time Inc. publications. As all the magazines had their own Research staffs and neither Luce nor Mary were ones to micro-manage their organization, Luce gave Mary the peculiar sideline assignment to discover how the people worked together. (McClintock Correspondence, 2011)

Mary kept the notes she made about how the staff interacted or reacted and it makes for amusing reading (Box 26, **Daniel Longwell Papers**, Rare Book & Manuscript Library, Columbia University in the City of New York).

This note was dated 1948 and perhaps was part of her work on thinking about how life at Time Inc. was in the post-war years.

- Lunch Habits: Jack Dowd, celebrating four years of service with the company, for three years of which he has been attached to J.S. Billings staff as legal counsel for the editorial department, says he has never been to lunch with JSB. It is not proper for him to ask JSB, must await an invitation from, his boss.

- Lunch Mores: Sept. 1, 1948 Lunch date with C. Thrasher, Mr. Luce's secretary, who reported with some amusement that just before we set out, JSB came and inquired whether HRL had found a lunch date—seems he had asked JSB who could not oblige, and there was some worry, HRL might have to eat alone. Thrasher reported that he had made a date with someone outside the company, but "would probably pump him on his business and come back with ideas," since lunch date with HRL is always a business occasion, not a social one, his lunches with members of the staff being for business talks.

- Dress: Aug. 27, 1948. Heat Wave on—N.Y. temperature at 100 for two days. Orders from Personnel Dept. to send people home at 3 if possible. Lunch discussion on clothes—two girls on TIME came in backless dresses with jackets, were told must wear jackets in hall. Sandals with bare feet generally deplored. Two LIFE writers came to work and changed to shorts (shortly thereafter were back in long trousers). LIFE Style editor came to work in low cut dress, confounded discipline of those who would keep bare backs hidden.

- Anniversary: On Aug. 23, 1948, Content Peckham said she was celebrating her 14th anniversary with Time Inc. No celebration for 14th. When she completed 10 years, Yi Sung, Chinese Researcher gave Chinese Dinner to celebrate "500 Monday nights."
- Should we address issue of who pays at a business lunch??? There are at least three refs to this.

From within the halls of Time Inc. Daniel Longwell saw a future in journalism that no one else was able to see. Lots of people were thinking about the future of pictures in print, but Longwell had what might be called "tunnel vision" about using pictures: photographs, art, maps and cartoons. In today's world, it seems childish to get excited about pictures in print. Today's youngster cannot grasp the excitement the black and white television brought us in the 1950's, or the utter amazement of color photos and color television coming soon after. Adults of the 1930's were yearning to "see" the world they heard about on radio and read about in newspapers. Longwell knew in his gut he could satisfy that yearning and feed people's hunger to see the world around them. Many talked about it over cocktails and in memos. But it was the former "Lt. Colonel" Daniel Longwell who knew that he himself could lead the cadets of journalism down America's Main Street and into millions of American homes. In fact he had once said to Henry Luce after turning down an offer to work at FORTUNE that if Luce ever wanted to start a picture magazine, he, Longwell, was the one man in the USA who could do it for him. Longwell believed in himself but Luce was skeptical.

I am reminded of the conversation between Winston Churchill's doctor, Lord Moran and the British author, poet and historian, John Masefield. Masefield's spoke of Churchill in the highest of terms: "Winston is a natural force, a volcano, big and dynamic" (Moran, page 348). We can adapt this description to Longwell whose internal force was about to energize the push toward photo journalism.

Longwell seemed to feel a 'moral' force within himself to give the American public a picture of itself. Longwell loved America as Churchill loved England. People who love don't hide what they love under a bushel. They set it out for everyone to see.

As Longwell reflected on the fact that at Doubleday he had worked with literary giants who just happened to be telling intimate tales of common Americans from all sections of the nation, their struggles and triumphs, he must have known there was an endless treasure of stories to photograph. Daniel Longwell knew where to set the lamp for those stories to be seen.

CHAPTER FIVE

LIFE MAGAZINE: *A WHOLE LOT OF BIRTHIN' GOIN' ON*

"...perhaps the book (Time, Inc.—The Intimate History of a Publishing Enterprise, 1923-1941) establishes beyond question that Dan was one of the architects of LIFE magazine and HRL told me many times that Dan deserved the greatest share of the credit." --Robert T. Elson (November 28, 1968 Letter to Mary Longwell on the Occasion of Dan's Death)

Henry Luce announced to John Shaw Billings that he was pregnant... with a new magazine. Of course he had already given birth to TIME and FORTUNE, but he had not had Daniel Longwell on staff during the gestation period of either of those. (Billings Diary, Feb. 28, 1936, Courtesy of South Carolinia Library, University of South Carolina, Columbia, SC)

Most publishing activity was happening in the east coast city centers. But like most Midwesterners, Dan Longwell was not myopic nor locked in on east coast expertise. His perspective saw an America filled with interesting people, buildings, events, colleges, rodeos, art work, Saturday nights and Sunday mornings. He was ready to share all this pride in the USA and show it to a hungry public.

Major news events had not been "seen" by the folks at home. The nation was ready for a weekly newsmagazine, a companion to TIME which would give them news in pictures. Television was only in an embryonic stage. There were news clips at the movies but what people would snap up for weekly visual information was the new Time Inc. magazine, LIFE, which was still in the "production womb".

Longwell stood by his assertion to Luce that he could create a picture magazine for the Time Inc. list. Luce was still thinking more along the lines of a supplement to TIME. But Longwell was thinking of a separate magazine that could stand on its own. In fact a picture magazine had become Longwell's professional passion.

Most people think of history being in words on pages from scrolls to books. Longwell noted that history was also depicted in pictures painted on cave walls, set in stained glass windows, religious icons on church walls, Sistine Chapel ceilings and epic sized canvasses filled with land and naval battles.

Those visual representations were based on stories which were common knowledge to people of long ago. Being aware of the people's "common knowledge," the artist could design his work. However, a picture magazine of *current* news did not have the advantage of telling a familiar story.

In the 1930's several groups outside Time, Inc. were working to develop a picture magazine. But it was Daniel Longwell who figured out how to *present* a "picture magazine" with the story in photographs and paintings arranged in such a way that the story line would become obvious to the reader who was seeing the story for the first time with no former reference to draw upon.

LIFE was first to develop the *"Picture Essay,"* a pictorial literary composition. This was a new journalistic tool which some declared as the greatest invention since movable type. (Memo to Elson, 1965, Time Inc. Archives; Box 81, **Daniel Longwell Papers**, Rare Book & Manuscript Library, Columbia University in the City of New York)

Longwell's first attempt at the picture essay was to send photographer William Vandivert to Emporia, Kansas, to create a literary composition in pictures showing the vestiges of the New England way of life and architecture as reflected in the western prairie of Emporia, Kansas. Longwell and Vandivert were helped in this endeavor by William Allen White[24] who was Emporia's Pulitzer Prize winning editor of the *The Emporia Gazette.* His editorial positions had put Emporia on the map. His son and daughter-in-law, William L. and Katherine White, had worked at Time Inc. and were prominent journalists in their own right. At any rate, the pictorial essay idea appealed to the senior White and he spent two days taking Vandivert around the town. (Letter from Longwell to Mary Alves, 1955, Box

---

[24] The University of Kansas Journalism School is named for him.

57, **Daniel Longwell Papers**, Rare Book & Manuscript Library, Columbia University in the City of New York)

They photographed a covered bridge, elm shaded streets, Beecher Baptist Church and a New England church called the Rifle. This story never ran; but Longwell sent out other photographers with the same instructions to "shoot" a story. The results were Margaret Bourke White's cover story on the Fort Peck Dam and the accompanying "essay" on the boom town at Wheeler, Montana. Alfred Eisenstadt's story on the girls at Vasser College followed. When those photos came in and were shown to Luce, he called in the Pulitzer Prize winning poet Archibald MacLeish to write captions for the set and to write a prospectus for what the *Picture Essay* should be. MacLeish later became Director Librarian of the Library of Congress. The *Picture Essay* became a permanent feature in the middle of the magazine. Longwell said this made LIFE different from the European picture magazines and was often the strength of an issue. The essay was a literary event, not a news event. News was in the section named *News Fronts. Speaking of Pictures* and *LIFE Goes to a Party* were sections or departments which Longwell credits Henry Luce with naming. Longwell admired Luce's ability to come up with titles that seemed to be the only right thing.

Like other natural gestation periods, this publishing pregnancy took its own time before the birth came to pass. Little did John Shaw Billings and Daniel Longwell know when they first became acquainted at lunch in 1934 that they would become the managing editors of the most popular magazine in the Time Inc. list. LIFE was launched on November 23, 1936. But there was a lot to be done between Christmas of 1934 and November of 1936. Proper photographers had to be found. The layout had to be formulated with acceptable type chosen. Photos and stories had to be found not to mention editors, writers, paper and presses. It was rather daunting to everyone except Longwell. He knew he had a strong brace of executives behind him and strong cast of characters beside him. But, in truth, Luce had not yet approved the venture as a stand-alone magazine. He was fixated on a picture supplement to TIME.

Longwell estimated that he was spending about $150,000 on the experiments for the picture magazine, but Luce could not yet "see" it. And Roy Larsen, Time Inc. business manager, was not convinced it would be good for the company to get too far from the promotion of TIME and FORTUNE. Most new efforts were going toward the Time Inc. cinema newsreels, *March of Time.* Moving pictures could easily tell a story because of the voice-overs speaking behind the images. Longwell had spent time in London promoting the newsreels. Later they developed a "coffee table" book with the title *Four Hours a Year.* This was a compilation of still photos taken from the newsreels. Longwell later felt that this effort really gave them practice at telling stories with photographs. But once again it was telling stories which the reading public already knew about. The challenge to tell new stories was still before them.

Longwell proposed the use of pictures with limited text though story text would not really be required. He admonished cameramen that the purpose of the pictures he had in mind was NOT to illustrate, but to tell the complete story without text. He set the challenge. "Cameramen may well ponder the possibilities in this form of pictorial journalism, use their ingenuity in finding subjects and methods of treatment." (Longwell, Dan, "The Pictures of Time", Time Inc. Archives)

Pondering and meeting this challenge created some of the greatest photographers the world has known. Most of them worked for LIFE magazine and many others reached for that golden ring.

It is retrospection that tells us that Longwell had his finger on the pulse of the American public. He sensed that the American public was hungry for pictures of current daily history which they could enjoy at the kitchen table after a day's labor or in an easy chair at hearthside. Not everybody went to the "picture show". Newsreels were just a now and then event.

What was going to surprise everyone was that the American public would enjoy seeing itself in print. Longwell had learned in working on *March of Time* and its subsequent book, *Four Hours a Year,* that common everyday people were the subjects of some very good photographs. Henry Luce was surprised to learn that the good news of a big wheat harvest was just as intriguing as bad news.

The experimental department was re-established in secret with more space and a bigger budget. Luce was interested now.

Besides the growing enthusiasm for a picture magazine, romance was in the air at Time Inc. In 1935 Henry Luce had fallen in love and was about to be remarried. And Daniel Longwell had met his love and future wife, Mary Douglas

Fraser, during the gestation period of LIFE. According to her Wellesley College Alumni files she had been assigned to the new experimental department in addition to her other substantial duties at Time Inc.

Both the new Mrs. Luce and the future Mrs. Longwell no doubt saw her own husband as "the" founder of the new magazine. In fact, Mrs. Luce saw herself as a major influence in its development. However, it might be said that the future Mrs. Longwell was at her desk in the Time Inc. building while the new Mrs. Luce was on her honeymoon in Cuba.

A picture magazine had been discussed in many quarters. Under Longwell, Luce's Time Inc. had secretly laid out several experimental issues called "dummies". They carried titles like SHOW BOOK, REHEARSAL and even DUMMY.

The Defining Moment

A packet with a new "dummy" from Longwell of what could become LIFE magazine had been hand-carried by Ralph MacAlister Ingersoll on a business trip to Cuba to see Luce who was honeymooning there with his new bride, Clare Booth in December 1935.

The following letter from Luce addressed to Longwell surely came back in a similar office packet, very much like a diplomatic pouch. The letter was a personal and exciting response to Daniel Longwell from his friend, Harry Luce. Longwell showed it to many people in the experimental department and certain other executives. No doubt to protect this letter which indicated the significant change in Luce's magazine mind, Longwell put it somewhere for "safe keeping", forgot where, and the letter was lost. When giving interviews to the Time Inc. historians, Longwell said he had looked through all his papers and could not locate the Luce letter. Eventually it was stored in Box 69, **Daniel Longwell Papers**, Rare Book & Manuscript Library, Columbia University in the City of New York, when Mary sent the materials to Columbia in 1970. And that is where I found it. Having read the Longwell interviews at the Time Inc. Archives, I recognized the lost letter/memo and knew immediately of its importance to the history of LIFE and the part Daniel Longwell was to play. This is how it read:

> Dear Dan'l[25]
>
> This is primarily to tell you that Clare sends you her love and that upon careful reflection, I am of the opinion that this the best of all possible worlds—thanks in some measure to your moral support at various moments.
>
> But you may, if you choose, believe that I write to congratulate you on your picture dummies— and you will also be right.
>
> The dummies plus the ideas with them were swell and they serve excellently the purpose of high-lighting the question of TIME's picture supplement. Of course from this distance I reserve judgment on the question. But I can tell you that once again my feeling is 100% for a

---

[25] His friends at Time Inc. sometimes called Daniel "Dan'l" as a nod to his Missouri roots and new frontier-attitude, like Dan'l Boone.

picture magazine. There must be a great picture magazine –fine pictures, excellent pictures, lots of pictures, excellently printed, etc, etc. There just <u>has</u> to be this magazine. Then why not this magazine by <u>us.</u>

So, here's to our meeting in the very near future—and to the long postponed birth of the inevitable magazine.

Cheers to you and for you from us both.

Yours,

Harry

This memo is THE defining moment when Henry R. Luce wrote from his honeymoon in Cuba, December 1935, to Daniel Longwell that he was now convinced that they could produce a picture magazine and that Longwell and the Experimental Department had finally gotten the formula right. This is the letter that excited Longwell and which he remembered and reported to all the LIFE historians, but which he could not produce as proof.

I accidently stumbled on the above undated note from Luce in a folder marked "LIFE Pre-publication" in Box 69, **Daniel Longwell Papers**, Rare Book & Manuscript Library, Columbia University in the City of New York in the spring of 2010. Written on the regular blue office paper in black ink, it is in Luce's hand.

The note from Harry Luce while he honeymooned in Cuba at Christmas of 1935 was surely the best Christmas present Daniel Longwell had ever hoped for and his New Year wishes would all come to pass.

Now a year of work of an unprecedented magnitude began. Today, arranging for the obtaining of photographs from around the world sources is nothing in light of social media today with every kid on a corner having a camera at hand. But in 1935 this was hardly the case. Just getting enough good pictures together for one issue was difficult enough, but now they had to plan for an issue every week in a world of changing news fronts and social behaviors.

TIME magazine, begun in 1923, employed writers who were adept at taking clipped articles from newspapers and rewriting them for amusement as much as for the news that made up TIME. FORTUNE magazine, a monthly publication, was made up of lengthy in-depth studies of major corporations in the business world. The picture magazine, a weekly, was going to be a whole new ball game.

The Corcoran Case Reveals How LIFE Began

For the enormous task of starting a new publication, we need to recognize that preceding the *effort* was the necessary ingredient, *enthusiasm*. Mr. Luce himself speaks of the stimulation and inspiration of Longwell when he testified in the Corcoran Case, 1942, before the Supreme Court, Bronx County (Box 56, **Daniel Longwell Papers**, Rare Book & Manuscript Library, Columbia University in the City of New York) to determine who owned the "idea" of a picture magazine. On pages 17-19 of the *Court Report* by J. Stuart Duane, the Court Reporter notes Luce saying:

And there were various people in our organization who had various degrees of enthusiasm about pictures. By that time, by March 1936, one of the people who had become most important in our company from the point of view of ideas—and, you might say inspiration—was a gentleman named Daniel Longwell, who had been a number of years in Doubleday Page— Doubleday Doran & Company, and was notable there as a young man of ideas. I forget just what year he came to us;...—it was a couple of years before this. But by the Spring of 1936 he had become a part of our editorial family, of our corporate life, and he ... had unlimited faith in the picture magazine field; I mean, if only the right magazine could be evolved in that field.

So far as I am personally concerned, he had a great deal to do with re-stimulating me on this thing because, as I said, I had gotten a little discouraged by what I felt was the non-success of the first Experimental Department. I still had a fundamental belief that pictures could be used even more than they were being used.... I certainly had a great deal of faith in the unexhausted use of pictures.

But the question was, to get this general feeling for pictures. And I may say that during the whole of that period, during the whole of the early thirties, ... the photograph was—I mean, as a photograph—was coming up a good deal in prestige. Advertisers were making more use of what might be called the fine photograph.

... it would be absurd for me to say I am primarily indebted to anybody, even to Dan Longwell, for my interest in pictures, because, going back a long time, it had been stimulated in many ways, in our work, in theorizing or vaporizing outside of the work.[26] But in regard to the second Experimental Department, I do have to give Mr. Longwell a good deal of credit there, at least in the sense that his and my enthusiasm for a picture magazine was probably the immediate cause of a determination to try once again to see if we couldn't work out the answer to our satisfaction for the kind of picture magazine that we wanted to turn out.

In 1965, when the Time Inc. corporate history project was getting underway the leader and editor was Robert T. Elson. Recognizing the wealth of information that Dan and Mary had in their heads, he sent them partial manuscript copies for their comments. In an August 16, 1966, letter from them which is located in the Time Inc. Archives files, Mary writes for Dan who could no longer use his left side because of his stroke of April 15, 1965. Dan says:

> I wish you could get someone to describe Luce as an editor—John Billings or Roy Alexander perhaps. Luce is of course one of the great editors of our time. At work he is amazing—he seems to stand like a ship's captain, one foot toward the

---

[26] This is Luce's language for how various conversations at places not necessarily the workplace led to momentous decisions at Time Inc.

pitch of the ship and the other toward the bow to steady himself….

Alex used to complain that although he got to the office at 7 o'clock, Luce always bobbed in about 8 and wanted to start a talk fest.

I recall an incident when we were all working on a dummy of the experimental LIFE one Sunday morning. …Someone said, about some story Luce was working on, did it belong in a mass circulation magazine. Luce whirled, saying 'The next fellow who mentions mass magazine around this office can take it and go stick it. We're not aiming for a mass magazine. If our feeling that pictures are a great story-telling force is right, what we're doing is right.'

Luce laid down a principle LIFE happily followed: that we do the best we can, tackle any subject and let the reader come along.

Somewhere in there my philosophy jelled with Luce's: my idea was that LIFE was just so much white paper—you could do anything.

I particularly remember Luce in his 'stick it' statement because he had not the gift of easy-flowing blasphemy or scatology of our Midwestern contemporaries (Time Inc. Archives).

Life at LIFE

Dan Longwell wrote to Roy Alexander on October 29, 1964, "LIFE was light-hearted. It was more fun to come to the office than to do anything else." (Box 57, **Daniel**

Longwell Papers, Rare Book & Manuscript Library, Columbia University in the City of New York)

We know that Daniel Longwell had taken to journalism like the pheasants he liked to hunt take to the sky. As much as he loved the people he formerly worked with, he had not been blind to the problems of the Doubleday Company—or book publishing in general. In a January 28, 1936, (Box 67, **Daniel Longwell Papers**, Rare Book & Manuscript Library, Columbia University in the City of New York) memo to the Managing Editors of *Fortune*, Eric Hodgins and Jack Jessup, Longwell comes up with more reasons why he had left behind the world of book publishing in favor of journalism.

> I give you my word, [book publishing] is a puny, conceited business. Affected with literary importance, a monument of hokum, by the gullible (including the press and some of our editors) it is given a standing that is really only a leaning posture.

No doubt Longwell had read the February 1936 issue of *Fortune* before it went to press. Notwithstanding that the country was in the midst of the Great Depression, the article's title joined with its subtitle read: "Doubleday, Doran & Co....which outsmarts, outsells, and outrages its competitors by breaking all the rules of the small but noisy book publishing business—How Nelson Doubleday finds $9,000,000 worth of uses for a press he didn't want, and makes a good living at it."

With everything behind him and a blank page in front of him, the true creation of what would be LIFE magazine began. The corporate histories and other books by devoted writers and employees have tread the ground of details of new sorts of cameras, new coated papers that could be printed without ink bleeding everywhere. The finding of photos and the hiring of LIFE's own first photographers is well-documented. The only unheralded point I wish to make is to take note of the explosion of the creative impulses by so many people bound together with only a singular goal in what I would call a monumental publishing task in the Time Inc. tradition but with no-organization-what-so-ever.

Longwell had hardly any organizational instincts. He seemed to just make suggestions or assignments to various people and their best results just bubbled to the top. It was never able to be defined, but it was called "Group Journalism." By-lines and egos were not so much a part of the process. A by-line at Time Inc. was as heady as being named a Pulitzer winner. The mast head was in small print. Photo credits were listed there by page number. It was an accepted and unwritten rule that the staff never appeared in their own picture magazine. It may sound trite today but the LIFE offices really had a feeling of "All for one and one for all." Of course this was enhanced by the fact that the skills of genius imbued and embraced everyone in the office.

In those publishing days, a newspaper or a magazine office was commonly a structure in which one person sat in front of a singular typewriter with one piece of paper, wrote an article or story and handed it to an editor who did his thing, sent it to the copy desks and they did their thing and the piece of paper went through the layout process and on to press; maybe with a by-line and maybe not. This is not to say there were no arguments, but no argument ever prevented an issue getting out.

A picture magazine was an all-together different operation. It is highly likely the production sequence has even been forgotten in today's world of websites, blogs, and tweets.

When the first issue of LIFE came out the masthead was a small print space beneath the long index and the Editors were listed simply, Henry R. Luce, John Shaw Billings, Daniel Longwell, followed by lists of photographers and then associates. They were a modest bunch, not throwing themselves at the public, just hoping the public liked their work. Their pride was in the publication of LIFE.

To produce the picture magazine, here is what had to happen: pictures were gathered from contracted sources and photographers were assigned to cover events in the news or just a common story thought to be of interest. Those several thousands of pictures came in, were looked at and consulted about and culled. The selected pictures were shown to the managing editor who then might consult the editor-in-chief but surely talked it over with the person who chose the selection in the first place. News and stories were decided upon depending on the illustrating strengths of the pictures available. The managing editor then made a suggested rough layout for each page with the pictures and sent the layout to the art people in the layout room to create the pages and fit everything in. The managing editor then gave it to writers who wrote captions for the pictures in the spaces designated by the layout people.

Meanwhile the writers and researchers were working to make the most minimal but still most interesting and informative captions. Here the old saying, "Brevity is the soul of wit," (Shakespeare, *Hamlet*) came home to roost.

This was a magazine that was "invented" even as it was being produced. The extensive corporate Time Inc. histories and the subsequent books about the development of the picture magazine all name persons who were involved. There is much discussion about who did the most and who claimed credit and who deserved credit. In all that I have read, Longwell never claimed himself to be a one man show. He gave a lot of credit to Luce whom he identified as the greatest of editors and he gave Luce the credit for titling the main sections of the magazine. This is taken directly from the deposition which was trying to nail down whose idea was LIFE magazine. This is Longwell's deposition from the *Court Report* of the Corcoran case:

> Luce invented the form of the magazine—Speaking of Pictures, the Essay, the text page, Picture of the Week, Life Goes to a Party—placed his first emphasis on pictures. I did the type and cover, page size, size of the magazine, contributed story-telling ideas in pictures which I had got from comic strips.
>
> Then Longwell was asked "Where did the idea for the size of LIFE come from?" Longwell answers,

Luce wanted it to be the size of *Vanity Fair.* I said it had to be as big or bigger than *The Saturday Evening Post,* and the change in size cost plenty— several million I believe. But I said the pictures had to be seen, and insisted on the larger size. The size was perfectly logical—A, the pictures had to be seen. B, competing against the *Saturday Evening Post* and *Colliers* at double the price, I knew enough about merchandising to know that we had to be half an inch bigger one way or the other than they were. Also, *L'Illustration, Illustrated London News* and *Berliner Illustirte Zeitung* were all big size. It was logical.

Another critical person involved happened to be Executive Vice-President of Macy's, Paul Hollister. It had become habit that the dummies printed for the experimental department would be sent out for comment. The first dummy was panned as amateurish. Paul Hollister told Luce "You give me a check for $1,000 and I will fix it."

Longwell continued:

One day Miss Thrasher (Luce's secretary) grabbed me and said Hollister wanted to discuss the matter with somebody on the phone. (Luce was away.) I had known Hollister a long time. He and I had done typographic work when he was an advertising man. I went up to Manchester, MA, where he was staying and one Sunday morning we laid out the typography of the magazine, designed the page size, etc. Hollister later helped

us with the layout on Rehearsal (the final dummy).
(Box 56, **Daniel Longwell Papers**, Rare Book &
Manuscript Library, Columbia University in the
City of New York)

Honing the product was in the hands of the copy editor. The copy desk made sure the words were fitted to the picture. If changes were made, and they usually were, the research and fact-checking of newly written and newly-edited copy began all over again.

Even before the first issue was out, the second needed to be underway. This included compiling of stories and organizing them into a press run sequence for publication. Little wonder that Luce decided to go ahead and publish LIFE and learn about it as it developed. Little wonder they were all scared to death of failure. Later in 1938, Longwell was known to buy up the left over copies at newsstands which Mary reported to Luce and Luce said he knew how Longwell felt.

But this was not often necessary. The first LIFE that finally reached the newsstands and the new subscribers was a jaw-dropping success. The first printing was 250,000 copies. News stand dealers were calling for 400,000, and that was just the beginning. Box 67, **Daniel Longwell Papers**, Rare Book & Manuscript Library, Columbia University in the City of New York holds a letter from Longwell to Luce reminding him, "I well remember your saying to John Billings and me on Tuesday after the first issue of LIFE had appeared on the stands Friday that, "We seem to have sort of a hit on our hands here—maybe we should get out another issue."

Two years later during the 1938 fiscal year, as Time Inc. losses were more pronounced, Luce once asked Larsen in the presence of Longwell and others who were discussing it, "Aren't you scared, Roy?" Longwell remembered that Larsen admitted to being scared but replied also, "Are you going to let go of what will turn out to be the biggest thing this country has ever seen?" (Time Inc. Archives).

Why was the popular LIFE in trouble financially? A main reason had to do with the cost of production and the demand for the magazine. Longwell explained that the cost of production was tied to the new inventions in printing which made LIFE so popular with the public as a picture magazine. Verification of this is found in a 1941 deposition of Longwell for the 1942 Corcoran trial.

> One other thing about LIFE you must remember is the prohibitive cost of producing a magazine (priced) so cheaply. I insisted on a price of 10 cents and the large size. Luce insisted on a good quality paper. …
>
> The techniques of printing we learned after we started LIFE are as much responsible for its success as any editorial ability we showed. These were inventions of printing and dry coated paper. LIFE is an invention of speed printing itself. It also represents inventions in inks and papers. It is a 50 cent magazine for 10 cents, and if we had not made these inventions, the magazine would not be possible because if we were operating on

costs of paper, printing and ink and at the speed of production of Volume 1, Number 1, we could not deliver enough copies to make the magazine a success and we would be losing more money than we are now making. LIFE is not just an editorial idea. (Box 56, **Daniel Longwell Papers**, Rare Book & Manuscript Library, Columbia University in the City of New York)

To a businessman the situation with LIFE during its first years was not amusing. They were in the precarious situation of losing money on a very popular publication that had a soaring public demand. In these cases it is only natural that the editorial side of publishing begins to fear and tremble in the face of the business side of publishing.

And yet it was really the early business decisions in 1936 that were responsible for this situation. These decisions were to set the advertising rates at "sale" prices in order to acquire a year's contract and assure advertising in the face of the unknown future of the new picture magazine. The money they lost was not due to the editorial side but due to the business side.

The advertisers had a near free ride and they knew it. Back page covers with Coca Cola ads are still iconic poster quality and often seen for sale by themselves without the magazine[27].

---

[27] In fact, in 2013, the Country Bookshop in Plainfield, VT, carried a set of LIFE magazines which had been privately bound …but the owner had torn off all the back covers and probably for profit. I was only able to buy two volumes which I now greatly value: Vol. 1, Nov.-Dec. 1936, and Vol. 17, Oct.-Dec. 1944.

There is one more thing to mention about LIFE coming to life during 1936, and that is, in the midst of it all, Longwell had to have an appendectomy. The photos taken of the office chaos, staged of course by the principals makes a picture essay in itself. They also invaded his hospital room and gained photos of Longwell editing copy or writing some sorts of instructions clothed in the pajamas and dressing gown which he had ordered for the occasion from Brooks Brothers. There are lots of photos on file of parties great and small, but my favorites are the ones taken when Longwell was hospitalized. One can see that the "Experimental Group" of youngsters had grasped the revelation value of the photograph.

What sort of creative thinking delivers a publication of this magnitude? Perhaps that is best answered by Longwell himself in one of the Alex Groner history interviews of Longwell on July 26, 1957. Groner was one of the earlier historians at Time Inc. working at preserving the corporation's history. The following is some historical philosophizing by Longwell.

Fun with the Staff at LIFE Magazine
(Billings Collection, Courtesy of South Caroliniana Library, University of South Carolina, Columbia, SC)

...Let's recall Melville Stone and his iron rules for Associated Press writing, and Adolph Och's and his "All the News That's Fit to Print." It was all too much and too dull for a rising literary generation.

Luce captured the right idea, with an assist from Hadden in early writing style, and Larsen in promotion. Larsen helped create modern advertising but it was with a literary approach.

Remember John Billings. He used to wander around New England with a copy of Vachel Lindsay's poems in his pocket, sleeping in barns, talking to farmers. He romantically joined the Ambulance Service in France, was a truck driver for the French Artillery at Verdun and crashed at Chanute Field, Illinois, as an aviation cadet after the U.S.A. entered World War I. It was that romanticism that Time Inc. was made of. ...

Now take the youthful Longwell, one year the junior of these great men we have been discussing. I ran across a letter Edna Ferber wrote me years ago. She was urging me to write the great American novel. She wrote that in descriptive writing, I could write around her a dozen times. But note the word "descriptive." Perhaps that was prophetic of the little American novel...I had a whack at in LIFE. ...

No publication in the world would have recognized instantly the chance Hemingway's *The Old Man and the Sea* presented and known exactly what to do with it.

Perhaps it's (LIFE) not the great American novel—but the great American *view* that urged so many of us inspired by Luce. How could you get the dandruff in Senator Hamilton's beard, the glory of Marion Anderson's voice, the maggot-eaten South Dakota boys reaching forward on the beach at Buna into a novel? I think I am right (Groner Interview of Longwell for Time Inc. history, 1957, Time Inc. Archives; also Box 26, **Daniel Longwell Papers**, Rare Book & Manuscript Library, Columbia University in the City of New York).

In Longwell's mind, the compliment Ferber had paid Longwell about his powers of description translated as photography.

As the formatting and construction of the magazine proceeded, Luce turned his attention to how the staff should be organized. While Longwell was given to loose organization, Luce was intent on structured positions which he could understand. When Luce wrote his first draft prospectus for the new picture magazine, he was continuing in the spirit of using the brightest and best to produce it. Reluctant as he was to give credit, he did pick out a few of the stars for proposed positions. I want to stress it was a draft prospectus dated "9/9/36" and is not the one that finally made it to the Board Directors to request the go-ahead for publication. In the memo's "Preface", Luce made it abundantly clear that no one was to get any special credit. "The Picture magazine is not the creation of any one individual, neither is it the pet baby of any individual. It is the creation of the large group of individuals known as Time Inc: and as long as it is a struggling child, it is the pet baby of Time Inc." (Box 69, **Daniel Longwell Papers**,

Rare Book & Manuscript Library, Columbia University in the City of New York)

Luce named himself as the Managing Editor for an "unstated term of months or years". The "Alternate Managing Editor" turned out to be a man dismissed before publication. For the purposes of this memoir the following information is in a memo from Luce to Kastner, Longwell, and Cort on Sept. 8, 1936, and is of special interest. ("Pre-publication Folder", Box 69, **Daniel Longwell Papers**, Rare Book & Manuscript Library, Columbia University in the City of New York)

A post of special authority on the Picture Magazine was that of Picture Editor and Office Manager, which was filled by Daniel Longwell. He would be solely responsible for the flow of pictures in and out of Time Inc. offices—including the flow of pictures into the hands of the appropriate editors and through their hands into the magazine-dummy and out of their hands to the printer. Every picture deal, every nickel spent for pictures had to go through him. He would be the traffic officer for all assignments to photographers and also for the work of layout men. The Managing Editor and other editors could short-circuit to photographers or layout men for the purpose of explaining and working out their ideas but all work of photographers or buying of photographs or laying out the photographs had to be regulated by the Picture Editor and Office Manager. (Organization of Editorial Staff of the Picture Magazine, Box 69, **Daniel Longwell Papers**, Rare Book & Manuscript Library, Columbia University in the City of New York)

Obviously Luce showed a lot of confidence in and deference to Longwell. But in this confidential memo (1936?) Luce also describes an almost killing amount of work. Luckily they were able to soon recruit Wilson Hicks to take on a great portion of this position while Longwell turned his attention to getting story ideas as he worked hand in hand with Hicks, a fellow Missourian.

The Luce memo continued to highlight other people who were to become legends of the new magazine: Associate Editors Cort, Kastner, and Thorndike.

John Thorndike was a strikingly handsome bright young man whom Longwell had convinced not to leave Time Inc. but to join him in the Experimental Department. As Longwell's protégé, Thorndike was trained with the idea of one day becoming the LIFE Managing Editor. In 1946, when Longwell was made Chairman of the Board of Editors, Thorndike was named to that position.

Later Edward K. Thompson, another protégé of Longwell's, was trained to be a future managing editor. He became Managing Editor after Thorndike and after his retirement from LIFE, he established the *Smithsonian Magazine,* for the Smithsonian Institute in Washington, D.C. My reporter colleague, good friend and bridesmaid, Sally Scott Maran, left LIFE to join the Smithsonian and later became its Managing Editor. She was significant in urging the writing of this book.

During Thorndike's tenure, Luce, trying to get a handle on "group journalism," reorganized and compartmentalized LIFE magazine into separate and competing departments. It may be that this was NOT what Thorndike had been "trained for" by Longwell who preferred the group journalism method. In 1949 Thorndike left to create the *American Heritage Magazine,* a hard-back magazine of American history and later *Horizon,* also a hard-back, geared to world history and art.

Joe Kastner, originally hired as a CBOB, was known to be able to write brief copy and later became Copy Editor of LIFE. Coming up out of the "old school," Joe was a bulwark for keeping "group journalism" in the ether of the halls and offices of LIFE magazine. The point is, there were a lot of "brains" in the birth of LIFE and the Longwells had a hand in bringing many of them along.

The first and confidential draft prospectus named Peter Stackpole and Alfred Eisenstaedt as Staff-Photographers with others to be appointed. At that time photographer Tom McAvoy was independent but was given assignments by Longwell and appeared in TIME while Margaret Bourke-White was with FORTUNE but also given assignments by Longwell. Luce himself spoke of Bourke-White's early connection to Time Inc. in the transcription of the Corcoran Case.

Perhaps the first American photographer of that particular period who became famous in journalism was Bourke-White. Since there had been no particular demand for her type of photography in journalism, she had tried to dispose of her pictures to advertising agencies; and it was in an advertising agency, for example, that I first learned about Bourke-White, and brought her over for FORTUNE,... ... the first issue of FORTUNE was February, 1930. I think we employed her the summer of 1929. (Box 56, **Daniel Longwell Papers**, Rare Book & Manuscript Library, Columbia University in the City of New York)

Bourke-White's photographs of the Montana Fort Peck Dam, and the story of the life of the town around it became the "lead" and cover of LIFE, Volume I, Issue 1.

Other photographers who joined the staff soon after its beginning were William Vandivert and Carl Mydans. Perhaps Carl is best remembered for his photograph of MacArthur coming ashore in the Philippines.

Of all the scribbling and pontificating about the construed new staff, hindsight reveals the prophetic placement of Mary Fraser in the mix. Luce wrote in a confidential memo on the organizational structure of LIFE:

> Acting directly under both the Managing Editor and the Picture Editor, will be the Copy Chief who will be Miss Fraser until she can get the job organized and train someone else to carry on. She will be in the unhappy position of having two bosses, but between the two she was more responsible to the Picture Editor than to the Managing Editor. Under the Picture Editor she sees to it that pictorial copy is dispatched to the printer on schedule. Under the Managing Editor she sees to it that research is obtained and word-copy is dispatched. ... Hence, with respect

to space and deadlines she was more closely accountable to the Picture Editor. (Box 69, **Daniel Longwell Papers**, Rare Book & Manuscript Library, Columbia University in the City of New York)

Two years later, the Picture Editor became responsible to the Copy Chief as he promised to "Love, Honor and Obey" Mary Douglas Fraser Longwell.

In those years before the war, LIFE magazine brought on a rebirth for Time Inc. and everybody involved. The ambiance at LIFE was delightfully full of enthusiasm and chaos. Journalism was its best and most fun in the halls of LIFE. Everybody was bright. Everybody was young. No one knew for sure what they were doing and yet they did get it done every week.

The comradeship that developed in this chaos was something never to be forgotten by those who participated and who could see the miracle of it all. It involved a lot of hard work, hard thinking, long hours and total absorption in the project. Some people thrived; some people did not. Some people were able to play it cool all the time and some people threw a tantrum now and then. But precious few gave up. Any person who came into this (what probably gave rise to the term "organized chaos") became very proud to say "I work at Time Inc." or "I work at LIFE," even though the outside world had not a clue of the basis of that pride. There was self-respect about working there; everybody experienced it from the highest editorial position right down to the mail clerks. Herein lies one of the foundational strengths of Time Inc. in general. Not only did they NOT publish down to the masses so to speak, they hired people with the highest of qualifications even for their lowest-on-the-ladder jobs.

Whatever was happening in the offices and corridors of this group of journalists, they were doing lots of something right. Longwell spoke of this unusual "happening" in his remarks to Alex Groner in an interview for the Time Inc. corporate history.

> You must recall that the men who played a large part in starting Time Inc. were a literary group representing a literary generation. Luce and Hadden were sensitive Yale poets. You will recall that Larsen was Editor of the *Advocate*, and thought of himself, when I first knew him, as more of a literary editor than a businessman. ... Even Mary Fraser had won the John Masefield prize at Wellesley. ... I was the only one in what Luce called "the literature *business*". (Later he described himself as being in that too), but that was what made the whole group so attractive to me.

> Now I am skipping dangerously here, unless I am understood.

> Although the great age of the American novel came to a sort of high in the 1920's, the novel was really done. The best writing talent was turning to telling what the world was like, and describing the actions and personalities on the world stage. That is about the time Luce and

Hadden and Co. walked in with a lively interest in attracting literary people to them. I don't say they fictionalized news, I simply say that they used the talents of novelists and poets to report the world as they saw it. ... (Groner Interview of Longwell for Time Inc. history, 1957, Time Inc. Archives)

In his preparation of the corporate history in the 1960's, Robert T. Elson sent manuscripts of the proposed history to Longwell for his perusal. The **Daniel Longwell Papers**, hold responses to Elson that Longwell dictated to Mary and I have tried to capture the essence here.

Longwell recalled being at a cocktail party with Charles G. Norris, known as C. G. to his publishing world friends. At the time of this party, statistics had come out showing that the subscription renewal rate for LIFE was at 90%. Dan said he knew that only the *Atlantic Monthly* had a renewal rate like that. Nelson Doubleday was also at this party and took Longwell by the arm, geared him over to Norris and said, "C.G., did you ever think this dumb bastard would be connected with a magazine of a million circulation? I understand your newsstand returns amount to as much as 20% some times." Dan records thinking to himself, "I was used to success with best sellers, but nothing as great as this." Those were early statistics. Subscriptions continued to rise. (Box 81 **Daniel Longwell Papers**, Rare Book & Manuscript Library, Columbia University in the City of New York)

A study later showed that for every one subscriber, eight other people read the magazine. Since LIFE's subscription list had grown to over five million, this tells us that actually forty million Americans were reading LIFE magazine. People loved it and watched and waited for it to arrive in their mail boxes. LIFE's stories, art, special features impacted people. Even today some people recall its weekly publication and the impact it had. My cousin chose to leave Missouri for California and Stanford University because of pictures she saw of that campus.

Daniel Longwell was the Managing Editor when that five million figure was reached. It had been his goal and dream.

And just how do such dreams come true? Dan Longwell said that you had to work hard and be alert—and if you worked hard, luck would break your way. That, in his opinion, was what happened when he, John Billings, John Thorndike and Roy Larsen decided to publish "Birth of a Baby" in LIFE's April 8, 1938, issue.

Longwell avidly read several major daily newspapers which is where he often found ideas for LIFE stories. He came across a newspaper story that stated a movie about the birth of a baby had been banned. He probably noticed this because at Doubleday he had published a book written by an old friend of his in Omaha, Dr. Palmer Findley. The Findley book title was *The Story of Birth*. It had hideous woodcuts of daunting images and was more a history than a current medical work. Longwell knew that TIME had given it a good review and that Doubleday had published it with no alarms going off. However, the movie about birth was a different matter. Today, no one would blink an eye, but in 1938, the moral standard of what the American public would accept was not really known.

Longwell took the little article to Joe Thorndike who was "handling movies" at the time. He told Joe to get the film and see what they might do. Thorndike got it, made a layout using some of the films' strips and showed it to Longwell. Longwell was hesitant. But as he recalled to the Time Inc. historians on tape (Time Inc. Archives), that night he recalled the Findley book and thought that perhaps the "real" story might work in LIFE magazine. The next morning he told Thorndike to get the movie back (they only had contracted for it for 48 hours) and to see what they could do. Thorndike got it back and Longwell took it in to Luce and Billings. He recounted for them the history of the work they had done so far. Longwell said to Luce, "I'm scared to touch it." According to Longwell, Luce walked out on it saying, "Don't put the responsibility on me."

Longwell then reports, "The two fellows who had the courage and did the job were Joe Thorndike and Roy Larsen." By now, Roy Larsen was Publisher of LIFE. Longwell reported that Thorndike and Larsen worked out a scheme of getting important people to approve it before it was published…even Mrs. Roosevelt. Much of the medical community supported it too.

At publication there was a wonderful uproar. In some places, LIFE was confiscated and Larsen was arrested and the news media did more advertising of LIFE than Time Inc. ever could have bought. It turned out that the public did not damn it as feared. It was hailed by many and LIFE was congratulated on their courage.

Longwell said,

> There is a time in the life of every magazine when something happens that sets it off. …We needed something like that…but you can't go out and get it. I mean, you've got to be alert and find it somewhere and be on the watch out, but that's what LIFE needed at this moment. Well, about a week after *The Birth of a Baby,* I said, "Who'd ever suspected that would be it? … This causes more talk than half a year's effort. (Time Inc. Archvives)

The confiscated magazines were all sold. Larsen was acquitted. The public had been given vital and life-saving information and censors were the only losers. LIFE magazine was out of its newsstand slump and while no one said so, Group Journalism had one fine moment of glory. And let it not be forgotten, it all started by an alert executive editor reading and clipping a newspaper story—and sharing it at the office. (Groner/Sugarman Interview, Part I, Time Inc. Archives)

Later, in 1961, Longwell elaborated on other initial people of LIFE magazine and their particular expertise that brought forth the magazine each week. The reader may feel they are re-reading material presented before but consider that time away from the trees can bring the forest into perspective. Also, the better a person knows their subject, the better they are at refining it down to its most salient and basic points. This is what I think Longwell has done while cogitating on his patio in Neosho, MO while he was retired. During my research hours, I wrote in the margins of this memo, "This is the best of Longwell in my opinion."

As I get perspective, it seems that several things get overlooked. One was that, at 36 and 37 years of age, Henry Luce, John Billings and I represented a new fund of divergent experience. Luce had founded TIME and FORTUNE. Billings had a journalist's career behind him including being a great Managing Editor of TIME. We were from Harvard, Yale and Columbia. Though the youngest of the three, I had put in fifteen years as a book publisher in the largest of the publishing companies, Doubleday. ... Doubleday's gave me thorough publishing training in all sides of the business, both in Garden City and in England. ...

All three of us were old enough to have been brushed by World War I. We knew what it was about. Larsen, our publisher was of the same age and the same experience. As editors Luce and I knew a lot about modern publishing. The picture magazine had been talked about for years.... Luce wanted one and he had the money. The point is that we knew where we were going (not how far), we had a pretty general idea of what we were up to, through Time Inc.'s shrewd use of pictures.... I had two years wandering around Time Inc., experimenting in the pages of TIME, getting acquainted with FORTUNE, working on *The March of Time*, etc. ... I knew we were going to have a big woman's appeal, and that there was our advertising revenue and said many times: "Girls will read boys' books, boys will not read girls' books." Those things we just knew, didn't need to discuss.

Luce and Billings knew the cast of characters on the news stage by heart. Luce was the greatest Editor I have ever known and Billings was a hand-in-glove operator. I was a fairly sophisticated guy in the literary and graphic worlds. I knew typography and design and advertising and the literary world. Billings and I were a unique combination, complementing one another and I could field a catch from Luce that he never knew he was throwing.

This was an experienced editorial team, but young enough so that we hadn't any rusty traditions. We actually didn't expect the success we had, we hoped for it in a couple of years. Our first efforts gave a lot of rise to a lot of talk which we accepted and fostered—that we were pretty innocent fellows who didn't know what we were up to.

The point is that editorially we were in a new and modern graphic field, and we didn't know any sure way. Our critics, now that I look back on it, were people who were eminently or slightly successful in their own fields and were certain if we'd just do what they were doing we would be all right….We took a lot of abuse and shed it. But if we had known editorially exactly what we were doing we never would have burst all the boundaries in ten years. We had to make our own pattern and not follow anyone's and "in publication" as Luce repeated somewhat wistfully when things got bad in 1938. ...

(Letter from Longwell in Neosho to Alex Groner, Feb. 13, 1961, Time Inc. Archives)

Again in an April 1965 response to Robert Elson for the corporate history, Longwell extended his thoughts about the difficulty they all had in actually realizing that telling a story in pictures was not quite as unique in history as they had thought. Longwell's explanation again relates to ancient and classical experience:

> It seems... the hardest intellectual feat in getting at modern picture journalism, so called, was to overthrow the 600 year old tradition of printing and book making, even manuscript, that pictures illuminated or illustrated the text. Sure if we had looked at Giotto's Life of St. Francis of Assisi, or Chartres' stained glass windows or the illustrated Bible books that just preceded Guttenberg or the Bayeux tapestry, we might have caught on sooner. (Robert Elson Interview, Corporate History, 1965, Time Inc. Archives)

As LIFE got underway with its emphasis on picture journalism, the literary community was not ignored. Longwell knew these people so well and had such fine personal relationships with them that he was able to bring the personalities into focus. He did this by capitalizing on their best-seller works which were made into popular movies. The public wanted to know more about these authors and stories and LIFE could show them.

Longwell had a great respect and interest in maps. Whenever a story would lend itself to maps, he had one made. The first issue carried a map of the continental USA showing a picture history of aviation trying to get above weather. This was a unique picture to show the public in 1936. The undeniable truth, often pointed out by anyone who knew Longwell was that he had unquenchable curiosity and a deep interest in anything that crossed his path. This weekly explosion of ideas in the pages of LIFE might explain why what was once on the newsstands for a dime, is now sold at ten dollars for common issues and up to one hundred dollars for issues of historical value.

LIFE Goes to the Movies and Broadway

The very first issue (Nov. 23, 1936) carried photos of Helen Hayes in her role as Queen Victoria in *Victoria Regina*. The background and rise of movie star Robert Taylor with Gretta Garbo in *Camille* was the Hollywood offering.

The movie of Christopher Morley's *Kitty Foyle* starred Ginger Rogers. Longwell was smitten by Ginger like a proud father. She too was from Missouri, Arrow Rock to be exact. Through LIFE, March 2, 1942, the public got to see where she grew up, the beginning of her career and her retreat from Hollywood in southern Oregon near the Rogue River. Her complete biography was in that week's Photographic Essay of nine pages.

When Kenneth Roberts' *Northwest Passage* was filmed, LIFE (March 18, 1940) ran photos of him at his fieldstone home on the Maine coast. LIFE showed *Northwest Passage* movie stills with Spencer Tracy portraying Robert Rogers whom history came to identify as the leader of Rogers' Rangers who fought Indians in an equally fierce environment. LIFE was able to show Roberts' home where he toiled for accuracy in writing about the French and Indian War, the Revolutionary War, and the War of 1812. Kenneth Roberts' books, *Arundel, Captain Caution,* and *Northwest Passage* won him a Pulitzer Citation for his body of work.

Authors and Artists

LIFE's spotlight on Kenneth Roberts' friendship with his neighbor, collaborator and mentor Booth Tarkington gave readers insight by "sight" into the lives of these literary geniuses. The LIFE issue featuring Booth Tarkington ran September 4, 1939.

Scoops of this nature were surely made available to LIFE by Longwell who had made these friendships while working at Doubleday. The celebrated authors had a trust in Longwell. He had legitimate and intimate knowledge of their work and the depth he could bring to the presentation was not shallow media mayhem. They trusted him and let LIFE into their homes and studios.

Not only was this true regarding the literary world, but Longwell was also knowledgeable and interested in the artists of the day. He developed friendships with Missouri's

Thomas Hart Benton, and Iowa's Grant Wood. John Stuart Curry of Kansas was featured in the very first issue of LIFE. These artists were known as the Regionalists. Their subject matter was "all American" and LIFE was delighted to show their work to the nation they were portraying. If art is truly a reflection of the society that creates it, LIFE was the perfect vehicle to show the population how simply beautiful and unique was their America.

One of the traits of Dan Longwell was his endless curiosity and varied interests. Public trends and reactions were like the morning papers to him. When World War II artists began to be printed in LIFE, there was reaction from other American artists.

Longwell from his own perspective as an art admirer and collector told the Time Inc. history archivists that there was some disgust on the part of the Abstract Expressionism painters toward the Representational Regional artists, also called the Regionalists. The Abstract artists did not feel it was necessary to be in the battlefield to grasp the realities of war.

After the Metropolitan Museum of Art carried a show with 123 works by LIFE's commissioned artists, the non-representational artists had a show of their own contending that war could be painted without going to the battlefield. In the June 12, 1944, issue, LIFE printed their works in a pictorial essay entitled *Studio War Art.* These were done by artists who had not gone into the battlefields but expressed war as they saw it from their vivid imaginations.

Some of the Representational Regionalist artists LIFE used were John Stuart Curry,[28] Grant Wood, Fletcher Martin[29], Aaron Bohrod[30], Byron Thomas, Peter Hurd and Thomas Hart Benton. As an aside, the Longwells' private collection included the works of these artists and many other noted American artists.

Among the American artists showcased by LIFE in the 1940's was Lauren Ford (1891-1973)[31] of Bethlehem, Connecticut. Ms. Ford's work graced the cover of the December 25, 1944 issue of LIFE, continuing the trend of regularly highlighting the work of American artists in the pages of the "picture" magazine.

Longwell's personal artistic taste ran to the Contemporary and Modernists, too. Mary had given him a Jackson Pollock, (*Number 23*) which hung in their home in Neosho until it was sold to the TATE Gallery in London. When LIFE ran a story on an artist, Longwell urged the photographers to

---

[28] Curry was the Kansas artist featured in the first issue of LIFE

[29] Martin painted the battles in North Africa

[30] Bohrod sketched D Day +6 behind German lines unknowingly

[31] Of interest: Lauren Ford eventually became a patron of a group of nuns who emigrated from France. Ford had studied in France where her style was influenced by liturgical Catholic art. As a patron of the Benedictine Sisters who emigrated from France to Connecticut, she helped them begin the Monastery of Regina Laudis on her farm, Sheepfold. Clare Booth Luce brought the story of the founding of this monastery to life in her short story, *Come to the Stable*, which was made into a motion picture starring Loretta Young and Celeste Holmes in 1949. Elsa Lanchaster was cast in the part of Miss Potts, the artist-patron based on Ms. An aside: The actress Dolores Hart, noted co-star of Elvis Presley in *Where the Boys Are, King Creole,* entered this cloistered monastery in 1963 and continues to reside there at this writing. At one time, she was its abbess. [https://suburbanbanshee.wordpress.com/2005; www.imdb.com/name/ nm0366247/bio; en.wikipedia.org/wiki/**Clare_Boothe_Luce**]

get pictures of the studio where he or she worked. "Artists are interesting people," he would say. Little wonder that at retirement from LIFE the American Federation of the Arts drafted Longwell to be their president and spokesman which he agreed to be for two years.

Through the years, LIFE featured major artists known at home and abroad. LIFE magazine was like a museum come to your home in your mailbox!

The LIFE Midwives

Mary Fraser Longwell had been with the development of LIFE from the beginning. Furthermore, she had been with Time, Inc. for several years before Daniel Longwell arrived.

Mary's insights have been recorded and she steps in with praise for the women who in their own way contributed to the respect gained for women in the work place. One must remember that Mary was a young woman at a major college for women during the height of the women's suffrage movement. Today young women probably cannot imagine what it meant to be born without the right to vote, not to mention other legal rights and opportunities. She came of age in the light of Elizabeth Caddy Stanton and Susan B. Anthony. She knew what they had endured and what they accomplished and she never let it be thought that the struggle was in vain. Mary always remembered that the Nineteenth Amendment was won by the women.

In proof-reading the Elson materials for the corporate history, she took umbrage at the fact that little attention was paid to the women at Time Inc. By the time I got to Time Inc. in 1962, women had gained ground and had even achieved being writers and department heads. My own immediate boss when I was in the LIFE Text department was Betty Dunn. The editorial head of the department and its first line editor was Dave Maness. Betty's boss was Chief of Research, Marian MacPhail. These women rode herd on the Researchers, and were powers of respect and accomplishment in their own right, but they had no reason to write a string of memos. If they wanted to tell us something, Betty came down the corridor to my cubicle or Marian would call me into her office. None of that is on paper in the archives. Knowing this work pattern, Mary knew why the women were easily overlooked in the drafts of manuscripts by the corporate historians. We must remember that "Fra" worked first with TIME, then LIFE and TIME again in 1940 and 1941. She wrote how that magazine worked, and how much it relied on the Researchers at the home office as well as the news correspondents in the field. The Researchers' work was background to the news and therefore provided a fuller report for the reader.

One of Mary's good friends and company cohorts was Patricia Divver. She had joined FORTUNE in 1930 when Mary was setting up the Research staff for that new magazine devoted to in depth stories from the worlds of business and industry. Divver had actually begun at Time Inc. in 1928, at a weekly salary of $22. She worked then under Kay Abrams. When Divver needed surgery for a goiter in 1929, her boss Abrams wrote Briton Hadden as asked if Time Inc. could loan Divver money for the operation and Hadden came right back with "Certainly" and it was on easy terms. In 1936 Divver was made Chief of Research for FORTUNE until the United States entered the war and she then went to TIME as Chief of Research. Twenty seven Researchers and Writers on FORTUNE sent Luce a petition asking him to keep her on FORTUNE. In 1944 Divver sent a memo to Luce, "I would like to collaborate with Fra on a manual for training Researchers." (Time Inc. Archives)

When interviews for the corporate histories were being done, the Divver interview described how life became what is was for Researchers at Time Inc.

> The women at Time Inc. were an absolutely extraordinary group of women. The pattern, in my opinion, was set by Kate Abrams and Mary Fraser, who were great friends. Kate was my first boss, Mary my second. And there was instilled in us in those early days: "You gotta work together. Because if you don't work together, you have absolutely no power and no influence." And we always did. (Robert Elson Interview, Corporate History, 1965, Time Inc. Archives)

Pat Divver added later, "Certainly, you worked all Saturday night and all Sunday night. But what of it? It was fun."

Peg Quimby agreed with Divvers in her own observation, "I do not think the current crop of Researchers have any sense of the fun." (Box 81, **Daniel Longwell Papers**, Rare

Book & Manuscript Library, Columbia University in the City of New York)

As the corporate history was being written, Researchers on that project began to realize the impact of Mary Fraser Longwell. In March 1968, Marie Crum closed one of the many letters sent to Mary with the following, "I think it would warm your heart to know how often we have wished during this project for 'a Mary Fraser.'" (Box 81, **Daniel Longwell Papers**, Rare Book & Manuscript Library, Columbia University in the City of New York)

However in my opinion the June 17, 1968, letter[32] to Mr. Longwell from Peg Quimby held the quintessential compliment about the corporate history's research staff's view of the Longwell legacy. It was hand written from her home at 39 Gramercy Park, New York City.

> Dear Mr. Longwell-
> The Company history is about to go to press. I'm writing to you from my home rather than from the office because this is really a "fan" letter.
> The pre-LIFE and early LIFE sections were mine to research, and in doing them I think I got to know you a little. I don't know if the sense of excitement and innovation and experiment—and fun even if exhausting—comes over. I felt it as I did the research, and I wished I'd been in the early days. ...

---

[32] This letter very much expresses my own feelings about working on this memoir. I am grateful to Peg Quimby for stating our feelings so well.

I'm a fairly "trained" historian—I've found myself marveling more than ever at the writers of history who take a handful of documents and then speak with "authority". We had so much and I, for instance, loved your directions (written from a hospital bed!) for how to get pictures for the unborn magazine without letting on that that was what you, (impersonal you) were doing. It was so decisive. But if all the things we had were used, this book would end up one volume longer than the *Britannica.*

I hope the sum of our work is right. I recall one of my professors pointing out that a map—"a curved surface made flat—is only an approximation of the truth".

Anyhow if I'd been there in 1935-36, I'd have beaten on your door. As it is, all these years later, I have in a way been enjoying those days. Thank you.

As for Mary Fraser Longwell—the number of times Elsa and I have said, "We need Fra", would reach from here to Neosho.

Our thoughts have, and our gratitude for your help. Speaking for myself, this book has been a labor of love—for people I've known and not known, but who created the company where I've spent an unbelievable number of years, so many of them happy.

Sincerely, Peg Quimby

> (Box 81, **Daniel Longwell Papers**, Rare Book
> & Manuscript Library, Columbia University in
> the City of New York)

Besides the Researchers, many women with other skills and knowledge influenced the magazine. Daniel Longwell noted that "the girls added taste and single mindedness." By that he was thinking of LIFE's art director and artist in her own right, Margit Varga. Her memos are in the archives and most are between the War Artists and their assignments and her compliments to them on their work. When Mary wrote Elson that the Time Inc. magazines "would not have had the editorial character they do without the women," she was not speaking from a vacuum of experience. She expressed her thoughts to Elson while he was doing the corporate history. It is not dated, but she refers to pages 335-365 of the manuscript copy [*Time Inc., The Intimate History of a Publishing Enterprise 1921-1943*], found in Box 81, **Daniel Longwell Papers**, Rare Book & Manuscript Library, Columbia University in the City of New York.

> I am of course somewhat bothered that there is very little attention paid to the female staff, and having battled for the ladies these 20-odd years of course I can't resist taking the platform again. ...
>
> Dan of course was used to working with women, and liked the system. Some writers and editors got into battles with the girls, some girls were entirely too rigid in their fixation on checking, but the majority developed a kind of

empathy with the writer, and then the joint results
in writing and research were spectacular. …

When one reflects on Mary Fraser Longwell's comments, one comes to know that hers was a personality that had no guile, only gravity. She was the perfect complement to that crazy mixture of "executive" men at Time Inc. and she was the one woman moved to the Executive floor. In a November 22, 1938, (Box 81 **Daniel Longwell Papers**, Rare Book & Manuscript Library, Columbia University in the City of New York), letter to her friend Nancy Ford, the one girl-Friday of the earliest Time Inc. days, Mary describes the phenomenal growth at Time Inc. and how she herself had been impacted by it. The letter invited Nancy Ford to Mary's now "monumental office" and recalled that Ford had been the entire "checking[33] staff for TIME magazine" in the early 1920's.

Mary Fraser's personal insights regarding the corporate history focus on the earliest days of LIFE magazine found in a file from the Time Inc. Archives.

> If I may be permitted a personal observation about D.L.'s part in the early experimental and trial days of LIFE: I have always felt that his book publishing background was invaluable, because he was trained by experience and gifted by nature with a feeling for long range planning.

---

[33] The term "checking" is what the Researchers did. In the very beginning, they were just called "checkers." The index in Vol. 1, of the Elson Corporate history does not have a listing for Checkers or Researchers.

Someone had to project way ahead, and he became the planner. The stories on Vassar, West Point, the wheat harvest in Eureka, South Dakota, for example, were his assignments. Perhaps if you queried a couple of the early hands, such as Eisenstadt or Carl Mydans on this you could confirm or explode my theory.

Billings and Longwell were a remarkable working team, with John Billings as the steady center of operations and Dan as the free-wheeling idea man and explorer. John was famous for sticking to his desk, and disliked travel; Dan did the traveling, the getting around, the seeing and projecting—everything he experienced or saw was translated into the visual and was the grist for LIFE's mill. They complimented each other in all phases of the operation. When Dan was made Managing Editor he said: "The thing I miss is myself. There is no one to do for me what I did for John." ("MFL [Mary Fraser Longwell] Comments on 'The Launching of LIFE'", Nov. 18, 1966, Time Inc. Archives)

However, the initial "disorganization" of the staff and the rather meaninglessness of the masthead titles was in hindsight one of the magazine's greatest strengths. When I began the research for this memoir, it seemed that Henry Luce was trying to subvert the importance of Daniel Longwell, and to some extent, perhaps that might be so. However, in fairness I do now believe that Dan's constant insistence that the multitude of players with their individual creative impulses was the major factor for the success of this magazine. He called it "group journalism." Longwell never took singular credit himself, but he also never placed anyone else on that pedestal.

I have always been tempted to compare the early LIFE staff to being like the American Founding Fathers, a group of geniuses the likes of which we have never seen again. I am prejudiced of course....but I also knew a lot of the original LIFE group and I offer them as a fair comparison. (I will admit though, LIFE was little less important than the *US Constitution*.)

CHAPTER SIX

LIFE Comes to Life

Longwell Leads the Way and Mary Joins Him

It can be expected that some readers, critics or scholars will take umbrage at my apparent braggadocio of Daniel Longwell. This deserves explaining as the production of LIFE magazine obviously could not be and was not a one man show.

The main characters involved became a quartet of men and one woman. From what I have read, this is now how I see office life at LIFE magazine with the interactions of this group of five.

The male quartet was made up of Henry R. Luce, John Shaw Billings, Wilson Hicks and Daniel Longwell. The woman was Mary Fraser. Of course there were others who would come along to play major roles, but for the early days, these were the key, long lasting editorial cast of characters in my opinion.

Luce was the boss but it is difficult to nail down what he actually did. He led with philosophical input but his hands-on day to day work was not of the deadlines-to-be-met variety. He was known to pop in during layout sessions, choosing photos or story choices. Luce was not heavy-handed, but Billings thought him something of a nuisance during these sessions, especially if he proposed changes. Luce was fairly happy in his private life, newly married to a pretty and bright lady, Clare Booth Luce, who became a playwright, Congresswoman and diplomat. Luce was Harry to his friends but they referred to him as "Luce" in memos. He wrote his own memos in a very large script and signed them HRL; important policy documents were typed. He seemed not to have been comfortable or adept in social situations. This did not keep him from being a sought after guest. Too, he was a successful speaker at official and company functions. This confidence may have been due to many of his speeches having been written by others, namely Allen Grover who was his special assistant as a Vice President. The January 24, 1938, memo explained that Grover's chief regular function "is to act as the President's Manager" (Time Inc. Archives). Grover was known in the hallways as "Vice President in charge of Mr. Luce".

Luce's having been born and reared in China rather cheated him out of having an American "hometown" he could call his own. This seems to have at once made him feel superior and yet inferior to the backgrounds of Longwell and Billings who were all "wool and a yard wide" American home-town boys.

John Shaw Billings was regarded by everyone at the office as being the most organized and businesslike. He made the deadlines and kept the magazine on track for press runs.\ with fine journalism and writing credentials which he had honed after becoming the National Affairs editor of TIME in January 1929. He was soon elevated to be a co-managing editor of TIME and he shared the title in the masthead box. As the deadline of the first issue of LIFE drew near, it became apparent to Longwell that the man acting in the managing editor role, John Martin, was not going to get the job done. Luce and Longwell lived in the same neighborhood and would sometimes walk home together. Longwell filled Luce in on how things were not going well at the new soon-to-be LIFE. According to Longwell, Luce asked him what he thought about bringing Billings in to begin LIFE. Longwell was elated. Luce did the dirty work of sending Martin from his place at LIFE back to TIME.

Billings records on October 23, 1936, that Luce called him into his office, shut the doors, and proceeded to explain that he was sorely needed to come from TIME to LIFE and Billings said he would do whatever Luce wanted, but in his diary he wrote, "the decision is Luce's: to wreck Time to launch Life." The shift to Billings occurred on October 27th, less than one month before the first issue of LIFE would appear. (Time Inc. Archives, Billings Folder; also Billings Collection Courtesy of South Caroliniana Library, University of South Carolina, Columbia, SC)

The first issue listed the LIFE Editors equally, though not in alphabetical order: Henry R. Luce, John Shaw Billings, Daniel Longwell. Later Longwell realized it made more sense to have Billings as the sole Managing Editor of LIFE and Longwell took the position of Associate Editor which he shared with Wilson Hicks. This made journalistic history, though it is probably unknown that a major player at LIFE "asked" to be demoted on the masthead. But it also proves that Longwell's priority was success of "his baby", LIFE, and keeping Billings happy was the key. Longwell's argument to Luce was that Billings deserved having the title to himself which he had not had on TIME.

Billings lived with his wife and mother-in-law in an apartment on upper Fifth Avenue in Manhattan. It was a straight shot from his residence to the editorial and business offices of Time, Inc. in midtown Manhattan at 135 East 42nd Street, the Chrysler Building. He was driven there every morning by his chauffeur, William, in a Packard. Power lunches were often held in the Chrysler Building's Cloud Club, other lunches were at Schrafts. He had trouble keeping servants at home. His personal relationships at home were challenging to him as well. (Billings Collection Courtesy of South Caroliniana Library, University of South Carolina, Columbia, SC)

Billings had been born in South Carolina but reared in New York City. His grandfather had become Director of the New York Public Library. However the family was of Southern stock and all his childhood vacations were at Redcliffe, the family plantation in South Carolina. The Billings family was living in Washington, DC when he was recruited to be National Affairs editor for TIME in New York January of 1929.

Uknown to many, John Shaw Billings and his wife Fredrica lost their three year old little girl to spinal meningitis just nine months after moving to New York. Naturally, this had a horrible impact on their lives.

Billings was as staunch a Republican, as was Luce, and initially the two men hit it off well. However, according to Billings who longed for more verbal praise from Luce, a camaraderie did not develop. Developing camaraderie did not seem to have been Luce's management style. Nonetheless, Luce had great confidence in Billings and regarded him as an editor who could manage any or all of the magazines in the event that something untoward might happen to himself unexpectedly.

Billings' diaries[34] indicate he loved his wife very much but she was understandably often unhappy at home. The amount of time her husband was required to be at the office left her adrift at home in the apartment. On many days William would drive her to the office, she would claim her husband for lunch and then they might continue on to a movie in the afternoon. Subsequently he often needed to work nights, weekends and some holidays. Apparently, the Billings were not comfortable in social situations. At least he was not known for socializing but the diaries also reveal he was often unhappy about being left out. In his defense, he did not want to go without his wife and while she was beautiful and had the clothes, she was not comfortable in office company. There were often "scenes" when he got home from work.

---

[34] Most of the material in this part of this chapter is found in John Shaw Billings' diaries, housed at the South Caroliniana Library at the University of South Carolina, Columbia, SC. The references within the text are to the year of the Diary and the page. Some notes from those diaries were taken by former Time Inc. Archivist, Lillian Owens, when researching for Loudon Wainwright's book, *The Great American Magazine.*

On March 25, 1934, (Billings Diary, Volume 10, pages 278-79, Billings Collection Courtesy of South Caroliniana Library, University of South Carolina, Columbia, SC) he recorded, probably with much sadness: "such scenes make me scared to come home".

Billings more often thought of "home" as Redcliffe, on Route 2 of North Augusta, South Carolina, where he managed to buy and restore the family estate. He later deeded Redcliffe to the people of South Carolina along with his scrap books and diaries which are archived at the University of South Carolina in Columbia. The Redcliffe is on the National Historic Register and can be toured.

Billings was a diarist who never lost his pencil. Each day of his life is recorded and he had a lot to say about every day at work at Time Inc.

When Longwell had first come to Time Inc. in 1934, one of his first assignments from Luce was to get more photographs into TIME. Longwell learned then of Billings' strong writing and editing skills and his businesslike manner of meeting deadlines.

Daniel Longwell and Mary Fraser liked Billings. After the first LIFE issues and Christmas of 1936, were past, Dan and Mary with Noel Busch surprised John at the office with a dachshund puppy.

Sometimes the measure of a man is in how he treats his dogs. This is what John Shaw Billings wrote in his Diary, December 28, 1936:

> In the afternoon Longwell led me into his
> office and there I was presented with a six-weeks

old dachshund puppy by him, Noel Busch and Miss Fraser as a Christmas present. She was very cute and charming-and I fell in love with her at first sight. I finished up my work & took the puppy home in a box. (She slept all the way.) Fredrika (sic) was in transports over the little lady-we call her Juliana Van De Grebelsburg, Julie for short.

The puppy was much beloved and despite good care, the puppy only lived about a month.

During their stint together on the lower LIFE editorial floors, Longwell and Billings, if one is to believe the Billings diaries, were the original odd couple. Billings claimed that Longwell often gave him the feeling that Longwell was the superior party as the "idea" man and "genius" behind LIFE magazine. Billings found this very irritating. On other days, Billings was grateful for Longwell's pulling good story ideas together and managing to get the pictures to go with them. Longwell often talked of how they enjoyed Sunday afternoons in the office competing with each other in choosing photos for the next stories. Longwell favored photos with the American flag and Billings argued for men with beards a lá Confederate faces. Aside from the humorous, Longwell and Billings were both men who had a sense of the importance of history and the imperative of understanding it. Of course Billings had more journalism background than Longwell, but Longwell was the one who had the literary, photographic, and illustrations background. Their differences made them like a perfect pie. Billings was crusty and held things together. Longwell had a new recipe for a new filling every week and instinctively knew what to serve up to the public palate.

Longwell was also the one man in the mix who was very social and he kept in contact with everyone he ever worked with which was invaluable to the production hunger of a weekly picture magazine.

Longwell was well-read, a fascinating conversationalist, and could carry his weight in any social situation at any level whether with the literati of England and the United States or the farmers and bankers in Midwest America. He liked people and took a true interest in them. They returned the compliment. It really was that simple.

For several years the Luce, Billings, Longwell combination would get the magazine to press and the public ate up. This trio of titans claimed they had no real idea of what they were doing that made LIFE so successful, so right. Longwell's touch on the public pulse had to be a big part of LIFE's credit with the purchasing public.

Wilson Hicks joined the Titan Trio which then became a quartet. Hicks had been born in Sedalia, MO, and had been a picture editor for the *Kansas City Star* before moving to New York City in 1928 to rise in the ranks at Associated Press. He brought specialized insight into what was a good composite of pictures.

When Luce first suggested hiring Hicks, Longwell threw a fit and spoke of resigning, according to the Billings' diaries (Billings Collection, Courtesy of South Caroliniana Library, University of South Carolina, Columbia, SC) Longwell's place in the group journalism scheme had been strongest in the gathering and culling of photographs. Hicks would take over this assignment which made Longwell feel he would ultimately be left out. When Longwell threatened to resign, Luce bent to Longwell's wishes. However, eventually Longwell saw the light that Hicks could handle the pictures and photographers. This would free Longwell to travel and find more stories. The natural juggling for position soon worked itself out and the men seem to actually have fun working and arguing with each other. Obviously in those days job descriptions must have been somewhat obscure. Then again, picture editing in the LIFE format was a whole new journalistic tool. In 1952, Wilson Hicks published his book *Words and Pictures: An Introduction to Photojournalism.*[35] In Part One of this book he thoroughly explains what made LIFE different and just how the juxtaposition of photographs with one another made the impact it did. He based his text on his experience at LIFE exclusively. In Part Two he explains in detail how LIFE magazine was put together on a day by day, story by story basis. He puts into words how LIFE was creating stories with pictures. Although he knew of the verbal tugs of war that took place during layout time at the office, Wilson's book reads like it was all calm and peaceful. But then, it is meant to be clear as a textbook, and no doubt he used it as such when he became professor of photojournalism at the University of Miami in Florida in 1955. What began as "picture essays" in early LIFE terms came to be called "photojournalism".

---

[35] Hicks, Wilson, *Words and Pictures: An Introduction to Photojournalism.* Arno Press, New York, 1952.

What was Mary Fraser doing all this time? From the beginning, she seems to have been a floating Jane-of-All-Trades. She was not the power behind the wheels but she surely was the oil that kept the machinery running smoothly. At any rate she was an early and necessary component to this journalistic operation.

She had been the number one researcher for TIME and then worked on a trial "Letters to the Editor" supplement for TIME before it was incorporated into the magazine. Sometimes she would fill in as Billings' secretary. She would also receive and route Longwell's story ideas and reports-from-the-road to proper people in the offices. Simultaneously she was interviewing new hires and organizing the research side of things. She was significant in making sure the women employees not only got a fair break, but she was interested in finding the right women for the jobs she saw as important cogs in the machinery of this magazine empire. And she took her vacations in Bermuda.

In this twenty-first century it is one thing to say that Mary Fraser fought for the women, but it is another thing to get a clear idea of what that meant in 1936. Billings' March 1, 1936, diary entry noted that Mary Fraser had invited herself to lunch with Billings, Longwell and 'Goldie'[36] to discuss replacing Cecelia Schwind, who had just died. To quote Billings,

> Goldie and I both resented this self-invitation.
> We have no social relations with the female staff

---

[36] Goldie was Laird S. Goldsborough, TIME's Foreign News writer/editor.

and don't want any. We made it quite clear to Miss
F. that her lunch with us was to be no precedent.

To know Mary Fraser was to know a woman who could hold her own. She was not intimidating nor was she intimidated. She was in a working climate of highly intelligent and creative people who were not ones to brook disagreement easily. Yet there had to be disagreement for the "thesis versus antithesis to equal synthesis" dynamic to play itself out and produce the best product. In a working environment that had press time deadlines, team work was imperative. Mary understood that and somehow her presence made a difference for the good.

She had bright brown eyes that told you she knew everything that had happened, what was about to happen, as well as what needed to happen. It can be said that she had her finger on the pulse of the office. She had highly developed insight. She was a good judge of character and could handle any sort of person that came along. Betty Morris, Dan Longwell's last secretary, gave a loving testimonial description of Mary: "Mary was equilibrium personified" (Morris Interview, January 25, 2015).

I have only known one other woman like her and that was Helen Walton, Mrs. Sam Walton, of Wal-Mart.

Helen spent a weekend at my home in Kansas City, MO, in the early 1990's. Thankfully, we liked each other. In face to face conversation over breakfast, she shared with me her personal background and what she felt she had added to the Wal-Mart success story. She said that often times she would make a suggestion to Sam and he would either not agree or pay no attention. Then a short time later she would learn he had acted on her suggestion. One instance was re-titling the employees "associates," drawing them into "ownership investment". She had the same concern of the personnel as she had for the business itself and her style of thinking was parallel to Mary's. Helen had that same all-knowing, sincere look of attentive concern in her bright brown eyes. I wish the two women had known each other; they only lived a forty-five minute drive apart. They were even both Presbyterians. And certainly both their corporate interests impacted a broad scope of the American public.

There have been scholarly works analyzing the impact of LIFE magazine on American society during its tenure from November 23, 1936, to the demise of its weekly issue, December 29, 1972. Art historians and social science scholars who study this impact are the flattering proof that LIFE was important to the people of the United States and in some instances to the world. Americans loved the new magazine in which they could see glimmers of their own lives reflected as well as the contrasts of the worlds beyond their picket fences or bustling intersections.

To most, LIFE just arrived in their mail box and they gave little thought to who might be the driving forces putting it together before it went to the post office. To my knowledge, this is the first study of the main man behind LIFE magazine. In my opinion, Daniel Longwell led this pack of lone-wolf journalists who managed to create and survive the democracy of "group journalism". I claim the right to name the catalyst in this office chemistry: Mary Fraser.

After Dan had died, I asked Mary who was Dan's best friend at LIFE and she at once replied, John Shaw Billings. Later, it was surprising to me to read the Billings diaries and his sometimes daily written harangues about Dan Longwell. But I also have the rest of the story in the latter-year letters of both men. Mary had them pegged as friends even as she saw them "fussin' and a-fightin'," as we say in the Ozarks.

Luce sort of disappeared from this scenario of creative journalism. Hicks became a major part of the pictures and photographers. His name appeared on the masthead first as an "Associate" in September 1937, as "Associate Editor" with Daniel Longwell in September of 1938, and in 1947 he was listed as an "Executive Editor." Hicks had taken the lead in the photographic department and he was on board in 1937 and 1938 which were the experiment-in-publication years.

The main characters were cast in their parental roles and the magazine began to grow in philosophy and personality. Twenty years had passed since the end of World War I which was to have been the war to end all wars, but there were activities in Europe that indicated all was not peaceful.

Americans felt protected and aloof from Europe protected behind the Atlantic and Pacific Oceans. We were a very isolationistic population. LIFE magazine in its infancy was NOT isolation-minded. LIFE had a more All-American confidence and curiosity of the world beyond the oceans.

LIFE's intention was to discover and show American citizens their many-faceted country. It was not a landscape magazine; it was to be a pictorial mirror of American culture.

This culture was not made up only of the great personages, but also of common men and women. People were as interested in seeing common everyday lives as well as lives of the high and mighty. LIFE in the beginning was elementary "show and tell", but unlike the single-subject magazines of today, LIFE was a surprise every week. The first full year of publication was 1937. Unlike the single-subject magazines of today, LIFE was a surprise every week. Readers learned that Main Street, USA, was interesting too. Main Street was a very long street and the girls were just as pretty.

In February of 1937, Longwell was asked to list some interesting developments that had become apparent in the short three months LIFE had been in production. His reply is found in a colleague's speech which was augmented by Dan's insights.

Longwell summarized what was happening on the editorial side of the magazine in a memo to Robert Johnson.

> We never thought that news photographs would be so popular as they turned out to be.
>
> Pictures to the Editor Department has grown by leaps and bounds. We started off with a Contributions Editor and one girl and now have five people working on this alone. ... LIFE Goes to a Party. When first suggested we wondered how we were going to get into the parties. Now we are swamped with invitations to go everywhere

from private parties to Yale proms, and industrial meetings.

We ran an article on Vassar and received invitations from 20 Universities asking us to visit them.

The way people like LIFE is what astonishes me. It is a magazine which has personal affection. Readers write in that tenor. (Box 28, **Daniel Longwell Papers**, Rare Book & Manuscript Library, Columbia University in the City of New York.

When I flip through my own 1937 files of Dan and Mary Longwell, the assignments they were dealing with reveal how far they were reaching. LIFE tapped a reading market that had not been discovered except perhaps by advertising firms and local newspapers. The center of the USA was an anomaly to most coastal city folk. But the fact was, and in my opinion Longwell and LIFE proved, that America between the coasts was the norm after all.

I believe one needs to have been born and reared in the Midwest before one really "hears" the coastal mind set. While I was on a Woodrow Wilson scholarship to Yale Graduate School (1961-1962), coming from Neosho, Missouri, and Tulane University in New Orleans, a Yale peer asked me one day at lunch: "How did you get out of Missouri?" When I asked him what he meant by the question he responded with, "Well, by wagon? train?... what?"

Even now, with the development of air travel, I've heard coastal folk call the Midwest the "Fly-Over Zone". I believe that in 1937, Daniel Longwell had realized that a huge amount of material had not yet been exposed to the average American reader. He had a win-win situation: The subscriber market for LIFE was also between the coasts. City folk bought LIFE off the newsstands.

Because of the differing life styles in the Midwest, Longwell could and would show the readers what they had never seen before. Readers came to expect to experience art from our Midwestern museums as well as the big city ones. Never-before-seen private collections were photographed. LIFE would show behind-the-scenes of the entertainments Americans enjoyed. Readers would see back stage on Broadway and movie sets in Hollywood. The rodeo in Cheyenne, Wyoming, was there alongside the parlor games "Charades" and "Bridge." LIFE was full of amusements.

LIFE readers would see the corn growing in Iowa and Illinois, cattle grazing in Texas, the amber waving wheat fields in Kansas, New England farming in Vermont, the first views of outer space through a telescope at Mount Wilson in California.

Readers learned of the renowned scientist, Edwin Hubbell who had published a book on the nebulae fifty-three years before the telescope named for him was launched. (Incidentally, Hubbell was born in Marshfield, MO. just ten years before Longwell was born in Omaha.)

And how was all this happening? Longwell had a mind that constantly churned out story ideas for photographers and reporters to cover. The chief legacy that he left with LIFE was his penchant for story ideas.

I talked with Ralph Graves, the last Managing editor of the weekly LIFE, who was a young man when Dan Longwell was nearing retirement. Quoting from an email Graves sent me March 20, 2010:

> I liked Dan, all of us younger guys did. We thought he was something of a yesterday figure and definitely a fussbudget and kind of a joke with all those newspaper scraps[37], but he was friendly, encouraging, nice to much younger men, and above all he still cared passionately about the magazine. (Graves Correspondence, 2010)

With all due respect to the young men joking about Longwell and his news clips, the reader should remember that TIME magazine began by rewriting news clips and the job of clipping newspapers for stories was the main training position when I was "the clip gal" for LIFE in 1962.

Before she died, Marian MacPhail[38] (d. 1993), my boss and Chief of Research for LIFE, told me about Dan and his story suggestions, some from news clips and some just

---

[37] Dan was famous for tearing out scraps of newspaper, stuffing them in his jacket side pocket, then fishing them out at group lunches or other gatherings, presenting them as story ideas for LIFE. He was sometimes momentarily puzzled when he fished out a scrap because he couldn't remember why he had saved it, but eventually he would remember.

[38] **Amenia NY Harlem Valley Times 1993 Jul,** fultonhistory.com/.../ Amenia%20 NY%20Harlem%20Valley%20**Times**/Ame; The Harlem Valley Tunes, Arneiiia. NY.. Thursday. September 2. 1993, p. A10

out of his head. She said that the output was constant and enormous. She admitted that many of the ideas were not all that great, but then there "would be one that was worth a million dollars."

Longwell had a strong knowledge and understanding of history. Not only was he strong about past history, he had a nose for noticing recent trends that would affect or become history. He saw history as more like a novel than a text book. Once he said that he would like to have written the great American novel, and after thinking a moment, he continued, "Maybe I did with LIFE." To him LIFE was the vehicular show-and-tell of everything. He said they all saw it as "just so much white paper" on which any story could be told. (Time Inc. Archives Interview for corporate history)

Longwell's penchant for keeping abreast of all stories that could be photographed, drawn, or painted led him to become acquainted with a lot of men and women whom we now know were destined to be leaders in their fields. The lists of young photographers who began with LIFE and those who came later are endless and they are legendary in the development of their skills. This was true of the artists and illustrators and writers as well. Longwell knew them, encouraged them, guided them with almost fatherly affection. Most of the material in the Columbia Longwell collection is correspondence with these many, many people. In today's vernacular, it could be said with a fair amount of truth that once you were on the Longwell radar screen, he never lost track of you. I believe he answered every letter he ever got. No wonder his last secretary at Time Inc., Betty

Morris referred to him as "the phenomenon that was Dan Longwell." (Morris Interviews, 2012-2015)

He made a point of tracking talent in journalism and publishing. He would engage their talents whenever he could. Some of these folks were in obscure places. A little-known publisher, was Vrest Orton in Weston, Vermont, who would later create the Vermont Country Store and its mail-order catalogue which many Americans receive today. He too was asked to assist with a major LIFE story.

In 1937, Mr. Orton was running a little printing company named The Countryman Press, He had published his own book, *And So Goes Vermont.* Orton was set up in a modest timber and brick building where he worked his press in a tweed jacket complete with leather patches at the elbows and plaid tweed trousers. He was slender with a full head of black hair, glasses and a bow tie. Longwell had spent some time in Woodstock, Vermont, and had recognized the photographic opportunities of that New England state. He thought Vermont would be a good picture essay to run with photographs and the paintings of local artist, Luigi Lucioni. Longwell asked Vrest Orton if he would be willing to escort the Japanese photographer Younosuke Natori whom Longwell hired for the story, around Vermont and interface for him with the local population. Orton agreed, the picture essay appeared in the July 19, 1937, issue of LIFE along with the paintings of Italian-born Vermont artist, Luigi Lucioni. (Box 19, **Daniel Longwell Papers**, Rare Book & Manuscript Library, Columbia University in the City of New York)

The article states that Lucioni had exceedingly sharp vision and that he could see individual leaves on a tree 300 yards away. This reported fact caught my eye because Longwell also had better than 20/20 vision certified by two military eye doctors. Though Longwell never wore glasses, he could even read the print at the bottom of the eye charts. Ogden Nash mentioned his eyes as the most extraordinary he had ever seen. "His eyes were extraordinarily clear blue with the long vision of eagles and hawks." (Nash, Reminiscences of Dan Longwell, "Columbia Library Columns", Butler Library, Columbia University, New York, New York, p. 4)

Interestingly, Longwell only hunted fowl because he said they were the only game which had a fair chance of getting away.

Mary Fraser was part of the priority LIFE staff as an "Associate Editor." and in fact she began to be a major "interfacer" herself. After the Vermont story ran, she wrote a letter to Vrest Orton explaining what happened to the photo copies they had promised him.

"Mr. Natori shipped all his negatives to Japan and started out after them a few days later." Interestingly, she also wrote that she was promising herself a visit to Vermont to "see some of that marvelous scenery, and if possible, buy myself a farm." She complimented Mr. Orton with "I hope you don't mind being the official Time-Life-Fortune guide to the state." (Letter, Sept. 3, 1937, Box 19, **Daniel Longwell Papers**, Rare Book & Manuscript Library, Columbia University in the City of New York)

Longwell himself was of the opinion that Vermont was on the verge of a cultural boom as artists such as Lucioni, Rockwell Kent and Byron Thomas along with writers Sinclair Lewis and his wife Dorothy Thompson had taken up residence there. The LIFE title of the Vermont article stated it was the "Last Stronghold of Early Americanism." (Box 19, **Daniel Longwell Papers**, Rare Book & Manuscript Library, Columbia University in the City of New York) In my opinion, that headline would still be accurate today and Vermonters are proud of it. They are still strong on independent thinking, being self- sufficient and neighborly. It has been my good fortune that the Longwells bought a farm in Missouri and not in Vermont.

Staying in the 1937 time frame, Longwell was travelling the country looking for picture essay material and photographic news spreads. He took two of his best buddies with him on one of these trips: Nelson Doubleday, who was very tall, and Theodore Roosevelt Jr. who was fairly short. As the press gained information that young Col. Roosevelt was traveling, it became a sort of whistle stop train tour trip with crowds gathering at the various stations. Once they arrived in California it became more of a celebrity tour including lunch with movie star, Myrna Loy, and meeting with movie producers like Daryl Zanuck.

Back in New York, the ship was being kept aright by John Shaw Billings and Wilson Hicks and Mary Douglas Fraser. In retrospect the July 26, 1937 memo from Longwell to Hicks is surely a foretaste of things to come.

Rather than bother you with a big general memo, I have written you miscellaneous ones from time to time and I have given a lot of stuff to Miss Fraser. She is getting out a general list for you and Billings. While I am gone, I think you had better let Fraser handle lists and Future ideas—coordinate that work. (Box 17, **Daniel Longwell Papers**, Rare Book & Manuscript Library, Columbia University in the City of New York)

No doubt Miss Fraser had her hands full coordinating between these three strong personalities.

We may suppose it was just a feature of journalism in general in those days of everyone being "in the office" that inner office harmony naturally wavered between humor and hubris. Longwell was not always "out scouting stories" and was more often "in the office." When Billings would be out of the office, Longwell would stand in as Managing Editor. He was very proud of how things were going and he was especially proud of his great big magazine that rather "held court" over the others on the newsstands.

One of the examples of pride overtaking common sense occurred in the April 26th issue of 1937. It was only the twentieth issue of LIFE. Ralph Graves' email told it this way.

He famously ran a cover of a rooster without the LIFE logo. His theory was that the magazine was already so successful and established— big size, big black and white photograph—the newsstand buyers would recognize it and buy it without the logo. Removing the logo would leave more room for picture display. Dan was wrong. The issue was a disaster on sales and the experiment was never repeated. (In fairness to Dan I think he picked a poor cover picture. Maybe the rooster would have sold badly even with the logo.) (Graves E-mail, 2010)

All I can offer to this story is that when I was giving a program in Neosho, MO to a women's club, one lady raised her hand to say she had framed that cover and it still hung in her chicken house. It might not have sold in New York City, but Daniel Longwell had his finger on the pulse of the Midwest subscriber.

Aside from editorial decisions, the organization of LIFE in general seems to have been taken in hand by Miss Fraser who had the ear of Mr. Luce. Box 71 (**Daniel Longwell Papers**, Rare Book & Manuscript Library, Columbia University in the City of New York) held the following memo of the standard blue memo paper used by Luce.

Dear Miss Fra-
Your memo of Nov 30 has been in a prominent corner of my desk-top ever since its receipt.

Now I'm going away for a long New Year's weekend with my kids. But before I go, let me say that all things which were in your mind when you wrote the memo are in my mind—And after Jan 1, I want above all to do two things.

1) Get LIFE established in some sort of workable routine.

2) Attend to the things you have in mind.

Your note is therefore very much in order.

(Signed with his initials). HRL

In September of 1937, Mary Fraser had suggested that she take over handling the research for both magazines. Luce, by return Western Union, wrote that her solution was "excellent and practical", and asked her to prepare a memo he could issue on Monday. There can be no doubt that Mary Fraser was a power to be reckoned with in the offices of Time Inc. She had a unique personality that was not threatening, but was clearly intentional. She could hold her own with any other wit or intellect and she could enjoy mutual decisions and discernments with grace and ease.

Eleanor Graves, Mrs. Ralph Graves and a future leading lady of LIFE, wrote me of being interviewed for a job by Mary over 50 years ago. Graves' impressions are worth adding to the Fraser persona. (Eleanor Graves' Correspondence, June 23, 2010)

> I recall she (Mary Fraser Longwell) was located in a very dark office on a high floor (very special) with only a desk lamp creating a small pool of light. I found this odd and a little scary. I do not remember why I was summoned to see her but I had been offered researcher jobs at both Time and Life from the trainee program and perhaps she just wanted to look me over. I was not intimidated by her but plainly this was part of her

modus operandi—the dark office, etc. As I recall we talked for a very few minutes—I suppose about my background—and I was dismissed.

I do not know whether this came before or after both my job offers—that was quite unusual, and although it sounds boastful, I believe I was the only one on the training program to get two offers before the program was completed. I was supposed to go on to training at Fortune and SI. But I never did, opting for the job on LIFE.

I interviewed at Time Inc. in 1962. The letter that I sent back to the Longwells who were then living in Neosho was saved by Mary and she gave it to my mother before she moved to California. I wrote the following on July 31, 1962, from Yale, in New Haven, Connecticut. I was twenty-one years old.

Dearest Longwells,

I am going to admit I have put off writing you because it is difficult for me to believe that I'm so very sold on Time Inc. Last Saturday I went to NY for interviews…I had lunch with Suzy Tooni who took me to see and meet my "peers" and also to show me the building (plus a sneak preview at Mr. Larsen's office since he had left for vacation.)

The girls seemed very much like my sort of people and how could I give a higher compliment? Then when I met Misses Taylor and MacPhail the whole image was reinforced. But just to add fuel to the flame, I read the biography of Britton Haden in which the author, Busch, gives a lot of character to Time Inc. I feel like a little germ just itching to get into the blood stream.

Please don't express all this allegory to your buddies up there, but I sure do like them. I'm to go in on Monday, Aug. 6, to see about being a "Clip Desk gal".

The people I met all ask about you and Miss MacPhail wanted to know if Howard Bush put out your seed catalogue and if you also lived in "Spring Hills"...Some man (whose name I was too flustered to remember) asked me if I knew Granby. Nevertheless he impressed me because he was in shirtsleeves, like he'd been working. MacPhail and Taylor were also WORKING. I also noted that everyone stays overtime. I was there 'til 6 PM.

I may be crazy but I think staying overtime is almost an opportunity and I wanted to ask if everyone really did it but I thought she might think I was afraid of the idea or was apple polishing. Somehow I have had the idea if you worked late, your colleagues would frown.

So what all this amounts to is, I want to work there and I WANT the clip desk. I don't ever remember wanting anything before. I do know I definitely follow images. I could name you exact moments during my short life when I felt like a young Mary Longwell.

Now that I've probably embarrassed you (hopefully not) I'll come down to earth and tell you salary was not discussed. ... I forgot how

much you said I need to live in NY. At this point
I'd almost pay them to let me work there.

Love from the pavement pounder, Judy

I did get the job and I was not disappointed. But at twenty-three I fell in love with a Yale peer in the International Relations department whom I married in 1964. We moved to Washington, DC, and I worked for *National Geographic* which was not nearly as much fun.

Wit, fun and energy-charged amusement was part and parcel of working at LIFE in Time Inc. Even the bosses were fun. It was if democratic comedy was the rule of the day. In December of 1937, Mr. Longwell's secretary at this time was Miss Roberta Locke. Longwell was a thoughtful and amusing boss and when she was hospitalized he wrote to her. This letter illustrates the general sense of office humor in that place at that time.

It seems that I told Eisenstadt to go to South Carolina to get Southern hunting, but he's gone to South Dakota to get Southern bunting instead. There's some misunderstanding in the research department but I can't find Fraser to discover what Southern Bunting is because she is waiting to see Mr. Hicks and Mr. Hicks is waiting to see Mr. Billings and Mr. Billings is waiting to see Mr. Luce and Mr. Luce is trying to find Mr. Barnett, who I know for a fact is looking for Fraser. So there it is, You better hurry back. (Box 17, **Daniel Longwell Papers**, Rare Book & Manuscript

Library, Columbia University in the City of New York)

While on the September 1937 trip Longwell sent back a constant stream of Western Union telegrams to Billings, Hicks and Fraser and his secretary Roberta Locke. These were full of fun and puns reporting that in playing golf at Pebble Beach, he had shot an eighty-six and was having it framed and stuffed for their office. A telegram two days later told Locke to tell Fraser he had shot an eagle, or seagull, which he was having stuffed for Fraser's office. Same telegram states he found a pair of eels for Roosevelt and Doubleday. (Box 17, **Daniel Longwell Papers**, Rare Book & Manuscript Library, Columbia University in the City of New York)

Apparently Mr. Longwell had more in mind for Mary Fraser than decorating her office with a stuffed seagull. On December 16, 1938, after a day at the office during which Billings reported they were "useless" they were married at the First Presbyterian Church in New York City with Mr. and Mrs. Ogden Nash of Baltimore, MD, as attendants. Rev. Wilbert Smith performed the ceremony. The newspaper articles were followed up by a proper engraved announcement on card stock that read "Mr. and Mrs. Caleb Douglas Fraser have the honour of announcing the marriage of their daughter Mary Douglas to Mr. Daniel Longwell, Friday the sixteenth of December, One thousand, nine hundred and thirty eight, New York."

Mary's father wrote to the couple, January 1, 1939, saying,

> Dear Mary and Dan, I just want you to know how happy we are to welcome Dan into our family. And wish for you a very happy married life, you know—Parent's chief concern is the welfare and happiness of their children. ...Thanks for TIME and FORTUNE> (signed) Father.
>
> (Box 17, **Daniel Longwell Papers**, Rare Book & Manuscript Library, Columbia University in the City of New York)

Unfortunately, Mary's father died October 29, 1939, at age sixty-nine. His obituary was carried in the *New York Times.*

Mary told me her wedding present from Dan was a shotgun and they went duck hunting for their honeymoon. This is not to say they spent all their time in a duck blind. Harry and Clare Boothe Luce offered them the Washington cottage on their Mepkin plantation in South Carolina. Mrs. Luce left copious notes of the particular duties of the seven mentioned servants, and that the butler, Reed, had the keys to the liquor closet. There was also a horse and buggy for sight-seeing around the plantation, thermos of coffee for early shooting and proper breakfast to be ordered for their late morning return. She closes with

> Please use Mepkin as your own home this week! Harry and I wish you much joy of it and of life too, now and forever.

P.S. The water runs awful hot. Don't scald yourself by accident. Silly reminder but people have done it."

She signed, "Affectionately, Clare and Harry"

Five more P.S instructions followed. The Longwells left a cigarette box for a gift to the Luces under their Christmas tree and a poem in the guest book.

They also spent part of their honeymoon at the Doubleday's Bonny Hall plantation in Yemassee, South Carolina. Ellen Doubleday later wrote them January 8, 1939: "We simply loved having you here and it was dear of both of you to share your honeymoon with us. All happiness dear Mary and Dan and as a parting shot, you are the only woman in the world who can possibly keep Dan in order." (January 6, 1939 Ellen Doubleday Letter, Box 70, **Daniel Longwell Papers**, Rare Book & Manuscript Library, Columbia University in the City of New York)

A similar reaction was written to Dan by Frances (Mrs. Ogden) Nash: "I want to congratulate you from the soles of my feet because both Ogden and I are mad about Mary. We always knew you were clever, but not that clever." (Box 70, **Daniel Longwell Papers**, Rare Book & Manuscript Library, Columbia University in the City of New York)

Mary received a gift of Steuben Glass from eighteen researchers with a card that read, "With Love to Fra from the researchers." (Box 70, **Daniel Longwell Papers**, Rare Book & Manuscript Library, Columbia University in the City of New York)

Dan received a letter from his childhood mentor, Dr. Palmer Findley saying,

"Well you finally succumbed to the wiles of Venus. …Hearty congratulations from the Findleys and our best wishes for all the happiness in the world." (Box 70, **Daniel Longwell Papers**, Rare Book & Manuscript Library, Columbia University in the City of New York)

Vrest Orton in Weston, Vermont was very quick to respond to the news of their marriage and his letter to Dan is classic.

> Dear Dan;
>
> Have you no pity on your friends and on Mary's? Is it not enough to have the excitement of Xmas and New Years without the additional excitement of receiving such a surprise as the news of your marriage.
>
> But good news! I always thought you were a smart guy! I didn't think you were quite smart enough to get a girl like Mary…but now you've done it.
>
> Of course she's vastly too good for you but aren't they all too good for most of us! Most of us get better wives than we deserve anyway.
>
> Seriously, it's grand news and I know you'll be very Happy. Do thank Mary for remembering us at Xmas with the subscription to LIFE. I hope now she is Mrs. Longwell, she won't forget Ellen and me and that you'll both come and see us this summer for a good visit.

Best of luck………yours, (signed) Vrest
(Letter, Dec. 28, 1938, Box 19, **Daniel Longwell
Papers**, Rare Book & Manuscript Library,
Columbia University in the City of New York)

After the honeymoon, their residence at 2 Sutton Place
South, an apartment in a beautiful building overlooking the
East River Bridge. Dan had moved from his 1937 bachelor
apartment at 433 E. 51st Street on Halloween of 1938. The
saved packing list shows scratched and stained end tables,
radio, the usual book cases, books and paintings plus a
desk. Packing and a month of warehouse storage cost the
nostalgic total of $70.37.

Mary must have taken charge of the new place because
it is all comfort and clean in the photos filed in Box 47,
Daniel Longwell Papers, Rare Book & Manuscript
Library, Columbia University in the City of New York.
Staffordshire dogs rested on a white art deco mantle
piece surrounding a black marble fireplace with screen. A
comfortable upholstered two-person divan and a chintz-
covered comfortable chair beckoned the viewer. Book
shelves to the ceiling and a magazine stand just for LIFE
issues revealed the interests of the residents. The bedroom
with white Venetian blinds and white sheers were gracefully
pulled back to allow sun on a potted begonia and vases of
fresh flowers. Quilted coverlets fitted tightly on twin beds
and a chaise lounge upholstered in a tight tufted fabric
revealed a cozy atmosphere. Mary's table space showed
expensive perfumes in lovely bottles, bookended by large
Steuben goblets with fresh flowers. Dan's table space

displayed toy soldiers and ships of WW I vintage. An early Grant Wood painting matted and framed appeared to be a collage of portraits including a youthful self-portrait. This was a work that Dan chose to hang over his space, not only in New York, but later in Neosho.

Dan seems to have truly taken to the married life with a companion like Mary and his correspondence to friends reflects his enjoying the newness of it all. In April of 1939, he wrote to C.G. Norris, "Mrs L. is as busy as can be surrounding me with frilly white curtains and making me varnish what-nots, and we even have a dog!" (Letter to Charles G. Norris, April 4, 1939, Box 1, **Daniel Longwell Papers**, Rare Book & Manuscript Library, Columbia University in the City of New York)

The dog was a dachshund and the first of several they loved. As time continued, they gave puppies to friends and guarded their pedigree.

Dan and Mary's circle of friends were somewhat surprised at their getting married in such a private and simple way, but then, that was their style more often than not.

February 1, 1939, Dan wrote to Kenneth Roberts thanking him for the Christmas card of his new house which Dan liked. Then he added:

> I would have written my Christmas greetings sooner, but I got married to a very fine girl and have been somewhat preoccupied. Marriage is something I've not done much, but tell Mrs. Roberts I think it is fine. (Box 20, **Daniel**

Longwell Papers, Rare Book & Manuscript Library, Columbia University in the City of New York)

January 12, 1939, Dan wrote to the Ogden Nashes who were their wedding witnesses:

> That was a mighty handsome coffee set you sent us, and what a splendid note Frances wrote us. I like being married fine, but I didn't mean to get such a comical wife. Every morning she clowns around and says, "Nasty old offices and teases me about –could she come down and see where I work, etc. I will be glad when she goes back to work! (Box 19, Daniel Longwell Papers, Rare Book & Manuscript Library, Columbia University in the City of New York)

The coffee set was not the only gift from the Nashes. Frances told Mary she wanted to buy her something special and so the two girls when to Greenwich Village in lower Manhattan to an antique store. Mary chose the miniature pair of Staffordshire poodles sitting on pink pillows which lived at the hearth ever after. After Dan died and a young couple dear to them were getting married, Mary gave the poodles to Tom and Peggy Pearl and told them how dear the poodles, and they, were to her. The Pearls have since given them to the Longwell Museum at Crowder College in Neosho. MO.

Indeed, Mary did take a leave of absence from work. This gave her an opportunity to travel with Dan as he sought story ideas and picture essays. Of course he took her to Omaha and introduced her to his high school English teacher, Sarah Vore Taylor. Miss Taylor remembered this meeting in a letter to Dan ten years later, March 1950.

> Dear Dan
>
> It has been a decade since you and Mary Longwell and a big camera and I stood at the study hall door of Central High School. You had then in mind a project of LIFE to publish pictures of certain teachers of English who had a happy influence over their pupils. To my great surprise and delight you included me in the list. Thus fate deigned us an hour together. (Box 21, **Daniel Longwell Papers**, Rare Book & Manuscript Library, Columbia University in the City of New York)

On that trip to Omaha, they continued down to Springfield, MO to meet Dan's family on his mother's side. They also drove to Dan's childhood stomping grounds around Ragan School west of Neosho. He showed Mary the farm where he had lived. The little house was run down (Mary told me an old outlaw used to live there), but Dan was taken by the nostalgia of his old school and the surrounding hay fields. Finally Mary said, "Then why don't you buy it?" And so he did. They would summer there and make friends with the neighbors, some of whom were Dan's old eighth grade classmates.

They would stay in the town of Neosho at the Big Spring Inn and in those summer vacations, they really became part of the community. At that time the Big Spring Inn looked like it had been transported from New England. Its porch overlooked a rock-sided pond filled with rainbow trout from the local "national" fish hatchery which produced them for supplying area streams. There were coiled ropes in the bedrooms for escaping fire by sliding down to the ground if such an emergency occurred. Dan was able to get all the newspapers he wanted to read. They had telephone and cable service to New York and trains in all directions. Across the street, a city park with a children's wading pool at the far end still beckons both tourists and the locals. The town square is two blocks away and the whole venue is embraced by bluffs with pretty houses on top. Dan called it a "hamlet." I think it was their hideaway. And in 1954 they would occupy the house on the bluff, up the some sixty-five steps which rose above the Big Spring and its park and pond.

They stayed at the Big Spring Inn, but they spent their time out at the old farm. This farm never had a name. It was just, "the farm" or "the place out by Ragan School." Dan went at domestic life like he did everything else: full steam ahead on developing and improving. He did the same thing at a New England country house.

Early in their marriage, they had bought a lovely place in Sharon, Connecticut. Like many people with careers in New York City, Connecticut was their weekend getaway. Dan later referred to this owning second homes as the "Time Inc. Disease". He described it as what might be called a "keeping up with the Jones' syndrome." While homes in the country had a certain cache at the office and were truly a way to "get out of town", they had a devastating effect on the paycheck.

The Longwells were different in that they had two paychecks and no children. Furthermore, being a frugal Presbyterian by nature, Mary had some money of her own which she was happy to invest in the home front. Dan would compensate from time to time by putting some of it in her name alone. Later the sale of the Connecticut property would pay for the town house in Neosho. The Neosho farm was bought by mortgage arrangement at the Bank of Neosho.

On both the Connecticut and Missouri properties, Dan began planting trees and hiring help. In Connecticut he started raising pheasants, stocking fish, and purchasing a tractor. In Neosho it was a truck. In Connecticut they raised flowers and vegetables. In Neosho it was clearing land and raising cattle. The Neosho farm was such lovely ground. Buffalo Branch waters ran along it and old tall trees shaded it. Gardens were behind the little house. The Neosho asparagus patch was still yielding beautifully when Mary moved to California and I moved to Kansas City, in the early 1980's.

However, one should not get the impression that they were never in the office. Dan's work is more easily defined than Mary's. Dan was to identify stories, culling or finding photographs to tell the stories, and his work was all under the editorial umbrella of LIFE.

Mary, on the other hand, was busy in all the magazines in what seems like all the departments—editorial, personnel—and what passed for technology in 1940: the "teletypesetter".

She naturally had a hand in developing budgets for each group. And she was active in the Newspaper Guild.

Over her long tenure at Time Inc., all her work had evolved along with the magazines and seemed to take on a combined horizontal and vertical description. Job descriptions don't read well when the description abstracts into horizontal plus vertical. The editors of each magazine seemingly did not quite understand how one person could handle so many situations but had no job description. Part of her work was in personnel and that was considered to be "horizontal" across the company. Other jobs were considered to be "vertical" responsibilities inside one magazine which could be a budget or personnel or research or training or labor problem. But then those problems were often horizontal as well.

Probably the chief concern was of course: What if she "went away"? Who could fill in for her? How would they be able to tell her replacement what to do? One solution for management was to ask her from time to time to report to them on how she spent her time.

In March of 1940, she wrote an "Office Memorandum" to Manfred Gottfried, Managing Editor of TIME with copy to Mr. Luce. The first two paragraphs highlight the generalities before she goes on to list several specifics:

> Some time ago you asked me to give you a memo on what my job consisted of. As well as I can define it, here it is:
>
> In February 1939 I was appointed by HRL to be Chief of Research for TIME, Inc. It was

a job in which I was to work "with heads of divisional research departments, of the Morgue[39], of the Personnel department and of any other departments concerned with TIME Inc.'s research." In other words, it was an appointment to create a job. (Box 81, **Daniel Longwell Papers**, Rare Book & Manuscript Library, Columbia University in the City of New York.

The answer to all this was that she was not "going away." The rumbling of war in Europe and Asia, the impending call for the young and smart to the military created a serious shortage in the office which meant she really had her hands full to get the routines established and the jobs defined regardless of how many or how few people it would take to do them.

In January of 1941, Mr. Daniel Longwell did a very wonderful thing for his wife. He did not choose to celebrate a birthday or anniversary. Instead he gave her

A TESTIMONIAL DINNER
Tendered By
Daniel Longwell
To
Mrs. Longwell,

---

[39] The "Morgue" was in-house jargon for the reference library which consisted of standard reference works and collected clippings of old news and anything else a writer or researcher might want to delve into. It was sort of the Google and Wikipedia of today, but was a major functioning part of Time Inc. research and probably more reliable than the internet in my opinion even though it could not be as extensive.

And her many patient friends. Jack &
Charlie's "21" January 16, 1941

The menu at this still famous and historical club/
restaurant now listed as Club 21 at 21 West 52nd Street,
in Manhattan was of course totally French. Wines were
vintage 1926, 1929, 1934 and champagne was served with
the dessert of Soufflé au Grand Marnier. The cover of the
menu is a pen and ink drawing of a sweet little girl sitting
next to her hunting dog on the pier of a small pond watching
a flock of geese flying overhead.

Guests signed testimonials of every description such as
"We the people" love Mary and Napoleon. The Doubledays
and McIlvains were among the guests, but probably the
tiny capital letters penned at the bottom of the menu was
Mary's favorite,

"And now I see with eye serene
The very soul of the machine"
(Signed) Wordsworth +D. Longwell
"Hope Springs Eternal"

And so it was that the "machine" that was Mary Fraser
Longwell moved on into 1941 with a January 28, memo to
Roy Larsen, Publisher of LIFE, keeping him posted on her
activities. (Box 84, **Daniel Longwell Papers**, Rare Book
& Manuscript Library, Columbia University in the City of
New York)

First, she was making changes in the Morgue to put it on
a self-sustaining basis with a budget of its own. Until they

found another supervisor, she would take care of editorial problems of the Morgue. Second she would spend three weeks on a report consisting of "research into research". Case histories of stories and a breakdown of the number of researchers, years at work, salaries, etc. Third and finally, she would be filling in for one of the heads of the News Bureau while he was on vacation.

The question could be asked, How many people would it have taken to supervise Mary Fraser Longwell? In this, Dan was the smartest! He won her heart and married her.

CHAPTER SEVEN

"AND LIFE OWNED THE WAR"

--Dan Longwell (1957 Time Inc. Interview)

The War Begins

Without provocation, charity or common sense, German troops under Adolph Hitler's command marched into Poland, and German planes bombed Polish cities. This was September 1, 1939. The previous year in March of 1938, Hitler declared Austria part of his government which he called the Third Reich. During *Kristallnacht* (night of broken glass), November 10, 1938, in Germany, 7500 Jewish businesses were looted, 191 synagogues were set on fire, 100 Jews killed and tens of thousands sent to concentration camps. March 15, 1939, Hitler annexed Czechoslovakia.

In May of 1939, President Roosevelt requested Congressional permission to grant aid to France and Great Britain in the event of war. The Senate blocked that permission. In June, the passenger ship *St. Louis* was refused docking privileges in the United States which caused the 907 Jewish refugees on board to be sent back to Europe. In August, Hitler lured Russia into a non-aggression pact which cleared the way for him to safely invade Poland in September. By November he had seized Belgium, the Netherlands, Luxembourg, Denmark and Norway. This was just the precursor of attacking and defeating northern French forces in April 1940. With Italy attacking the south of France in June, France surrendered to Germany on June 22, 1940.

The paragraphs above are just a skeleton report of what was happening in the places far away from American shores. The aggressions had been masked by Hitler's appeasements and promises not to do what he intended—but finally did.

In the Pacific, Japan was making strides into China and had taken the northern territories. Polls were showing that Americans were less opposed to a possible war with Japan than they were about war in Europe. (Based on World War II Timeline @ www.shmoop.com/ wwitimeline)

As Hitler's armies marched into European countries, Luce, Longwell, and Billings pretty much saw American isolationism as wishful thinking. This trio of men was well acquainted with war and all that war, any war, meant. Billings had driven a French ammunition truck during World War I. Luce's family had been forced to evacuate their home in China during the Boxer Rebellion. Longwell had prepared for the military in his high school Student Army Training Corp and as earlier stated had declined an appointment to West Point as World War I ended. (Box 27, **Daniel Longwell Papers**, Rare Book & Manuscript Library, Columbia University in the City of New York.; Brinkley Alan, *The Publisher*, p. 11-12; see Chapter 1)

In 1939, Luce, Longwell and Billings also knew that the United States was only just coming out of the Depression. The economic depression had also led the American population into a general sort of mental depression. Luce brought up to Longwell and Billings a discussion he had heard at a Wall Street luncheon where the Wall Street bankers had said that the whole world was going to have to accept a lower standard of living for several decades. Luce wanted to know if Longwell and Billings agreed. They did not. They maintained that the US was coming out of the Depression, industry was firing up, babies were being born, people were optimistic. Evidently they convinced Luce, and this optimism became the core and continuity of the magazine. Longwell said,

> This was where LIFE came out with a belief in the United States, a tremendous belief…. We put a whole lot of faith in the United States, and that was a spiritual change in the magazine. We built on that for an awfully long time, and we believed in it, believed completely. And we edited it that way—you can go back and look at it today— the magazine reflects that tremendous belief in the United States and its capacities. (Time Inc. Archives Interview II, August 1957, page 15, Alex Groner and Celia Sugarman, interviewers.)

There was another side to the coin however. Lynne Olson, in her fine book, *Citizens of London: Americans Who Stood with Britain in its Darkest, Finest Hour*, discusses the August 1941 Roosevelt-Churchill Placentia

Bay, Newfoundland, meeting. Londoners had prepared for siege. They were desperate for help from the United States. Churchill made a plea. Olson states,

> The President, however, rejected Churchill's appeal, explaining that Congress and the American public were in no mood to enter the conflict. Indeed, during the week of the Placinta Bay meeting, legislation mandating a one-year extension for a limited military draft, instituted in 1940, came perilously close to defeat in the House of Representatives, surviving by only one vote (Olson, p. 122).

Olson continues reporting Churchill's response which he put in writing to his son:

> The President, for all his warm heart and good intentions, is thought by many of his admirers to move with public opinion rather than to lead and form it (Olson, p.123).

Obviously this was not said directly to Luce, Longwell or Billings. However they had earlier determined this in their own journalistic, history-minded thinking.

Longwell, the LIFE editors, and other outside commentators were pretty sure the US would have to join the conflict and they were agreed that it would more than likely be a two ocean war, but when the Japanese hit Pearl Harbor, the historian turned journalist was ready for them. Longwell and LIFE "had done their homework."

Their next "spiritual" challenges and goals for LIFE magazine were to raise American awareness of the war in Europe and to create a confidence in public resources and military matters. This in the long run would serve to build national patriotic feeling which is required in a democracy to wage a war. The editors of LIFE were convinced American involvement was going to be required. (Groner Interview II, August 1957, pp. 17-18, Time Inc. Archives).

Continuing the Time Inc. interview with Groner and Sugarman in 1957, Longwell pointed out that LIFE had paid a lot of attention to the military from its beginning. LIFE "believed" in the American armed forces. Longwell said it was "like church or religion." The very second issue of LIFE has a West Point cadet on the cover. Following issues of LIFE showed Admiral Arthur Japy Hepburn and the fleet and the North Carolina National Guard on maneuvers. (Groner Interview II, August 1957, pp. 14, Time Inc. Archives).

As LIFE was begun, it did many stories on U.S. military preparedness, building awareness of the men and women in all our Armed Forces. Patriotism is born of pride and LIFE built that pride while at the same time showing what yet needed to be improved. This task became the driving passion of the LIFE editorial department led by Daniel Longwell and John Shaw Billings. Furthermore, it had the blessings of their boss, Henry Luce, who wrote of the future of patriotism in his classic 1939 essay, "The American Century". (Brinkley, p. 265-269)

LIFE had become the mirror image of a public America thinking positively about the future with photo essays of factory workers, soldiers, sailors, farmers, miners, dam builders, college students, and the children of every type of citizen. If ever there were a time when the USA approached being a perfect democracy, it was in the pages of LIFE magazine. As public pride grew, public patriotism grew.

In the mid 1960's, at the time of the writing of the corporate history of Time Inc., the author, Robert Elson, was sending questions and draft texts on various points to the Longwells. Time was of the essence because neither Luce nor Longwell were well at the time. Regardless of their physical condition, their minds were in very good order. The **Daniel Longwell Papers**, Rare Book & Manuscript Library, Columbia University in the City of New York, Box 81, holds a memorandum to Bob Elson written by Mary Longwell as she took dictation from Dan as he wrote for the history. Mary's memo, which follows, liberally quotes Dan on putting together the issue of LIFE which followed the Polish invasion, September 1, 1939.

> Dan was in Nantucket when the Germans started the war in Poland. He phoned John Billings and asked what was the color for the next week? —It was eagles. "Fine, leave it the way it is—I think we ought to have a war manual." D.L. caught a train to New York, "went to [the hotel], spent an entire day making a dummy, sketching in the pictures I hoped we could find. Took it to the office Monday, Billings accepted it and we went to work. Billings and I knew this was the outbreak of a world war, but the rest of the staff rejected this. We had to change every writer's story to

the present tense of war. That issue tended to
copyright the war for LIFE and gave our readers
a background for everything that was to come."

In 1957, nine years before the above memo, Dan
Longwell had granted interviews to the Time Inc. company
historians. He had elaborated then more on the disbelief of
the young people in the office who did not think world war
was eminent.

However the young staff on LIFE could not believe that
a world war was developing. There were lots of arguments
between the writers and researchers (sometimes called
checkers). When Hitler marched into Poland the possibility
of this now becoming a world war loomed in the editorial
offices for sure.

> I worked that whole weekend to work out that
> issue and we had a horrible time editing it. It
> was odd, --the pictures fit in and all that kind
> of stuff—but the staff insisted it wasn't a world
> war. And everybody who had been at least a
> private in World War I knew it was a world war…
> everybody under that age didn't realize it. And
> we had to check and check and check to keep the
> researchers from saying that England was not a
> democracy. We were lining up the democracies,
> England, France and the United States, and so
> forth. And we had to put *that* back into copy about
> three times—that England was a democracy. And
> we had to keep putting in that there was a war.

I had done more homework in Washington than any editor in my position in New York; I just spent an awfully lot of time with the Army and Navy. And Billings … was wonderful.

And LIFE owned the war. There is just no denying the fact that that was one thing we owned. We had done our homework, we knew the people, we had travelled, we got around. (Longwell, Time Inc. Interview II, August 1957, pp. 17-18, Time Inc. Archives).

LIFE editors had decided to do a defense issue for its July 4, 1941, number. Actually the issue was dated July 7th, but it was clearly labeled, "DEFENSE ISSUE. U.S. ARMS." Ed Thompson got the cover photo which was General George S. Patton, Jr. standing in the turret of his special tank painted with his own red, white, blue and yellow color scheme wearing his shoulder holster with his pearl-handle pistol. The accompanying story was of Patton leading his troops and those of the First Armored Division on maneuvers in Tennessee.

As this issue was being put together, the seeds of future issues were planted with poetry and paint. LIFE painters who would come to be known as "War Artists" first used in this issue were Tom Lea, Peter Hurd, and Henry Billings, the brother of John Shaw Billings. Lea had been an illustrator for the books of J. Frank Dobie during Longwell's Doubleday days and Peter Hurd was the husband of Henrietta Wyeth, sister to Andrew Wyeth. Later, Longwell invited Andrew

Wyeth to join LIFE artists. March 16, 1943, Wyeth sent a hand written letter in response.

> Dear Mr. Longwell,
>
> I was delighted to receive your letter containing the remarkable opportunity for me, and I'd jump at the chance to go but less than a month ago my draft number came up and I took an advanced Army physical and came through with a 4F. However I am under a doctor's care and hope to overcome any trouble in the near future.
>
> I've been waiting just for such a chance such as you offered and am terribly disappointed to have to reject it now that it has come along. …
>
> Many thanks for giving me this chance.
>
> Sincerely, Andrew
>
> (Box 7, **Daniel Longwell Papers**, Rare Book & Manuscript Library, Columbia University in the City of New York)

For the "Defense Issue" (July 7, 1941), Longwell drew from his Doubleday days. He hired the poet Stephen Vincent Benet to produce his five LIFE-size pages poem, *Listen to the People.* There was also a heart-rending story of a little girl orphaned by the German bombing of London which killed her parents in the blasting of their home.

William L. White, son of William Allen White of the *Emporia Gazette,* Emporia, KS, was on the Time Inc. staff and was sent to the London office. His wife Katherine, who also worked for Time Inc., had urged him to look for a child they could adopt. In London he found an exceptionally bright young girl named Margaret at an orphanage. LIFE carried the story of the Whites adopting her and the challenges of her war syndrome behavior. Finding refuge in a loving home environment and renamed Barbara, she came to be their darling daughter. She also followed in the family's journalistic endeavors as she and her husband, Paul David Walker, are retired as Publisher and Editor Emeritus of the *Emporia Gazette.* Their son, Christopher White Walker is now Editor of the *Emporia Gazette.* Katherine White was a cherished friend of Mary Longwell's whom she often visited in Emporia.

Additionally, Mrs. Luce, who was then signing her work as Clare Boothe had made a trip to the Philippines and had written a "Close Up" article on General Douglas MacArthur. She had also suggested a cartographer to Longwell who had

> …some theories on air attacks on Japan from the Aleutian chain. The Art Director of LIFE at the time, Worthen Paxton, worked those plans out and added the maps of the traditional invasions of the Philippines. These were to prove historic. We were well aware of Japanese attacks but we did not expect Pearl Harbor …. (1956 Longwell Memo to Sugarman, p. 6, Box 81, **Daniel Longwell Papers**, Rare Book & Manuscript Library, Columbia University in the City of New York)

Preparing for War

America was a very lucky country when LIFE began to gear up in preparation for the coming war which the editors were sure would require America's participation. The first job was to tell the military's stories. The gathering of all these stories began in the usual way a LIFE story began. Ground work was laid, assignments were made, people were sent out. Longwell tells it best in the July 18, 1957, memo to Celia Sugarman for the Time Inc. Archives.

Ed Thompson, John Field and I went to Washington, spent the evening with General Richardson, then Army Public Relations Officer and he mapped out inspection tours for all three of us to scout out material. John Field took the southern camps, Ed Thompson took the Midwest industrial district and I was sent to Fort Sam Houston to learn something about the Army— then to Randolph Field [both in San Antonio], then on to Elliot Field near San Diego to look at the Marines and finally to Fort Ord, California, where General Stillwell was in Command.

I quickly realized that you had to do something in color to show what the Army was really like and telegraphed back for Thompson and Field to watch for possible places to use artists. General Simpson, later Commander of the Ninth Army, was my host at Fort Sam Houston. He, General Lucas and I picked out an old Army First Sergeant in the Regular Army (Top Sergeant Bruce Bieber)

as a good fellow for a close up in that issue. I asked
Holland McCombs to get Tom Lea to come over
from El Paso and paint the sergeant's portrait.
(Time Inc. Archives)

It was from that trip that Longwell and LIFE began to
hire their first war artists, Tom Lea, Peter Hurd, and Aaron
Bohrod, from across the country. Lea was the one Longwell
chose for first assignments. No doubt the clean, calm and
steady character of Tom Lea, who was also a gentleman
of good character, made him the sort of civilian artist the
military people would be comfortable having in their ranks.
This was probably why Longwell chose him for what we
now would call an "embedded" assignment.

Continuing in the same July 1957 memo to Sugarman
(Time Inc. Archives), Longwell wrote,

> …I believe Lea was the first combat artist
> assigned by private industry or the Armed Forces.
> One thing to remember about the war artists was
> that Eastman Kodak had not yet developed fast
> color film and the color film procedure was too
> slow to report a war in action.

Pearl Harbor

Longwell, the LIFE editors, and other outside
commentators were pretty sure the US would have to join
the conflict and they were agreed that it would more than
likely be a two ocean war, but when the Japanese hit Pearl

Harbor, the historian turned journalist was ready for them. Longwell and LIFE "had done their homework."

Japan bombed Pearl Harbor on December 7, 1941. LIFE appeared on the stands dated December 8th, but had gone to press December 5, 1941. Nevertheless, it had the look and talk of a post Pearl Harbor issue and this is the background of how that happened. It was one of those instances where prophecy mingles with knowledge and instinct which are the trademarks of true journalism.

In October of 1941, LIFE had published an article with the title, "Over the Hills in October." The soldiers who had been drafted were not seeing any war action, and they used the acronym "OHIO" which meant that when their drafted time was up, they'd be "over the hill in October". However, Congress had extended the draft by only one vote in the House. Morale in the Army and the country was not high at that time and Longwell was looking for a way to change that.

On one of his trips in Washington a Navy chaplain suggested to Longwell that while morale in the Army might be low, it was very high on the Navy's air- craft carriers. Longwell followed up on this and was able to get a LIFE crew of photographers into Pearl Harbor. They took lots of photos and had them into the New York offices about a week before the war began.

Longwell had remembered the history of the Japanese attacking Port Arthur, Russia, February 6, 1904, when peace negotiations had been underway. He suspected they might try that ploy again. Longwell recalled this in the 1957 interview for the Time Inc. Archives. Additionally there was the memo to Celia Sugarman of Time Inc. on the same subject dated 1956 in Box 81, **Daniel Longwell Papers**, Rare Book & Manuscript Library, Columbia University in the City of New York.

The following material draws from both sources. But the words are Daniel Longwell's.

> Now, it's a funny thing on the outbreak of the war—on Pearl Harbor. You remember that Kurusu, special envoy, was coming to this country. I don't know how I had the brains, but I did remember the surprise attack on Port Arthur, and there were maneuvers of Japanese diplomats towards Russia at that point. (Sugarman/Groner Interviews, Part II, p. 26, Time Inc. Archives)

Henry Luce was getting anxious about LIFE running Clare Boothe's article on General MacArthur and he was hounding Longwell about it. Longwell recalled to Celia Sugarman (1956, Box 81, **Daniel Longwell Papers**, Rare Book & Manuscript Library, Columbia University in the City of New York).

> Luce even called me off the tennis courts Sunday morning at the River Club to check on when I was going to run Clare's article with MacArthur on the cover. I persuaded him to put if off for another week. I kept saying Kurusu, the special Japanese Ambassador, had to reach Washington. Kurusu was just approaching the west coast. The next Tuesday I said, 'Let's go", Kurusu was in the USA.

Mrs. Luce's article went in the early closing forms, and I built the issue around that and a Naval Air Force essay (photographic) that Peter Stackpole had taken as part of the *March of Time* crew.

I dug up a stock picture of the Japanese Emperor's youngest brother and his bride and some current newsreel pictures of Japanese industry to make a three page lead for the December 8th issue.

I had three facts. FDR had been annoyed over the news that the Japanese were pouring more troops into Indo-China. Winston Churchill had said that if steel were essential to modern war, then Japan with seven million tons of production was reckless in promoting a war against the USA with a ninety million ton production. And the Gallup poll for that week had come out with the survey that a war with Japan could be pushed through Congress with the ease of a minor appropriation.

To come out with an issue that strongly suggested war with Japan before Pearl Harbor was a pretty gutsy statement by LIFE and Longwell probably felt like he was, as we say in the Ozarks, between a rock and a hard place. On one hand it read like war-mongering. On the other hand he had bet on an immediate Japanese attack based on nothing other than knowledge of Japanese historical practice and his own journalistic gut instinct. Longwell elaborated his story to Sugarman (1956, Box 81, **Daniel Longwell Papers**, Rare Book & Manuscript Library, Columbia University in the City of New York).

It looked bad. I was a war monger. Kurusu was only approaching Washington and was to call on Hull that Sunday. Mary Fraser Longwell and I were sharing Edward McIlvain's house with his wife that winter in Kent, Connecticut. Sunday, December 7, we had just come in from dinner and had turned on the radio for the Philharmonic. The announcer's break through came in seconds after, telling about the attack on Hawaii. F.D.R came on the radio a few seconds later and said the Japanese attack was on the island of Oahu. It took me several seconds to translate that from Hawaii, Honolulu to Pearl Harbor. Then I disgracefully said, "Oh my God, I was right!"

I quickly apologized to the company, but immediately broke into a sort of hysteria and told everyone what a terrible thing had happened. My host told me to pipe down so I walked around the yard a couple of times. I then came in and called the office.

It was press time for the December 15th issue. Longwell continued.

John Billings, bless him, answered the phone and said that everything was under control. I made only one suggestion. I said run the word WAR in as big a type as he could find on the lead and if I remember rightly, he did....

Oddly enough the December 15th issue was the one that got the praise. No one had gone back to read the December 8th issue which had the

full story three days in advance. Later Walter
Winchell said that LIFE was the only periodical
that hit Pearl Harbor on the nose, praised Mrs.
Luce for her MacArthur article as he should
have. I never received a memo from anyone on
the issue, (December 8th) nor did any of the staff
so far as I know. I suppose that was the greatest
compliment of all. We were supposed to be right.
We had, after all, put in two years of work on
that project and if we were three days too soon,
still we had the back stop material for another
notable issue (1956 Memo to Sugarman, p. 10-11,
Box 81, **Daniel Longwell Papers**, Rare Book &
Manuscript Library, Columbia University in the
City of New York).

Now America was in the war for sure and the next
four years revealed that LIFE did indeed "own" the war
with all their reporting and illustrating people in place
from the beginning. They owned the war because LIFE
was positioned to cover all the unfolding events. Of course
Longwell was not acting alone, but one might ponder
what the coverage might have been without his leadership.
Besides the legion of photographers, LIFE had twelve
artists painting *in situ* and Longwell was about to gain
seventeen more.

Longwell had been going to Washington, DC, on a
weekly basis and he did some bragging about that in the
1957 interview. It was during this period that the Longwell
sense of historical perspective intersected with his keen
observation of current events. Daniel Longwell really

became a "priestly prophet" figure to his profession. His weekly trips to Washington in search of stories, photo opportunities, and to maintain those ever-important friendly "connections" with people in important military positions paid off many times over. He was never blind to the news of the day. It was his habit all his life to read several daily newspapers from across the country. One of these Washington train-trip-newspaper-reading days, he really hit the jackpot. He told the story in the same Time Inc. Interview II, August 1957, on pages 27 & 28, Time Inc. Archives.

Well, I was riding to Washington one day and I picked up a *New York Times* and I read about the biggest appropriation bill in history—140 billion dollars had gone through the day before, and there were just two little items they had knocked out of that. One was they had wanted to stop so much traveling by the soldiers—so they cut down on the appropriation of that. And the other was 140,000 dollars for some artists that the Army had hired. ...Some Congressman said, "They're just going to send those fellows to paint portraits of the generals."

So I breezed into the Assistant Secretary of War's office and said, "Now you've done it; you're in trouble. I will take all of those artists right off your hands—everyone you've got there—and fulfill the contracts."

I spent all day there, right smack in and around that office until I finally got an agreement. One

Army lawyer finally said, "Well, I guess you win." So we sent a cable out to 18 different artists in different parts of the world, all but one joined us—seventeen joined LIFE—and then there were some who hadn't gone to service yet.

The artists had casualties just about like the troops: There were two wounded, one nervous-wrecked, and one killed, and out of about 34-40 fellows, that's about the average. And they were brave men. They went to lots of places.

Longwell was just not an "employer" of these artists and photographers. He was not just an admirer of the military. He had a deep and constant appreciation for their bravery and courage. Long after World War II when he was living in my Missouri neighborhood, he was at a party where the Viet Nam War was being discussed. As the pros and cons of debate overcame friendly discussion, Mr. Longwell summed up the situation with a conversation-stopping statement.

He said firmly to the gathering, "You cannot insult the troops!"

It is also impossible to go much further in this story without emphasizing the part played by Wilson Hicks. As written before, Hicks and Longwell shared the title and duties of Executive Editor which basically tells the reader nothing. But the two men understood it and Longwell was anxious that Hicks get his accolades.

Longwell explained how Hicks played his part in getting LIFE positioned to have photographs for the war. They sent

Hicks to England to observe how the British journals got their photos with a "pool system." Obviously all photographers were in competition with all other photographers just as all publications were in competition with each other. Longwell was concentrating on getting permissions for artists and photographers to get to where the action was and Hicks was concentrating on getting those photographs for LIFE.

Longwell suggested that Hicks spend time in Washington, DC to check out the competition and to meet with Longwell's contacts. While there, Hicks came up with the idea of a "pool of photographers" very much like what he had observed in London. Hicks, having been with Associated Press had a lot of contacts of his own and the "pool" he arranged was made up of LIFE, Associated Press, United Press and INS[40] (Time Inc. Archives, Longwell Interview II, 1957, pages 22-23).

> Longwell relates,
>
> We were the pool—we covered the war. There were some other photographers, but we had first choice. And it was pretty wonderful that the big three—once we got into the pool, we did a better job than anyone else...The LIFE photographers were very brave men. And Wilson Hicks has never been given the credit for covering that war that he should deserve. He did a beautiful job of getting the right men in the right places at the right time.

---

[40] INS: International News Service but just called International

During the war years, the war art in LIFE became an historical record of significance. One of the things the American public appreciated about LIFE was the emotional balance in the magazine. Not only could the reader study the heart- stopping art pieces or battlefield photographs taken *in situ,* there was also what a psychologist might call "comic relief" from the terrors of war. LIFE always had a balance of stories and pictures of civilian life displayed in fashion, science, sports, modern living, regular events in the fine arts, politics, agriculture, labor, and entertainment show-stoppers from Broadway to Hollywood.

LIFE on the Homefront

Dan Longwell was especially fond of Mary Martin in the opening night production of Broadway's 1938 hit, *Leave It to Me.* She sang the song, "My Heart Belongs to Daddy," making it a hit as she did so. Longwell was at the opening night performance and immediately arranged for Alfred Eisenstadt to do a photography session with Miss Martin the next day. She graces the cover of the December 19, 1938, issue. Longwell told the story that he wanted the cover title to be "My Heart Belongs to Daddy," but the other editors did not think that was appropriate so the cover title reads "Mary Martin: From Texas to Broadway."

However in the Uncatalogued Correspondence Files in Box 46 **Daniel Longwell Papers**, Rare Book & Manuscript Library, Columbia University in the City of New York, is a 3 X 5 engraved gold frame. The picture is a photo of Mary Martin in costume and signed "A wonderful guy, Mary

Martin". The frame is engraved at the top with a musical measure which looks to be notes for "My Heart Belongs" and where "to Daddy" would be is engraved, "To Daniel Longwell."

The D-Day Issue

The June 12, 1944, issue has a history of its own. The reader will need to understand that issues were always dated for Monday, the day when it was expected the issue would be on the newsstands. However, color had to be printed much earlier and if big news broke before the Monday, the big Donnelly presses had to be stopped in Chicago. D-Day, the Normandy Invasion, was one of those occasions. The office knew such an invasion was coming, but they did not know when.

John Shaw Billings was at his home in South Carolina and Longwell was filling in as Managing Editor. It is interesting that he finished a story on the studio war art (productions by artists who did not work *in situ*) and had sent it to press earlier. The Robert Elson corporate history and the Wainwright book do not tell much about what was happening at the office when the Normandy invasion was anticipated. The Time Inc. interviewers don't seem to have asked Longwell about it during their time with him. I had not focused on it either though I had looked in the Longwell diaries.

Early spring of 1944 for the Longwells was all about completing the little Missouri farm house restoration and getting furniture moved in to make it livable. They then returned to New York so that Billings could go to South Carolina which meant Dan was to be Managing Editor for a while. Actually, Billings was soon to leave the Managing Editor position to be made Editorial Director. Soon after June 1944, all issues were finished by Longwell. (Time Inc. Archives; Box 81, **Daniel Longwell Papers**, Rare Book & Manuscript Library, Columbia University in the City of New York)

In Longwell's June 6th, 8th, and 13th (1944) letters to Billings (Box 27, **Daniel Longwell Papers**, Rare Book & Manuscript Library, Columbia University in the City of New York) the excitement of a big news event leaps off the pages. Longwell's devotion to Billings and his desire to share office action details with him about everyone working together starting with a false alarm Saturday afternoon, June 3rd. There was "a hell of a ringing of bells" from the Associate Press teletype machines. After realizing that none of the Saturday news was making sense, Longwell sent everybody home saying he and Joe Kastner, copy editor, and Bernice Shrifte, chief of senior researchers, would come in Sunday and fix things up.

Longwell and Wilson Hicks had been taking off alternate weekends and on this Sunday night, Wilson called to say he was coming back to town so Longwell decided to go to their place in Connecticut. Monday night, June 5th, the Longwells came back to New York. They listened to the radio until 11:00 p.m. but there was no invasion news so they went to bed. At 4:00 a.m. Mary answered the phone and learned they had been trying to reach Dan for an hour thinking he was still in Connecticut. The Invasion had been officially announced. Wilson Hicks (Executive Editor) and Andrew Heiskell (General Manager) were at the office and they had ordered the presses stopped in Chicago. Fortunately, Longwell had sent some material in late so the presses were behind schedule. This immediate issue would be dated June 12th. Longwell had also sent materials for the June 19th issue: a cover of Eisenhower and a three-page spread of text with space left for photographs.

The text written for the June 19th issue by Charles Christian Wertenbaker had been written in the past tense but was already in New York. When Longwell cabled to ask if they should plan to run it next week, the answer came back, "Run it this week." This gave Longwell a clue that the invasion was imminent but that the exact date and time was still unknown.

Weather was the problematic factor and weighed heavily on Eisenhower's decision for the exact date and time for crossing the English Channel into Normandy on the French coast. Unfortunately weather did not coordinate with press schedules in Chicago. Furthermore, transmission of text and photos was by wire. This worked fine for text, but photos did not transmit so well. Trains and planes carried those treasures from Europe to New York to Chicago. Remember, this was 1944.

One has to recognize that the people running the huge presses in Chicago were just as intent on putting out a good issue as were the editorial people in New York. As the invasion photos began to come in, they had to pass the censors in Washington, be sent to New York City, laid out for the magazine, sent to Chicago, and put to press. Rome fell June 4ᵗʰ and the Normandy invasion began June 6ᵗʰ. The "Contents" listings in the LIFE issues of June 12ᵗʰ and 19ᵗʰ, read like a "Who's Who" in war coverage.

Longwell reported it all to Billings and his letters give us the best picture of news coverage under siege itself. The first letter was written June 6, 1944 (Box 27, **Daniel Longwell Papers**, Rare Book & Manuscript Library, Columbia University in the City of New York).

> I got here at 4 a.m. and found everything in good order. The Daily News trucks were tearing up the streets like ambulances and people, even at 4 a.m. were standing at newsstands trying to hail them.
>
> I came in Sunday morning with my papers all read, ready to re-edit the lead. Fortunately, I did because nobody else had any papers, so seeing the newsstand wasn't open this morning but had a stack of the Times, Tribune, News, etc., I stole them and brought them upstairs.
>
> Wilson (Hicks) had already officially got together a wire photo spread on the fall of Rome and arranged for its transfer to Chicago with a deadline of 12 o'clock.
>
> This is a hell of a good staff you've got here. Everybody was at the appointed place, even at the false alarm...You journalists like Wilson and yourself like these crises, but with my temperament, I'm a book publisher type and I confess I'm glad it's all over now.

The next letter, (June 8th) is short but has an interesting closing paragraph, (Box 27, **Daniel Longwell Papers**, Rare Book & Manuscript Library, Columbia University in the City of New York):

> By the way, you'll note that the cover[41] on the invasion issue is up-side down. I did it deliberately. I just wanted to see what would happen if you did print a picture up-side down.

Longwell's final letter as temporary managing editor before Billings returned to the office, summarizes with pride what made the Normandy and Rome coverage well done under nearly impossible circumstances.

> I'm proud of Wilson and his photographers for their coverage of the historic events in Normandy and Rome, proud of our relationship with the Army that enabled us to get these pictures back within the week, proud of our Washington office because they got the Army to expedite the clearance, proud of Wertenbaker because he gave us a piece that will stand up as a revelation of news even the next week, and now that it's over, I am a little impressed with myself for taking such chances on late closing.
>
> The Army expedited their clearance and gave us priority on a plane. Miraculously the plane got here. Wilson and I made a record-breaking layout

---

[41] The cover of the June 12, 1944 issue of LIFE (Author's Collection), the "invasion issue" was of bombs dropping in Italy.

in ten minutes from contact prints. We put the layouts and pictures on wire photo and somehow wangled the originals on a plane. The weather was very bad so I came to the office Sunday morning to find that the plane was grounded in Pittsburgh. A little later it got up again and got to Chicago at 10:50. At one o'clock I talked to Fred Love (Chicago) who said the originals were so much better than the wire photos that they had caught the whole issue with originals.

P.P.S. Covers have been hard to come by. Finally in desperation late Saturday I put the Statue of Liberty to press [as the cover]. It was a picture of her D Day Evening, first time she has been flood lighted since Pearl Harbor. It's not a very good cover, but "Hell" I said, "We've got to get a girl on the cover sometime. (June 13, 1944, Box 27, **Daniel Longwell Papers**, Rare Book & Manuscript Library, Columbia University in the City of New York)

In a box in the Columbia Archives that I had not seen until my last visit (Spring 2015), I found a framed picture of a dummy page of Eisenhower sitting in the middle of six officers, no text identification, just the mock-up of the layout and the header "Hold for Invasion" (D-Day). There were many signatures on the page and in white ink someone had written, "For Dan Longwell". Many of the signatures had faded, but Mary's accompanying typed note revealed that this page from the dummy of that week's LIFE had been signed by every member of the LIFE staff who had turned out at 4:00 a.m. on the day of the Normandy Invasion when Dan was Managing Editor.

This was proof of the old esprit d' corps that still lingers in the hearts and minds of TIME-LIFE Alumni Society members. I was fortunate to experience this same sense of get-the-story, get-it-right and get-it-to-press when I worked during the editorial leadership of Ed Thompson and George Hunt, 1962 to 1964. Even at that late date, it was an all-for-one and one-for-all organization. The "one" for all of us was LIFE itself. (As I write that sentence it comes to mind that when asked where I worked in those days. I did not say, "I work at Time Inc." I did not say, "I work for LIFE magazine." I simply said, "I work for LIFE." Everyone knew what that meant.) (Box 1, **Daniel Longwell Papers**, Rare Book & Manuscript Library, Columbia University in the City of New York)

One of the traits of Dan Longwell was his endless curiosity and varied interests. Public trends and reactions were like the morning papers to him. When the war artists began to be printed in LIFE, there was reaction from other American artists.

Most of the war artists traveled, sketched, made notes and then painted in their studios back home. However, Woodstock, Vermont, artist Byron Thomas painted in the upper floor of a guest house in a village northwest of London. Time Inc. had rented it on the advice of Walter Graebner who was in the London Time Inc. office. Employees, traveling photographers, artists, and correspondents in general could go there for rest and relaxation away from the blitzing of London by German air attacks. The studio was in the village of Beaconsfield and the guest house was lovingly called "Luce Acres." There is in the files of Time Inc. Archives a cable from Mr. Luce to Mr. Graebner who had written to Mr. Luce about the house. One will see a bit of comic relief in the Luce play on words "Lend Lease" which was the American support to the British Navy.

> HAVE GREATLY ENJOYED LIVELY ACQUAINTANCE WITH LUCE ACRES THANKS TO BYRON THOMAS' EPIC ACCOUNT OF HIS WEEKEND THERE STOP AM PROUD TO BE DESIGNATED AS HOST IN ABSENTIA AND WISH IT WERE POSSIBLE TO LEND LUCE YOU ALL A GREATER MEASURE OF PEACE AND QUIET. (Time Inc. Archives)

Byron Thomas and Aaron Bohrod were two LIFE war artists who decided on their own to go across the Channel and sketch the Normandy invasion. They did this without having been assigned and without any authority whatsoever. Thomas had purchased a neutral looking military uniform from a second-hand shop in London. The two literally hitch-hiked by two boats on D Day+6[42]. The October 9, 1944, issue carries three full pages of Thomas' sketches of his and Bohrod's adventure and seven full paintings of British life during the war. The painting that opens the

---

[42] The "D Day +" designation indicates how many days after D-Day itself (June 6, 1944) that the incident took place.

spread is of the bombed Coventry Cathedral. It is proof that the drama of painting is equal to the reality of photography. Bohrod's sketches were published in LIFE August 28, and six of his paintings in the October 30th issue. After their harrowing experience of being in a warzone without proper papers or weapons, the two retreated back to London. Thomas returned to the USA and Bohrod went back to the battlefields of France. No wonder Daniel Longwell was concerned about the artists and photographers in harm's way.

Byron Thomas had earlier painted a portrait of Mary Longwell which was featured in the *Art Digest,* January, 1943, from the December (1942) 460 Park Avenue Show of portraits. The show title was "It Looks Like Me." Mary's portrait later hung in her bedroom in their Neosho home but its whereabouts now are unknown at least to me.

Byron Thomas and Longwell were friends for years and Thomas introduced him to the work of modernist painter, Herbert Katzman. Katzman was not a War Artist but his works, *Bowl of Fruit* and *Red Fish* hung opposite each other in the Longwell's Neosho home. In fact Mary used one as a subject of their Christmas card in 1956, drawn by Mary. Peter Hurd and his wife Henrietta Wyeth were also special friends of the Longwells. They vacationed together in Mexico after the war. His work, *Dry River,* of the New Mexico landscape hung in the Longwell parlor of the Neosho house.

Indications of the care Longwell took of his artists are found in the letters from wives and children. Longwell wrote to Sarah Lea when he had word from Tom. Censorship and security kept private letters to people at home pretty blank about what was really being experienced, so when he could, Longwell filled in the blanks.

Peter Hurd's young son, was the happy recipient of toy tanks, guns, and planes. His mother wrote Dan that he could not possibly know how utterly delighted the youngster was. Young Peter wrote a letter to "Dear Dan" which is a picture itself of an American child during WW II. He wrote:

> Thank you a lot (underlined twice) for the mechanized army. I really like the little field howitzer very much…Everything is fine here at the ranch. I miss my father very much because I won't see him for at least six months, but I am helping my mother around the place…I couldn't go (to school) the last day because I went to Roswell to see my father off to you know where… Love, Peter
>
> (Box 66, **Daniel Longwell Papers**, Rare Book & Manuscript Library, Columbia University in the City of New York)

Longwell's personal appreciation of art and artists did for him at LIFE what appreciation of writers and literature did for him at Doubleday. He did not simply hire and assign these people. He became engaged in their processes. He made them understand and believe that what they were doing was important to LIFE magazine and its readers. Nothing about working with Dan Longwell was a shallow experience. He brought his whole life to LIFE and while that was very obvious from the beginning, it grew in magnitude during the World War II.

There is a fine example of the Longwell ability to recognize happy coincidences and turn them to LIFE's advantage. After the arduous trip to army bases in the west and production of the "Defense Issue" (July 1941) finished, Mary Longwell insisted they take a rest in Bermuda. They sailed on a Canadian ship which zigged and zagged around oil slicks from sunken oil tankers which were the target of German submarines which patrolled the Atlantic. An American base was being built in Bermuda with U.S. Navy Captain Jules James in command. Longwell knew that Mrs. James was a niece of Henry Stimson, Secretary of War. Captain and Mrs. James had three daughters who loved dachshunds. The Longwells shared this sentiment as they had two of their own. That same year the Longwells would send a Dachshund puppy to the James daughters. There are charming letters between them in Box 17, **Daniel Longwell Papers**, Rare Book & Manuscript Library, Columbia University in the City of New York)

On January 5, 1942, Daniel Longwell took the time to write a letter and send a belated Christmas gift to the young pup, Wiggles. The following short excerpt from Longwell's letter to "Wiggles" yields a literary personality profile of a man who goes the distance for those he loves and appreciates.

Dear Wiggles:

I enclose a little identification tag your Mother, Cissy, wanted you to have for Christmas. I am sorry it is so late, but the engravers couldn't deliver it in time. I don't suppose you know how engravers are, but that's the way they are. When you wear this little identification tag, you will exactly match Cissy and your brother, Penny.

Dan Longwell with One of His Beloved Dachsunds, Date Unknown (Photographer: Possibly Alfred Eisenstadt)

Give our best to your good family. We still think you were the best of your litter and only those three nice little James girls and their nice parents deserved you. I hope you've been good—given up toad eating—and don't bark too much. Also, don't chew on things.

Tell your master that I have given you a signal for war times. It is this: America Expects that every dachshund this day will do its duty.

Thank Captain and Mrs. James for that nice photograph of you and their family. It is in your dogs' picture album—the history of your family—....

P.P.S. If I may suggest, Wiggles—in that picture Mrs. James sent us, you were looking a little too intently at the toast and things on the tea table. I thought you were a little obvious. Cissy

227

and Penny have the same fault too. I somehow wish you had improved on the manners we have taught them. But you look exactly like Cissy or Penny at tea. (Box 17, **Daniel Longwell Papers**, Rare Book & Manuscript Library, Columbia University in the City of New York)

No doubt this bit of comic relief was welcomed by the Captain and his family and for all we know, Wiggles got the message and eschewed toads and toast ever after.

While on their Bermuda vacation in 1941, the Longwells gave a dinner party for the Jameses and they brought along Admiral Robert C. Griffen who was just in with a convoying task force. Longwell reported,

> I learned from Griffen about the rugged undeclared war in the North Atlantic and particularly the roughness of life at the Canadian-British-American base at Argentia.... When I returned to New York, one hot day in August, I persuaded Admiral Hepburn, then in charge of Navy Public Relations, to send artist Tom Lea to Argentia. (1956 Longwell Memo to Celia Sugarman, Box 81, **Daniel Longwell Papers**, Rare Book & Manuscript Library, Columbia University in the City of New York)

These were the sorts of things Longwell and LIFE were doing to show America's threatened status in the Atlantic before war was declared. No doubt, daughters and dachshunds helped with the atmosphere between military men and a trustworthy big-time journalist.

It has been my rare and treasured memory to hear first-hand about the war from a wartime photographer, Carl Maydans, or second-hand from War Artist Byron Thomas's daughter, Murray Thomas Ngoima, or even, shall I say, third-hand by reading the letters between the war artists and Longwell. These connections reveal that Dan and Mary Longwell carried great concern for the Time Inc. people throughout the war and beyond. In fact, my acquaintance with those connected to the War was by way of a Longwell introduction.

When I worked at the TIME-LIFE Building in 1962, LIFE people sat in offices or cubicles on the 29th and 30th Floors. The two years I was there the offices had doors, but they were always open. The secretaries sat outside the individual offices. There were interior corridors where editors and writers could easily consult with each other. Researchers or reporters had more of a cubicle arrangement but the walls were floor to ceiling, not the half walls seen today in huge bullpen arrangements. In a nutshell, the writers and editors had offices with windows. The head of a department might have a corner office with a secretary. Only the interior corridor separated the researcher from the writer. All of this was enclosed by an exterior corridor that went all around the floor with exits to the elevators, stairwells, rest rooms and the through-way where the Associated Press teletype machine was clicking away typing up to the minute news. That is where I sat for my first few months at the clip desk.

I had come to work at Time Inc. in the summer of 1962. Friends of the Longwells would stop in to meet me.

Knowing I had no family in the area, Carl Mydans invited me to have Thanksgiving dinner with him and his wife Shelley at their home in Larchmont, NY. Conversation centered on the time they had spent in Russia.

I learned the Mydans' story some years later at a supper in Texas at the ranch of Holland McCombs. It was in this setting that Carl and Shelley Mydans talked a little about their experience of being interred by the Japanese in Manila, the Philippines. They and 2000 other civilians were crowded into the compound of Santo Tomás University. Carl and Shelley were imprisoned there for eight and a half months before being taken to Shanghai, China, and from there released to sail home on the last trip from China on the neutral Swedish ship, the *Gripsholm*. They were part of civilian prisoner exchange and in the letter Shelley wrote which was published in the LIFE November 29, 1943 issue, she describes how starved and pitiful the American and British men and women looked and how very healthy, well fed and dressed the Japanese looked.

Shelley Mydans wrote a novel (*Open City*, Doubleday Doran, 1945, en.wikipedia.org/wiki/**Shelley_** Smith_ **Mydans**) which was a story of the many truths played out by fictional characters as a result of the experience of internment. Probably everyone at the table had read her book with the exception of myself. As we enjoyed the feasts before us at the Texas ranch, Carl began to talk about hunger in the camp.

He said the women and men were separated. For evening's entertainment, the men took to telling bedtime stories as a way to settle down and fall asleep in their hungry and crowded conditions. He said that in the beginning it would be a story of a great evening out with a beautiful woman. She would be described in minute detail. They would go somewhere opulent that would require having an elaborate description. They would have dinner and perhaps dance. The whole imaginary evening's date would be a long and desirable fairy tale in this place of every deprivation.

Carl said that as the food got worse and less, hunger and starvation began to set in. The stories changed. At first the elaborate evening got shorter. The descriptions of food grew longer. Then the places dropped out altogether. Finally the girl was also dropped from the stories and more elaborate descriptions of food remained.

While Carl and Shelley were incarcerated, Longwell kept Shelley's mother, Mrs. Everett W. Smith at Stanford University, informed of the possibility of an "exchange of nationals". The information proved to be true and Carl and Shelley were soon home by way of India. The Longwells gave them their Sharon, Connecticut, home for rest, recovery, and Christmas.

Dan wrote to Mrs. Smith about Carl and Shelley, "They were such close personal friends of Mrs. Longwell's and mine that we feel deeply about them."

Shelley wrote to me years later about the Longwells. "How important they were in our lives. Dan hired Carl and Mary hired me for that fledgling magazine LIFE so long ago. They started out as our bosses and grew to be our friends. Wonderful couple." (Letter of January 12, 1997 from Carl and Shelley Maydans to author)

Longwell's Style at LIFE

Early in 1944, John Shaw Billings decided he did not want to be LIFE's managing editor any longer. The in-house newsletter, *F.Y.I., June 26, 1944,* announced that John Shaw Billings was appointed Editorial Director of all Time Inc. publications and that Daniel Longwell would be the new Managing Editor of LIFE. Longwell in turn gave new duties to Wilson Hicks as the Executive Editor and stated that Joseph Thorndike would fill in as M.E. for the magazine from time to time. He also permanently appointed Joe Kastner as Copy Editor. Longwell explained that it was his goal to develop a new younger team to take over and manage the magazine. But until then, he finished out the war as Managing Editor. There were a few more major battles and few more major decisions.

One overriding decision was that there were to be absolutely no faking of photographic events. There was not much trouble with this until the photograph of the flag raising on Iwo Jima came into the office. Longwell reasoned that it was a contrived photo because the fighting there was so close and severe that no commander would send men up an exposed hill to raise a flag. "This ain't a flag raising war. You get behind things in this war," Longwell said. He was right about constant enemy sniping and throwing of grenades from Japanese soldiers in caves on the hillside.

The first flag was raised February 23, 1945. However, the first flag was a small one, 54 inches by 28 inches, and was not so dramatic. The men raising that flag did draw fire but successfully beat back the enemy. A second larger flag, 8 ft. by 4 ft. 8 inches was sent up the hill. The first photographer, S. Sgt. Louis R. Lowery for *Leatherneck* magazine, was shot at and slipped down the hill breaking his camera along the way. The second photograph was taken some hours later by Joe Rosenthal, an Associated Press civilian photographer. It was the second photograph that became so iconic and was the model for the Marine Memorial at Arlington Cemetery. When the Rosenthal photo came in, Longwell said it was phony and did not run it. However, every other newspaper and magazine did. This brought Roy Larsen, President of Time Inc., down to Longwell's office to find out "What happened to that terrific picture? You didn't run it and everybody's running it." Longwell knew it was originally a Marine publicity shot. But he also had come to realize that "Our country needed that picture." (Groner Interview II Daniel Longwell, page 33-34., August, 18, 1957, Time Inc. Archives)

But when he did run it in LIFE, it was March 26, 1945, and it ran with a photo of the painting "Washington Crossing the Delaware" by Emanuel Leutze. Leutze had used German models on the Rhine River. Longwell kept to his standards and stood his ground.

Longwell was very proud of LIFE's support of the US Armed Forces and he had every right to be. In August 1942, he wrote to Major General A.D. Surles, Bureau of Public Relations, War Department, Washington, DC, that LIFE had run and continued to run more pages on Army, Navy and Air Force activities than any other general magazine.

In a book such as this, it would be foolishness to try and list all the ideas Daniel Longwell entertained for the sake of entertainment in the pages. He had a knack for finding fun where ever it was to be found. One of my favorite stories is in one of his letters to Mary explaining that at a base for practicing parachuting, lost or damaged parachutes were gathered up by kids, sold for $10 to wives who in turn made dresses out of them…even a wedding dress. They couldn't run the story because the practice was, of course, against regulations.

Another fun story was connected to an Army base in northern California. The infantry fellows were looking for a way to lighten their loads and had a couple of burros which ran wild in the area. Someone discovered that area Mexicans could catch them and would sell them to help out the Infantry. After returning to New York, Longwell raised some money for the burros by telling "the boys" that they could give a name to the burro their money would buy. He raised $150 from the LIFE office. (Box 21, **Daniel Longwell Papers**, Rare Book & Manuscript Library, Columbia University in the City of New York.

The Wartime Relationship between Dan and Mary

As busy as Daniel and Mary Longwell were with the magazine during these years of its phenomenal growth of influence with responsibility, they were never too busy to express their devotion to one another. Knowing them both and how reluctant and reserved they were, it was a surprise and joy to come across personal notes, letters and telegrams. Personal with a capital "P" would be apt. Existing inside this huge Time Inc. news and social apparatus was a couple who kept their own life together compartmentalized like a private room in a Pullman car on a fast moving train.

Trains were important transportation in those days and for those who had second homes in Connecticut they were more like a requirement than just "important." When gas rationing was imposed during the war, the train trip became more arduous. Pullman was selling standing room only tickets. Mr. Longwell applied for reserve seats for himself and Mary as they had such an arrangement prior to the rationing. I have only found letters to the Manager, Pullman Bureau of the New York, New Haven & Hartford Rail Road. I hope they were successful because what they were doing in Sharon, Connecticut, on weekends was as much for the war effort as their workdays in New York City.

They were growing vegetables and melons, and canning for winter; they would load this produce into duffle bags to take back to the city for themselves and other people at work. The diaries speak of this activity in detail, probably

Mary at Their Home in Connecticut, Date Unknown (Box 47, **Daniel Longwell Papers**, Rare Book & Manuscript Library, Columbia University in the City of New York)

because Mary was not known for her cooking skills and they always engaged people to help out in the kitchen and the gardens. Dan was used to farm life but it seemed like a new and rewarding activity for Mary and it delighted Dan that she took to it as she did. In Box 25, **Daniel Longwell Papers**, Rare Book & Manuscript Library, Columbia University in the City of New York, there is a letter from Mrs. John Shaw Billings undated, but probably 1943, in which Frederica is thanking Mary and Dan for the potatoes, cucumbers, squash, string beans and onions. She writes, "I couldn't be more enthusiastic about your vegetables—and truly thank you for being so thoughtful and generous for letting us share your fine crop."

The Connecticut home was a lot of work, but it was also a place to be "away." And they were fond of each other. I do not believe I am encroaching on their privacy by sharing some of the letters Dan wrote to Mary. Mary surely won't mind or she would not have placed them in the Longwell Collection at Columbia. My favorite, because it is funny, is one he composed as if he were the cartoon character, L'il Abner (which was also featured in an issue of LIFE) writing to his girlfriend, Daisy Mae.

"Letter to Daisy Mary"

(Box 32, **Daniel Longwell Papers**, Rare Book & Manuscript Library, Columbia University in the City of New York)

Dere Daisy Mary,

I aint got no flowers for you all this mawning. But Ah got a secret. Ah loves yo ????? Thas all I cain give yo this mawning. Ah mean ah show does aprechiate yo honey. Ahm tired naow.

Yrs cincerly xxxxxxxxxxxxx
[Little Abner Longwell- hisns mark]

In a more serious vein a letter address to "Darling Mary" from the Del Monte Lodge in Pebble Beach, CA. (They always addressed each other in letters with "Darling.") Dan writes,

I've made a huge circle since last I was here [at Pebble Beach the last time]. I made a job for myself, the magazine has proved stable, I've got married, a bloody war has broken out and I've met Ginger Rogers. Golly. It's funny what marriage does to you. Here we are a couple of saps who lived alone more than is normal for people who live alone and then we get married and I want you to share every pleasure I have and miss you when I am away and get awfully sentimental xxxx when I xxxxx think of you x, Dan. (Box 70, **Daniel Longwell Papers**, Rare Book & Manuscript Library, Columbia University in the City of New York)

In July 1942, he wrote her from Washington, DC, while waiting to call on a congressperson. He wrote Mary from the Carlton Hotel but mailed it later in New York's Grand Central Station.

Dear Sweetie-

I often see you get your mail in the morning when you only get ads. I want to get up and go around the corner and mail you a letter quick. At the moment I am in Washington waiting to see if I go out to the Shoreham and see [the Senator] tonight or go to bed and see him early in the morning.

So it was a dandy chance to write you a letter—for Virginia to bring you in the morning. Know what I always want to say in those letters I want to write quick….

I love you—that's all, xxx, Dan (Box 72, **Daniel Longwell Papers**, Rare Book & Manuscript Library, Columbia University in the City of New York)

On another train trip across country in April 1942, he writes Mary as the train passes through Missouri. He was on the Santa Fe's Grand Canyon Ltd. Mary and Dan had bought the Newton County farm which he had shared with his brother some thirty years earlier. Buying it was her idea but while he loved the area, he was not sure how life would be there for her. (Box 70, **Daniel Longwell Papers**, Rare Book & Manuscript Library, Columbia University in the City of New York)

Darling Mary,

It's a lovely spring day. I meant to type my reports right through but got lazy and just watched Missouri roll by. It's very pretty with the apples and dogwood in bloom and the trees just getting green. I read in the K.C. Star that the old telegraph operator in Neosho had died and that they had trouble getting enough strawberry pickers for the Monett Neosho District…I rather wish I had arranged things so that you could have met me in Neosho and I wish the devil we could get off for a week end down there. I do want you to see it when it is pretty. I worry about you and that little farm. I wish it were a richer place and not such a rock pile…It's really a lovely place just beyond the barn. There are nice cottonwoods along the brook …the creek there is all a rock ledge and very pretty. The layout is perfect and if we rebuilt the barn it would make a very cozy place. Just below there is a little marsh on our place where I hope someday to throw up a small dam that will catch our big springs water and attract egrets, cranes and even some ducks. Then if we rebuild the little old house we can be snug as can be… xxxxxx!darling, Dan

All these letters I have shared were typed by Dan. Once he spoke of having gotten settled in his Pullman car sleeper and putting some pictures around. He was a very sentimental man and I am sure those pictures would be of Mary and their dachshunds. If he did not have time to write a letter, he would send a telegram. The telegrams had precious little news, but precious lots of love and attention.

CHAPTER EIGHT

POST WAR Life at LIFE

July 11, 1949
Dear Dan,
Many, many happy returns of the day!
Here's a small memento of your 50th year.
It's a long way from "playing with pictures"
to being the impresario of Churchill--and
everything. A long way and a lot of fun.

Yours, Harry

(Fiftieth Birthday Greeting from Henry Luce
to Daniel Longwell, Box 73, **Daniel Longwell
Papers**, Rare Book & Manuscript Library,
Columbia University in the City of New York)

LIFE magazine was glorious during World War II and reached a zenith in publishing history with a circulation of 5,200,000. Dan Longwell had been Managing Editor from June of 1944 through the end of the war and well into 1946. The magazine was in its tenth year and though a few people were concerned about its future, worrying about the future was not on the minds of the LIFE staff. They were a proud rambunctious group who had thrived under the group journalism methods of their managing editor and its challenging chaos.

Mr. Luce decided that Daniel Longwell should come to the executive floor as Deputy Editor (HRL Memo to staff, Oct. 26, 1946, Time Inc. Archives). A glance at the Masthead in those days did not give any more of a job description to the title than the list of ingredients described in pharmaceuticals. Henry R. Luce was Editor-in-Chief. Roy Larsen was President. Editorial Director was John Shaw Billings. They were all on the "executive" level. At LIFE specifically, there was the Managing Editor, the Executive Editor and the Editorial Chief. An editor was an editor and the only hint of importance was in the chronological listing down the masthead.

It was rather creative of Luce to later change Deputy Editor to Chairman of the Board of Editors. Indeed this October 19, 1946, letter to Dan Luce once again verifies the importance of Dan's ability to "get around", and that he has leeway to create his own job.

> And now as to you—and your new job which, as you said, you have to invent (as indeed you may be said to have invented your previous jobs in the course of the invention of LIFE itself…One weakness of LIFE's top staff is that the editors do not get around. They do not have enough opportunity to expose themselves to the trends, fads and evolutions of this world. This means you must allow yourself enough freedom to get around in New York, make trips in this country,

and occasionally abroad. I believe in that way you can best serve LIFE. (Box 29, **Daniel Longwell Papers**, Rare Book & Manuscript Library, Columbia University in the City of New York)

When Longwell's promotion was announced, his LIFE staff immediately set to surprising him with a party. They made a big star as a name tag for the new "Deputy". Later Longwell's masthead title was changed to read Chairman of the Board of Editors[43], but there never was a designated or limited set of people for his "Board of Editors."

Dan Longwell, "Deputy Editor" at Time Inc., 1946 (Box 46, **Daniel Longwell Papers**, Rare Book & Manuscript Library, Columbia University in the City of New York)

The surprise farewell party was appropriately organized and created by the Modern Living Department and held at cocktail hour in the offices. It was well known and cheerfully accepted that Dan was partial to girls though it was also well known he was not the typical ladies' man. As he wrote to Sid James years later after reviewing a dummy for the experimental *Sports Illustrated*, which was seemingly short of women's sports, "Remember, Sportsmen also like girls." (Memo to Sidney James, April 30, 1945, Box 69, **Daniel**

---

[43] When Longwell retired in August 1953, the Board Chairmanship was "herewith terminated". (Retirement Announcement, August 10, 1953, LIFE Magazine, p. 13)

Longwell Papers, Rare Book & Manuscript Library, Columbia University in the City of New York)

The ladies of the department attired themselves in outfits that related to stories carried in the magazine under his direction and there was much laughter as they read their poems of favorite insights and good wishes to their Editor 'N Friend. One of the long standing memories was the poem composed by LIFE writer Donald Marshman. There is a photo of him dressed in white shirt with sleeves rolled up standing next to Dan who is trying to keep from laughing so he can hear all the lines. Dan was dressed in a three piece suit sporting his cardboard Deputy badge with its rootin' tootin' wildwest cowboy on a buckin' bronco. It seems they had nailed their Managing Character. Marshman's poem survived in every archive and Betty Morris gave me her sixty-eight year old copy. Three of its four stanzas are shared here under the title, *GUNGA DAN.*

We're awaiting rye and beer
While we're standing by out here
And Longwell's at his fav'rite occupation
Acting bashful, shy and silly
While he winks his eye at Millie
And offers her an extra week's vacation.
When I used to earn my pay
Under Longwell's weekly sway
I discovered that a girl's career was freer
Than a man's, for Dan will menace
Any act from Cal or Dennis
Once he gets a pitch from Margit or Maria

So it's Dan, Dan, Dan,
Won't you ever use a story from a man?
Foreign News is in a tizzie
While you cock an eye at Lizzie
And remark, "I'm much too busy,"
Don't you Dan?

I say, "Dan, Dan, Dan,
Though you never gave a break to any man,
Though misogynists deride you,
And the wiles of women guide you,
In my heart I'll be beside you---
Gunga Dan.
(Box 46, **Daniel Longwell Papers**, Rare Book
& Manuscript Library, Columbia University in
the City of New York)

Mary was also on hand to enjoy the humorous honors to her husband. Dressed in her feminine suit, looking like her own executive self as head of Personnel, about to become Chief of Research for all the magazines with an office on the executive floor.

That August, after union problems had settled down, Mr. and Mrs. Longwell embarked for a trip to the United Kingdom of Great Britain to lay a foundation for the next stages of their stellar careers in the colossal company they had helped to create. But first they had to pack.

Unremembered by most Americans today is that while World War II was disrupting farming and trade and everything else, the UK and the USA governments had imposed rationing. When the war ended, US rationing very soon became unnecessary. However it continued well into the 1950's in the UK. When the Longwells went over in 1947, shortages were still acute. So now instead of taking duffle bags of vegetables into New York City from their Connecticut farm, they began to plan taking gifts and supplies to their friends in the UK in a duffle bag and foot locker.

This group of friends was very much like their counterparts in the USA. The Henry Luce of the UK was probably Lord Beaverbrook who had introduced Longwell to Randolph Churchill in 1928, who in turn introduced Longwell to Randolph Churchill's father, Winston Spencer Churchill. Walter Graebner at the LIFE London office had established a wonderful liason relationship with the Churchills. A key British person during this period was Lord Camrose, Churchill's friend and literary agent. Even though these were high ranking British individuals, they too faced and shortages and had to have ration cards.

LIFE's man in London was Walter Graebner. In June of 1947, he wrote to Mary in answer to her query about what sorts of things should they bring over from America. His answer displays what it was like to live in London in 1947, and what was required to entertain guests.

> I might suggest a dozen or so bottles of Scotch and gin,(the duty will be heavy, but the total will be no more than the black market price in London, Some Cleanex (sic) (which is unobtainable here),

soap and soap flakes (for washing silks), chocolate (if you like it), cigarettes unless you don't mind English, and possibly fruit juices. If you spend a weekend with someone, they naturally like anything that you bring, such as marmalade and jam (most difficult to get here), tinned ham or an assortment of tinned meats, tinned fruits, rice, chocolate, olive oil, butter and fats of any kind… also much appreciated are nylons, lipstick and nail varnish…I forgot SUGAR! There is very little to be had…MILK is very short so you may want to bring some powdered or evaporated with you.

…the chances are there will be no duty on food stuffs but you will have to pay on tobacco, nylons and liquor. (Box 2, **Daniel Longwell Papers**, Rare Book & Manuscript Library, Columbia University in the City of New York)

Dan's response to Graebner warned him that their luggage consisted of a foot locker, six bags, a duffle bag, a book bag, a paint box, a hat box, cameras, a typewriter and a couple of bundles. Everyone was anticipating their arrival and they would stay at Claridge's from July 25 into September. This was a working trip as Dan was to line up all of the illustrations to be used in the Churchill history of WW II.

The preceding year, in November of 1946, the race to capture the Churchill memoirs of WW II, led to enormous investigations into copyright laws, tax laws and the difference between newspaper, magazine and book publishing. Complications abounded as LIFE dealt with two sets of national laws and tax codes. Longwell had experience with this from his time at Doubleday and he was more aware than most of what could be done and what might not be possible.

On November 20, 1946, Walter Graebner sent a nine page personal and confidential cable for Luce and Longwell to C.D. Jackson, a Director of TIME-LIFE International in New York indicating that Churchill (coded as "our friend") was casting about for a publisher of his memoirs and would welcome an offer from LIFE. As carrots on a long stick, LIFE had already published Churchill's paintings and had bought and published some secret speeches which he had delivered to Parliament during the War. (Interview with Groner, Part III, p. 5 and 6, Time Inc. Archives)

The Prime Minister had been duly impressed with the way LIFE handled his work and their attention to detail. Graebner also stated that Lord Comrose was coming to the United States and only he would have the final decision regarding who would win the memoirs.

Longwell reasoned that though Churchill was known as a politician and statesman, he really was an author and Longwell knew the velvet gloved ways publishers treated authors. Hopefully the reader remembers that Christopher Morely had pointed out that Longwell at Doubleday had maintained that authors were always disgruntled and so Longwell "gruntled" them. Longwell decided to "gruntle" Churchill. (Groner Interview, Part III, p. 7, Time Inc. Archives)

Churchill had come to America in 1946 and went straight from the boat to catch the train to Florida. So

Longwell got the British Consul to take the proof sheets of the Churchill paintings with a little note saying perhaps he would like to see his paintings as they would be appearing in LIFE magazine. Churchill wrote a little note back. Then Longwell sent him a note about his upcoming publication of the Secret Speeches saying they would buy all three but only planned to publish two. Discussions about this and copyright laws and other odds and ends had to be taken care of and Churchill got in the habit of phoning Longwell everyday. He even called him on weekends in Connecticut much to the delight of others on the party line.

When Churchill came to New York, Luce told Longwell to approach Churchill about the memoirs. On a casual Sunday afternoon, Longwell called on him. Others were expected but Churchill took Longwell aside and said he was not quite sure what he was going to do with his papers but that whatever he decided, Lord Camrose would be in charge of it.

Shortly word came from London that Camrose would be coming to the United States to "dispose of the memoirs." (Groner Interview with Longwell, Part III, August 27, 1957, p. 7-14, Time Inc. Archives) Therefore Longwell was watching out for Camrose but another fellow showed up, an associate of Comrose, touting the memoirs but Longwell knew that only Camrose had the final authority to deal. Luce then authorized Longwell to find Camrose and see what could be done.

It was at this point that Longwell's good relations with the heads of *The New York Times* came into play. The secondary agent had come to talk to Time Inc., but

Longwell learned at a private dinner with Charlie Merz of *The Times* that Camrose had been to see them. That was the first Longwell knew Camrose was in town. He immediately went to Luce who told him that General Adler of *The Times* had called him and Luce sent Longwell to see Adler. Not long before this Longwell had run a piece by *The Times* drama critic, Bruce Atkinson, and had paid him for it. Adler had been surprised that LIFE would pick up a *Times* story, and it gave him the idea that maybe LIFE and *The Times* could coordinate a deal on the Churchill memoirs. (Groner/Sugarman Interviews, Part III, p. 11-13, Time Inc. Archives)

Longwell reported the conversation to Groner and Sugarman in Part III of his interviews, page 11-13, Time Inc. Archives:

> He (Adler) said, "I wonder why we couldn't do something of the same thing with Churchill: we'll publish it weekdays and not in our Sunday edition, and you publish it weekly." And I said, "I don't see any reason for not doing that, at all. It seems to me a perfectly wonderful idea..." So I came back to Luce and said, "What do you think of that as an idea? I can't see anything wrong with that." And he said, "No, I think it's a good one." So we put our bids together and no single house could possibly have thought or had the courage to bid what was bid by the two of us....
>
> When Camrose came in, Larsen named the price. Lord Camrose nodded a couple of times – none of us understood what the nod meant—and

we were very excited when he said, "That's fine," and we got it….

We were the major fellows and *The Times* was really a dream from then on—the best people I ever did business with—do anything on the phone with them, adjust anything—they were perfectly wonderful.

And so it was that the contract was worked out in London and Longwell was in charge of choosing the illustrations for the Churchill texts and it was during that mission that the Longwells embarked for the UK in 1947.

There is a half-page typed note in the Columbia files which must have been a note typed by Dan to place in a printed essay by Churchill, *Painting as a Pastime.* It reads, "This book is autographed to Mrs. Longwell. At luncheon at Chartwell, (Churchill) discovered her hobby of painting, gave her a lecture on the art and this copy of his little book. "You must paint in oils," he urged, "You can lay it on so thick."

Working with any author is toil and trouble and Mr. Churchill was no exception. In the Daniel Longwell Papers at Columbia, Longwell explains some of Churchill's habits with editors, in this case, namely Longwell.

An editor was granted the privilege of following the work through its various stages. The author greatly appreciated prompt attention to the galleys. When I first went to see him about the book, *The Second World War,* in the summer of 1947, he promptly phoned me on my arrival at Claridge's and suggested that I might like a glance at a few things before coming to discuss the publication with him. A messenger arrived with more than a half million words in galleys. I advised Mrs. Longwell to seek out friends for a day or so and promptly started reading, lunching at my desk. I am a fast reader and I made notes. But I had just finished the last galley about forty eight hours later when my phone rang and Mr. Churchill's husky voice was asking had I had the opportunity of glancing at the few things he had sent me." (Box 4, **Daniel Longwell Papers**, Rare Book & Manuscript Library, Columbia University in the City of New York)

Thus began the arduous task of six years of dealing with six volumes of Churchill's memoirs of WW II. The editing for an American audience was no small task and most of this fell to LIFE editors, though Longwell was at their elbows. Oddly enough when the sixth volume came in summer of 1953, Longwell was the one man not on summer vacation. So he worked on it for a month and a half which was probably a month and half too long as his retirement had been announced.

But Longwell had had a special attachment to Churchill since having met him in 1928. From their first meeting they discovered that each of them enjoyed military history, art, and Ogden Nash poetry, and that each of them had phenomenal memories. That foundation of admiration and amusement was something Longwell was loathe to let go. He had long been collecting and would continue to complete his Churchill first edition books until he gifted it to Columbia University along with notes and letters between the two men. Longwell may have said he had "never worked so hard" but more than likely it was a labor of love like a loving mother tucking in her daughter who was would be leaving for college the next morning. This is why when the magazine went to press, we said we were putting it to bed.

Other staff in the office may have found the retired Longwell disruptive. One editor was heard to say, "Oh to be in England, now that Longwell's here." Such is the fate of persons who work to make something wonderful for the world and the world then runs right past them. It happened to Churchill after his leading England through the war. He was voted out of Parliament. It happened to Longwell after his creating and leading LIFE magazine into publishing history.

Longwell remained a friend and admirer of Churchill's works. In 1946 when Churchill gave the historic "Iron Curtain" speech at Westminster College in Fulton, MO., Longwell managed to get the final transcript with Churchill's last notations. At Longwell's suggestion the editors of LIFE gave it to the College Library. Longwell presented it to the college on behalf of LIFE at the 1952 commencement. (Box 22, **Daniel Longwell Papers**, Rare Book & Manuscript Library, Columbia University in the City of New York)

1952 was an odd year for Daniel Longwell. In fact after leaving the everyday working days of LIFE, all the years seemed odd. As Chairman of the Board of Editors he had authority to choose and define what that might mean.

What he chose to do was to bring in special celebrities into the offices for lunch with an editor of his choosing. Dan Longwell had always been the standard "Man about Town" and he knew that most of the editorial people just came to the Time Inc. offices or commuted and didn't go out much at night. In other words, they were just out of touch on a personal basis with other movers and shakers. It was his idea therefore to bring some of these people in for informal luncheons and discussion. A few of the people he brought in were Richard Rogers and Oscar Hammerstein, Nelson Rockefeller, Alfred Knopf, Ogden Nash, Jean Monnet and the Duke of Windsor. (Box 14, **Daniel Longwell Papers**, Rare Book & Manuscript Library, Columbia University in the City of New York)

It was to one of these luncheons that Leland Hayward was invited. Hayward had been in the theater business and had been an agent.

It was in farewell conversations after this "Editors'" luncheon at the RCA Building that Hayward was telling the current Managing Editor of LIFE, Sid James, about a new book by Ernest Hemingway. According to Longwell, (Groner Interview III, August 22, 1957, pages 19 – 25, Time Inc. Archives), James deferred to Longwell as the guy interested in books. Longwell deferred to James who was filling in as the Managing Editor while Ed Thompson was on vacation. Hayward sent James the manuscript to read, but he did not have time to peruse it, so gave it to Longwell the same evening.

Longwell took it home and read it that evening and after finishing it he simply gave it to Mary and asked her to read it and give him her opinion. Her opinion was, "Gee, that's a terrific story." Dan was more effusive, "There's never been a short novel as good as that." Longwell took it back to James and said he was not going to tell him anything about it, but to read it. James' opinion was "Say, that's quite a piece." (Groner Interview, Part III, p. 18-25, Time Inc. Archives)

Longwell was determined to buy it for LIFE and to publish it in LIFE and treat it as a real little book in LIFE. He wanted to decorate it with illustrations that did not interfere with the text and he wanted text on full pages, no half pages. And he wanted it bought immediately. James told Longwell he wanted him to handle it but that he also wanted to wait for Thompson to get back. Longwell was fearful LIFE would lose out and told James to get it. James did contact Hemingway's lawyer who was acting as agent. James gave the manuscript to Billings to read and Billings didn't like it and didn't think Longwell had read it when in fact Longwell was the first to read it. There followed a delay which Longwell dreaded but Thompson returned and somewhere in the thrashing things out, LIFE bought *Old Man and the Sea*. (Groner Interview, Part III, p. 18-25, Time Inc. Archives)

Photographer Alfred Eisenstadt was sent down to Cuba to shoot Hemingway and the sea. Mildly stated, the two men did not get along. Dan reported. "Scribners suddenly called me up and said 'Gee, he got mad at Eisenstadt.

He's pretty vicious on this thing, and he hasn't heard from anybody on LIFE.'"

Longwell promised to write him right away and did. He was again "gruntling" an author and wrote what he called a "pretty mushy letter." He sent his letter over to Scribners with the question, "Now, you know this fellow and I don't so how will he accept a letter like this?" (Groner Interview, Part III, p. 18-25, Time Inc. Archives)

Overnight, upon reflection, Longwell decided the letter was too enthusiastic. The next morning he called up Scribners and asked if he could send over a second version, but they replied, "No, we were just remarking, it's perfect, it's just what he needs."

Longwell sent off the letter to Hemingway which began a remarkable correspondence between the two men. Looking over the expanse of Longwell's lifetime, it is remarkable that his last major works at LIFE magazine were not in photojournalism of a picture magazine, but harkened back to his first love, literature in print, the thousand words won out over the single picture: The Churchill Memoirs and *The Old Man and the Sea.*

I had not realized this at first. It was only in reading again the letters between him and Hemingway. It was apparent that Longwell had sensed the fear of a writer having his carefully crafted word pictures turned into one of the photographic essays for which LIFE had become famous. Just as the artists and photographers evoked emotion from the reader, the writer's tool is a story with words and they are obsessively possessive about it. One has to wonder if this was the basis of the conflict between

Hemingway and Eisenstadt. At any rate it seems to be Dan Longwell who figured it out. Longwell assured Hemingway that the purpose of Eisenstadt's visit was to take photos for the artist, Noel Sickles, to be able to fit the illustrations to the text. Sickles was not to really illustrate the text, but he was to decorate it symbolically. This meant that there would be no drawings of the Old Man's face, but always turned aside and the hands would be the repeated symbols decorating the text. The art was "not to get in the way of the words." (Groner Interview, Part III, August 1957, Time Inc. Archives)

Hemingway wrote Longwell that he and his wife Mary had had a nice note from Eisenstadt indicating that Hemingway had wished they could have shown him a bit more fun but that they were all pretty tired at the end of the day.

Longwell knew from his days at Doubleday that authors were defensive about their work. He knew that the really gifted writers were more interested that their work be read rather than "recognized".

In fact, Hemingway expressed this very thought himself. In one of his letters to Longwell, he expressed his gratitude that the expansive readership of LIFE would have people reading *Old Man and the Sea* who might not be able to afford the book or might not be able to find the book available where they lived. He said he was more pleased to have it in LIFE than for it to win a Nobel Prize. (Groner Interview, Part III, August 1957, Time Inc. Archives)

This of course created the possibility that the LIFE publication might undermine book sales. But Longwell addressed this issue too. He held a meeting with Scribners, Hemingway's publisher. From this meeting came forth one of the oldest tricks in the publishing trade, but also one of the most effective book promotions in history.

Habit was that six galley proofs might be sent out to newspapers or magazines hoping for promotional reviews to introduce the upcoming book to the reading public. It was Longwell's idea and Scribners agreed, outside of the contract, to print five hundred confidential galleys. He had noted that all the people, husbands and wives, who had read it had all experienced its strong impact. He knew also that the greatest advertising a book could have was by word of mouth. So they stamped all five hundred "CONFIDENTIAL" and gave them to salesmen, reviewers, editors, other writers and they did not say anything about the material, just handed it out secretly. Stories came in of people reading it behind locked doors. Two people missed their communter stops they were so engrossed in the galleys. One salesman got thirty advertising guys to read it, each one handing it to another. The "inside-dopester" in all of us became a huge sales "whispering campaign". Longwell is here quoted, "You had every intelligent person in the United States talking about *The Old Man and the Sea* before it came out…People right here in the office would go out and pay three dollars for that little book instead of waiting five days to get (their complimentary copy) of it in LIFE." (Groner Interview, Part III, August 1957, Time Inc. Archives)

An astute young man I knew bought two copies as an investment when the book came out in 1952. In 2005 he sold the two to a dealer for a thousand dollars. I do not think Longwell was so astute about investments but he certainly knew a winning literary piece when he read it.

The Longwell and Hemingway correspondence did not end with the LIFE's September 1, 1952, publication of *Old Man and the Sea.* A trust and affection grew between them though they never met.

Having finished with the Hemingway book, the Longwell's took a trip looping through North Dakota, Wyoming, Alaska and Washington. Dan had a friend doing large construction projects and he filed research and stories suggestions back to New York about the huge road building projects, hydro plants, military installations, housing, and the boom town of Anchorage. In his energetic enthusiasm gathering ideas for photographs, he caught pneumonia.

He was hospitalized with a second bout of pneumonia in New York in October of 1952. The first bout with similar symptoms had been in February of 1952 when he had spent five days in Doctors' Hospital in New York. The October illness got his attention and he agreed to a rest and recovery time over Christmas with Mary at Squaw Peak Ranch near Phoenix, Arizona. Afterward they had plans to visit the Peter Hurds at the beginning of 1953, and join them for a holiday trip into Mexico before returning to New York.

January 14, 1953, Mary wrote to Holland McCombs that the Arizona weather had turned cold and Dan had begun to cough. She had entered him in St. Joseph's Hospital in Phoenix. After several x-rays, doctors found a lung abscess and noted that an operation was called for. On New Year's Day it was suggested they return to New York.

So—back to New York we came. Dan had an operation on Friday, they found a lung abscess and removed part of the lung. No malignancy, thank goodness. He's coming along fine, and the doctors are pleased with him. (Boxes 13, 29, and 72, **Daniel Longwell Papers**, Rare Book & Manuscript Library, Columbia University in the City of New York)

This was a four hour operation which would be a life-changing event for anyone. To someone with the activity patterns of Dan Longwell, it brought home what he referred to as "grim realities." There was a bit of a shock wave through the office. Harry Luce wrote two letters of concern and sent a bouquet of roses, Churchill sent a note, Hemingway sent an inquiry and best wishes flowed in as a person with this broad an acquaintance group might expect. (Box 73, **Daniel Longwell Papers**, Rare Book & Manuscript Library, Columbia University in the City of New York)

With the abscess removed, Mother Nature was able to restore strength and health if perhaps to a lesser degree than Longwell was used to. Furthermore, a lot of his work place world had changed as well as his personal physical world.

1952 had seen the election of President Dwight D. Eisenhower, and he named Clare Booth Luce as United States Ambassador to the Vatican. Her husband and Dan's friend, Time Inc. Editor in Chief was in absentia in New York but *in situ* in Rome. Perhaps the executive office suites lost some of their status.

The recuperating Daniel Longwells decided to take a slow boat to Japan in March of 1953, and believe it or not, the retired-from-office Harry S. Trumans decided to do the same thing. Both couples sailed on the "President Cleveland" though the Trumans were only going as far as Hawaii. LIFE and Longwell had already approached Truman about his memoirs. Two men from Missouri with a world of history in their heads and accomplished careers behind them must have made for relaxed but stimulating dinner table conversation. They enjoyed each other's company and they would see much more of each other in New York for dinner in June and in Missouri for years to come.

Bess, Harry and Margaret Truman disembarked in Honolulu. After a brief visit there, the Longwells continued on to Japan. The Department of Defense, Office of Public Information gave Daniel Longwell a letter certifying him "as representing TIME-LIFE with extended accreditation to the Department of Defense for two months beginning March 20, 1953 in connection with his assignment in the Far East Command." This no doubt was a courtesy Longwell thoroughly enjoyed and the military did extend to him every courtesy.

Returning to the United States, Longwell learned that *Old Man and the Sea* had won Hemingway the Pulitzer Prize. He wired his secretary, Betty Morris, to send the following cable, May 5, 1953.

MR LONGWELL WIRED ME FROM SAN
FRANCISCO TODAY ASKING ME TO CABLE

YOU AND CONGRATULATE YOU ON
WINNING PULITZER PRIZE WITH MOST
COMPLETE BUT SHORTEST NOVEL THAT
EVER WON THAT RACE. BUT HE SAID
IT WAS ONLY A TRIAL HEAT FOR THE
NOBEL STAKES WHERE HE CONSIDERS
YOU ALREADY IN. MR LONGWELL
ALSO SAID TO SAY HE HAS SENT YOU
JAPANESE EDITION OF THE BOOK WHICH
WAS NICELY PUBLISHED WITH MUCH
ENTHUSIASM WHILE HE WAS IN TOKYO.
(Box 8, **Daniel Longwell Papers**, Rare Book &
Manuscript Library, Columbia University in the
City of New York)

And again, Dan was right; Hemingway did win the
Nobel Prize for *Old Man and the Sea*.

As was his habit, Dan had also sent back research,
story suggestions and photographs on all things cultural
and social in Japan. The Longwells thoroughly enjoyed
themselves and apparently there were no health problems.
They returned to New York after a one week stopover in
Missouri. Drought was plaguing the farm and the tenant
farmer was having a hard time. Dan was sympathetic and
put more money in the bank to tide things over for the farm
and the farmer.

The return to New York meant thinking about the
future. Dan had spent some serious time thinking about
new magazines for Time Inc. and new ideas for improving
LIFE especially. He sensed that photojournalism was
changing and he was not sure he was comfortable with it.

He held discussions with Luce before he left for Rome, and the result of all that is best is found in a July 14, 1953, letter to his college fraternity brother, close friend, and attorney, Tom Chrystie. (Box 30, **Daniel Longwell Papers**, Rare Book & Manuscript Library, Columbia University in the City of New York)

The letter to Chrystie notes that Longwell and Luce discussed the possibilities and consequences of Longwell leaving Time Inc. They agreed on a financial severance agreement which enticed Longwell to retire.

Dan had also written a letter to Luce July 9, 1953, which seemed to be a farewell to the office life he had known.

> I am glad you are writing the announcement for next week. I have a few things to tidy up before I close up shop, and after Aug. 1, I will become very inconspicuous. I'll send you a note about a few projects next week. Yes, we should have a long talk about LIFE. I admire much of what the boys do but I suspect picture journalism is changing—or should change.
>
> I think you have been generous and understanding, and I am most grateful. I hate to leave—but it may well prove that you have done me a great favor in starting me on my own. Always remember that I am a friend, and one of your greatest admirers. (Box 30, **Daniel Longwell Papers**, **Daniel Longwell Papers**, Rare Book & Manuscript Library, Columbia University in the City of New York.

There was the usual going back and forth about contracts, retaining Dan as a consultant when needed, and the formal announcement appeared above the Table of Contents, LIFE, August 10, 1953. The title read, "17 Years Behind the Masthead". The text read, "Missing is the name of Daniel Longwell—the first time since the first issue of LIFE (Nov. 23, 1936) that his name has been absent. Dan Longwell has resigned his post as Chairman of the Board to turn his creative abilities to the development of other projects in which Time Inc. is engaged." (LIFE Magazine, August 10, 1953, p. 13)

There was no fanfare. He wrote to Luce December 14, 1953, "I don't want to have a party given nor get a watch for old times' sake. I've been telling my personal friends of my leaving, but that's enough." (Box 29, **Daniel Longwell Papers**, Rare Book & Manuscript Library, Columbia University in the City of New York)

For as social an animal as Longwell was, he was also shy and reticent, and may have discouraged any event. Perhaps it was because Luce was away until September and perhaps because Longwell was very soon back in the office helping to get the Churchill Volume VI edited down for LIFE publication. Churchill was glad for this and wrote Longwell in September, 1953, saying how sorry he was that Longwell was resigning his Chairmanship of the Board of Editors. Churchill stated, "Our association has always been a very pleasant one to me." (Box 1, **Daniel Longwell Papers**, Rare Book & Manuscript Library, Columbia University in the City of New York)

Mary Longwell did not resign when Daniel did. Luce wanted her to continue to work and she did until later in 1954. Dan on the other hand did decide to leave the offices in December of 1953. December 29 he wrote Luce from the Big Spring Inn in Neosho, MO.,

> I hope I have left Time Inc. with great friendship for all the people who have worked with me. In return, I wish I could express my gratitude to them—but I cannot. What I want you to know, though, is that the privilege and honor of working for you, as one of the greatest editors in my time, has been one of the greatest rewards I have ever had.
>
> With all best wishes for the New Year...
>
> (Time Inc. Archives)

On January 12, 1954, Dan's friend and "boss" Harry Luce responded with recollection and reflection about their relationship which he described as "richly different from all others." As is often the case in reflections such as this, one becomes poetic, and Mr. Luce did.

> Looking back years ago to long talks en route to Pennsylvania Station and elsewhere beneath the wandering moon, I think of all those youthfully assertive works of ours. They were not wholly lost on the night air, but indeed, they had a number of consequences,--one consequence especially, a working companionship. (Time Inc. Archives)

And so it was, the ways of friends were parted. The Longwell era at LIFE magazine had come to a close. Dan would still send in the occasional story about the happenings he was creating in Neosho, Missouri. He would be in New York May of 1954, and he and Mary would be treated to a luncheon by "the boys." There Dan was given an enormous Presentation Folio bound in blue Moroccan with gold leaf reading ***Dan Longwell and LIFE***. Inside the portfolio are forty-four mounted photographs of the stories special to Dan. This huge presentation volume measures 16 ¼ inches by 12 ¼ inches. It is signed by Henry Luce, John Shaw Billings, Ed Thompson and Joe Kastner. One can find it preserved at Columbia University's Rare Books and Manuscript Library, Longwell Collection, in an archival oversized flat box. It seems fitting that this was my final "find" in my search for the real Daniel Longwell. (Flat Box 3, **Daniel Longwell Papers**, Rare Book & Manuscript Library, Columbia University in the City of New York)

CHAPTER NINE

From Manhattan to Missouri

May 19, 1954
Dear Mr. Longwell,
I am glad that you and Mrs. Longwell
are coming to Neosho. That is at least within
visiting distance on short notice. Neosho is a
lovely town.

Sincerely yours,
s/ Harry S. Truman,
s/ My best to Mrs. Longwell
(Box 7, **Daniel Longwell Papers**, Rare Book
& Manuscript Library, Columbia University in
the City of New York)

We are both thinking at the moment of doing
an article, "How to Retire and Take it Easy";
New York was never as strenuous as Neosho,
Missouri.

(March 4, 1958, Letter from Mary Longwell
to Raoul Fleischman, *The New Yorker Magazine,*
Box 65, **Daniel Longwell Papers**, Rare Book &

Manuscript Library, Columbia University in the
City of New York)

Now the Longwells enter a new era of their lives and
it becomes a new era for Neosho, Missouri, too. Dan had
background here clear back to 1914. He had maintained
the friendships made in his eighth grade year at Ragan
School. His father had owned two hundred acres around
that school and in 1941, Dan and Mary had decided to buy
back the original farm. They spent summer vacations at
the Big Spring Inn across from the Big Spring Park and
built up a dairy herd and some beef cattle which Mary
was proud of because they "matched". They renovated the
little house and Mary had it painted yellow. They bought
a house in Neosho on the bluffs overlooking the Park and
Inn. Mary had it painted "that muddy grey color like the
houses in New England." At the time the Longwell's set up
housekeeping in Neosho, the population was about 6,000.

Most of their East Coast friends were curious as to how
they could move into such a remote place which provided
so little entertainment to such a sophisticated pair. Marian
MacPhail wrote her friend and mentor and asked what in
the world she did all day. Mary wrote a long list of activities
to Marian who read me the letter as we sat in her office of
the new TIME – LIFE building…which had never housed
the Longwells.

Mary wrote that after fixing breakfast at home she
drove to the post office for the mail and then to their office
which was just off the Neosho Square behind the New
England Hotel. Dealing with the mail was no small matter

as they were training a secretary, the new football coach's wife, Mary Beth Lane. She would be typing letters to the likes of Harry Truman, Ogden Nash, Winston Churchill, and the Duke of Windsor. (Lane Interview, 2010). Part of her instructions were to never again mail foreign letters with regular domestic stamps. Mrs. Lane told me that Mary was really Dan's best secretary and "ooh was she smart!"

Most of the local population was not aware of the Longwell's array of friends and correspondents. They simply embraced them as new, bright and probably influential people. This small town in the corner of the Ozark Hills always needed someone with outside connections and Dan Longwell would certainly fit that bill.

In fact, it was through Dan's connection to the War Department in 1941, that he learned ahead of the announcement that land just south of Neosho was to become Camp Crowder for an Army Signal Corps. The May 26, 1941, LIFE magazine had carried a very flattering photo essay on Neosho as a "small and peaceful town". There were nine pages with text and sixteen photographs of our town and its citizens. The citizens were interviewed by the LIFE Reporter as to what they thought of US intervention in the war. The richest man and the poorest man were quoted for their opinions.

There was an unintended consequence to this. The story was that a person working for the IRS looked up to see how rich the richest man was and apparently had no file for him which turned out to be embarrassing for our richest citizen of the time who will remain unnamed in this tome!

This however did not deter the Longwells from moving to Neosho in 1954. TIME, January 4, 1954, announced that Daniel Longwell had retired from the company last summer for reasons of health. His retirement contract said Luce could call him in for consultations but Dan had lined up some independent work for himself. The *Readers Digest* had him on a retainer basis as their man in the Midwest. They provided funds for office space and an expense account for travel with the understanding he would be writing stories for the *Digest*.

As for Time Inc. involvement, former LIFE editor, Sid James was sending Dan dummy mock ups of the anticipated new sports magazine to get his advice and ideas.

Dan sent back four and a half pages of criticisms and suggestions. On page two, under Pictures, he wrote, "You are not yet a very girlie magazine and I'd frankly suggest that your last page be a picture of the prettiest pin up character. Not a naughty picture but a pinup picture to appear every week." Sid James response is classic Time Inc. good humor written May 6, 1954.

It was real good of you to take the time to put down the specific irritations in the dummy. I found it most helpful and all the more valuable because of your unique background in this sort of adventure. If you will promise to be sharp always, I will send you some things from time to time— and profit enormously from your sharpness. All the best to you and Mary, s/ Sid (Box 69, **Daniel Longwell Papers**, Rare Book & Manuscript

Library, Columbia University in the City of New
York)

Mr. Longwell had also accepted the Presidency of the
American Federation of Arts. Because their headquarters
were in New York, Longwell made several trips from
Neosho to get financing, schedule small shows and solidify
a major convention that was already scheduled for October
1955. He was able to get Henry Luce to speak to what
turned out to be a fine audience comprised of members
which included major museum directors from across the
country.

Meanwhile back in Neosho, having settled into their
vintage office and home, Dan's ideas on a way to do
something for the community began to bubble to the top.
In the spring of 1954, they read in *The Neosho Daily News*
that the Missouri State Junior Chamber of Commerce
of Missouri was joining forces with UNESCO and the
Foreign Policy Association to sponsor a train trip for high
school seniors from every state in the Union. The chosen
students were to travel to New York to visit the UN and to
Washington, DC in order to acquaint the students with the
Federal Government and US participation in the United
Nations. Mr. and Mrs. Longwell determined they would
like to offer a "special New York City experience" to the
Neosho students who were chosen to go. The Rotary Club
sponsored Fred Clark, Anne Bush (now Cope) and Janice
Robinson. The Lions Club sponsored Darlene Hills. The
Neosho Junior Chamber sponsored Dallas Kelly from
Fairview, MO, a nearby town.

Mary Longwell phoned Anne's mother, Ruth Bush, inviting them over for afternoon tea and presenting them with the idea which was met with enthusiasm. Having received parental approval, the Longwells moved right ahead planning how to show some bright young people from their new "hometown" what it was like to live in New York City. Mr. Longwell made the arrangements through his former Time Inc. secretary, Betty Morris.

The entire group of students got to tour the UN, but the Neosho contingent had an additional experience of lunching in the Ambassador's Dining room. Later they were taken to the Frick Art Gallery and Saint Patrick's Cathedral. They were treated to two Broadway shows, *Wonderful Town,* and *Ondine* with Mel Ferrer and Audrey Hepburn. The trip only lasted a week and the Longwells chose highlights that could be experienced in that short time. However, the highest light of all was being taken to the apartment home of Ogden Nash. Mrs. Nash was not there as one of their twin daughters was hospitalized with an appendectomy. However the students were served tea and cinnamon toast by a butler wearing white gloves. Anne said Mr. Nash made a good effort at trying to relate to them and asked them lots of questions. He even gave them a tour of the apartment. Fred Clark said it was a "life changing experience to be able to get into places like that." Fred and Dallas recall that they went out for a night on the town by themselves. They stopped at a place which had a sign on the door, $5 Minimum. They didn't know what that meant so they moved on. Fred said he felt "grown up" when he got back home to Neosho. (Clarke Interview, 2015)

Dallas Kelly remembered "It was quite a learning experience. I had only been to Jefferson City." (Kelly Interview, 2010) Anne Bush recalled her mother told her she did not have to wear a hat, but she must wear gloves to meet Mr. Nash. Anne wore her gloves and saddle oxfords with ankle sox. (Bush Interview, 2010) (The cover of LIFE, June 7, 1937, WAS a pair of legs resting on a chair rung wearing ankle sox and saddle oxfords).

The students were ushered around by Betty Morris and she found them to be delightful saying years later that they were "quite exceptional." She also talked about how this was another illustration of Dan's great feeling for others. "He was as thorough at planning this excursion for them as if for Winston Churchill."

John Shaw Billings had taken his leave and retired from Time Inc. also in 1954. He and Frederica moved back to the plantation home, Redcliffe, in Augusta, GA and while they were very glad to be away from New York and Time Inc., they were having more trouble adjusting to retirement than were Dan and Mary. In an exchange of Christmas letters, Billings listed all the challenges he was facing with the big house and the fields, etc. closing with the statement, "Well, there's no help for it when you haven't got any money and have to do for yourself." (Box 60, **Daniel Longwell Papers**, Rare Book & Manuscript Library, Columbia University in the City of New York.

The Longwells were working on a much smaller scale than the Billings and for Longwells it was considerably less expensive and more comfortable. Even so, I am sure the two men missed each other's company. Dan wrote John that he "was one of the great friends of my life." In his letter of Dec. 28th, Dan described how it was for him and Mary living in Neosho.

We have left New York as completely as you have. Everything we possess is here. I am sitting in my small but high ceilinged room on Spring Hill as I write this. The house is gaunt, grey and Confederate. It was built by some Jewish banker some 80 years ago. We have painted and refurbished it, put in closets, new wiring, a new furnace... But we possess it free and clear, the Connecticut property having been sold at just the right moment.

MERRY CHRISTMAS
from
MARY & DAN LONGWELL
Neosho, Missouri   1956

The Longwell's 1956 Christmas Depicting the Hearth in Their Neosho Living Room (Drawing by Mary Fraser Longwell; Author's Collection)

I moved in about eight tons of books, put a couple of steel beams in the cellar and the old house is settling into its weight...The room I am writing in looks down Spring Hill. I own as far as the park with grey stone walls fortressing the place right to the huge basement and wide back porch that overlooks the town...We are sometimes described as living on High Street or even Presbyterian Hill because there are so many Presbyterians surrounding us. I can see the square from my hill top.

My office is just half a block off the square. It's elm shaded, a brick extension of the England Hotel, which is the old headquarters of the Scottish Land Co. which settled so much of this county, a New Orleans fellow is moving in with me. We have a pert secretary who I hope will work out.

We are planning a trip to Europe this summer...sailing August 9 from Montreal to Glasgow, and expect to spend a leisurely three weeks in England and Scotland, then fly to Italy to look at some art, and back home by boat. All arranged this way so we won't have to go to New York to get to Europe...Mary joins me in much affection to you both. She is typing this letter, and says she will send her version of Life in the Ozarks in the next installment. (Box 60, **Daniel Longwell Papers**, Rare Book & Manuscript Library, Columbia University in the City of New York.

The Longwells eased themselves into the Neosho community in an exemplary way. In their years of visiting in summers they had become acquainted with the banker, Arnold Farber, the lawyers and editors of the two newspapers, Howard Bush of *The Neosho Daily News* and Joe Taylor of the weekly, *Miner-Mechanic*. They also had relationships with business owners such as A.E. "Adelburt" Weston of Neosho Nurseries, Russell Hunt with the Southwest Lime Co., stone quarry and civil defense cave. Other civic leaders who had become their friends were R.W. "Bob" Anderson, Superintendent of Neosho Schools, the doctors at Sale Memorial Hospital, especially Dr. Harold Lentz and their neighbor, Dr. George Olive. Of course other neighbors were my parents, Bob and Lucille Haas. My father's family had been here since 1855 and had contributed to the community with love, loyalty and a building here and there.

The Midwest is often referred to as the Bible belt of the USA, and in the 1950's that was pretty much true. The businessmen of Neosho had created an organization open to all men and they called it the Laymen's League. Their main activity was a week of daily church services during Christmas season. The Layman's League had invited the Chaplain of the US Senate, Dr. Peter Marshall to come preach in Neosho and he had done so in December of 1947, two years before suddenly dying of a heart attack in January 1949. Twentieth Century Fox did a movie of Marshall's life in 1955. Charles Einfeld, the NY Advertising man for Fox, was contacted by Longwell's Neosho office partner to engage Marshall for the 1947 Layman's League pre-Christmas services.

Longwell brokered the story of Marshall's appearance in Neosho with LIFE Magazine and on March 30, 1955, Einfeld sent a telegram to Longwell reading, THE PETER MARSHALL LAYOUT IS IN LIFE THIS WEEK AND MANY THANKS ARE DUE TO YOU.

Einfeld also arranged for the showing of "The Peter Marshall Story" to open in Neosho and Joplin at Easter time that year.

However that was not the big story for Neosho in 1955. Of the one hundred years my family had lived in Neosho there were events like fairs and harvest shows and May Days with the winding of May poles and Easter Sunrise services in the Big Spring Park. With the establishment of Camp Crowder during World War II, we had experienced economic success. The Camp brought soldiers, jobs and many new families with students for our schools. We had such a surge in the student population in the public school district that we received what was called "impact aid" from the federal government. This enabled the district to build a big new high school in 1954, the same year the Longwells took up residence.

Set in the rolling hills of the Ozarks, Neosho is lovely town. Topographically it is almost perfect. The residential areas radiate from a flat center surrounded by a horse-shoe pattern of hills. The Longwells and my family lived on the western hill named Spring Hill. We look down onto the Big Spring Park, and at the time, the Big Spring Inn was across Spring Street to the east. Two blocks beyond that was the Newton County Courthouse. The squared-up grid of streets around the Courthouse were filled with businesses and movie theaters supporting our population of a little over 6,000 at that time. We were a sweet little town with a middle class population and we were really middle class in every way. This was the world that the Longwells had chosen to embrace. Mary once wrote that the town had about the same population as Time Inc. One might therefore draw the conclusion that working with the entire population was not a daunting task for them.

We know from Dan's work with garden books at Doubleday and from his youthful farming experience which he carried on later at his Connecticut and Missouri properties, he had a passion for flowers. He had even expressed a wish he had for Neosho on one of their summer visits. He was talking to Bradie Metheny, the young high school student who was the desk clerk, bell hop and multi-tasking employee at the Big Spring Inn. One of Bradie's jobs at the Inn was feeding the rainbow trout that lived in the dammed-up pond which ran from the Big Spring under the street and then under the Inn and out to Hickory creek north of town. Mr. Longwell loved to join Bradie in feeding the fish and Bradie instructed Longwell to throw the stinking combination of raw kidneys and bread out high so the fish would jump for it. One evening Mr. Longwell mentioned that he would like to see more flowers around and flower boxes.

During my interview with Bradie I mentioned that I had read that Dan had something to do with the plantings on Park Avenue in NYC, but I had not been able to confirm it. He responded with a conversation he had had visiting a friend, Charlie Strauss, at his parent's home on Park Avenue. Bradie commented that he liked the hanging baskets of flowers on Park Avenue and said, "We have flowers in Neosho. Mr. Longwell started that." Charlie's father responded with, "He started it here too." (Metheny Interview, May 2010, page 3.)

Dan Longwell's city beautification project in Neosho was supported by nearly every home and business in town. The idea was to have flowerboxes everywhere possible. I lived through this era and it still astounds me how it caught on and how everyone had such a good time with it. Never has less money been spent on a city project that had such far reaching results. It was like a Fibonacci sequencing[44] of participants.

Dan Longwell contacted his friend, Ralph Hayes, a Director of the New York Community Trust. At that time, one of the goals of the Trust was aiding communities in self-improvement. Longwell, not one to be out front with a project, chose his office mate, Ted Bethea to head up a committee to assess what Neosho might need and to write the Trust. Neosho asked for $2,500 but was awarded $5,000 to be used as prizes for businesses and homes who planted flower boxes. The two newspapers helped build enthusiasm. Three Neosho lumber yards said they would provide lumber at cost. The Neosho Junior Chamber of Commerce built flower boxes. Three floral companies gave seed or seedlings for the boxes. Southwest Lime provided plant food and the city dispatched trucks to get loam out of Hickory Creek and a community soil pile was "established." I will never forget the day everybody set a bucket at their curb for probably the only "Manure Day" ever held anywhere. Trucks came along and filled the buckets and put a little yellow, I think,

---

[44] The Fibonacci sequence is a series of numbers in which each number in the sequence is the sum of the two preceding numbers (1, 1, 2, 3, 5, 8, etc.). (Compact Oxford English Dictionary of Current English, 3rd Edition, Oxford University Press, 2005, p. 369)

flag in it to designate that it was now filled with manure for the flower boxes.

The upshot of all this cooperative activity was that once a flower box was on the front porch, the resident noticed that it would show up more if the porch were painted, then the porch would look better if the house were painted and the lawn were mowed. Trash on streets and gutters just disappeared. This ripple-effect clean-up campaign was amazing.

Some of the businesses around the square were very creative. I recall Newton Country Hardware planted a canoe which sat out front on the north side of the square. The Evans Drug store built a waist high apothecary mortar and pestle on the west side. The banks had fancy wrought iron boxes on the west and south side. All thirty-six windows in the Courthouse had a planted box of red geraniums. The hospital and the schools also participated. As time went by, Longwell noted that new houses being built included flower boxes of brick or stone added as part of the original architectural plans.

The first flower box was just next to the Longwell office at JoAnn's Beauty Salon. Dan had come over and asked if she would put boxes on her two front windows and she did, planting begonias. JoAnn McGrane Daniels married the next year and still has the long stemmed goblets the Longwells gave her as a wedding present. (Betty Lane Interview, 2015; Kiewit, Fred, April 10, 1955 article in Kansas City Star, Box 82, **Daniel Longwell Papers**, Rare Book & Manuscript Library, Columbia University in the City of New York) Because of the success of this enormous beautification effort, Neosho adopted the name of The Flower Box City.

Everyone knew Dan Longwell was behind this project but Mr. Bethea, who was the public face, was in charge of the public presentation. Neosho was nominated and won an All American City designation in 1958 based on the complete community and citizenry participation in the clean-up and beautification project. The Longwells themselves planted their front lawn and bluffs above the Big Spring in daffodils and jonquils. Their sidewalk on High Street was lined with exquisite iris of all colors.

Part of Dan Longwell's retirement was invested in articles for *Readers Digest*. His March 1958 article on the Neosho Flower Box project was printed in ten international editions of the *Reader's Digest*. This brought in letters from forty five towns in the US and even one from Mosel Bay, South Africa. *Ford Times,* a little magazine which is no longer published, paid Charles Banks Wilson to paint a long postcard of the Newton County Courthouse with all its boxes for their April 1958, issue. Who can doubt that Longwell was behind that, too. (Boxes 65, 77, **Daniel Longwell Papers**, Rare Book & Manuscript Library, Columbia University in the City of New York)

It is amazing what this kind of pride can do for a town. In 1956, some of the land that had been Camp Crowder was now owned by the US Air Force. North American Aviation chose this area to build a plant for building rocket engines for the Air Force and NASA programs. The Neosho division was Rocketdyne. This brought in more people and our population doubled. The community gained a lot of top level engineers and skilled people who moved from surrounding areas and from Rocketdyne's California headquarters.

I was in high school at this time and all of us students were convinced we were special. All the teams from debate to football won their conference championships.

The band and choir were outstanding, due in part to having outstanding instructors at the time. Longwell tried very hard to get the high school choir on the Ed Sullivan Show.

In February 1960, Longwell arranged for Suzette Morton Zurcher, (whose grandfather J. Sterling Morton established Arbor Day and whose father established the Morton Salt Co.) to come plant one of several trees at Neosho High School. Longwell knew her from her support of the fine arts especially the Art Institute of Chicago. (Box 83, **Daniel Longwell Papers**, Rare Book & Manuscript Library, Columbia University in the City of New York)

The Longwell legacy was not just at the heart of publishing and journalism in New York City, it crept into the hearts and minds of people in a little hamlet in southwest Missouri, too.

We learned that if one wants to get something accomplished, there were some guidelines one might follow. First, you don't lead the parade yourself. You find the best place and person for the job and build all the support you can. This followed my father's (Bob Haas, Neosho businessman) belief that more was accomplished by being the power behind the wheel than by being the wheel. Second, if you want to know something, you go to the top of the list of people in the know. Third, the more people you can entice into your "parade", the louder the band will play. These were not Longwells words, but these are guidelines I and others came away with by living in a community which the Longwells brought to life in a way we had not seen before.

In 1957, Ogden Nash came to visit Dan and Mary. He was on a lecture tour and came through Neosho from Minneapolis en route to Lubbock, TX. Mary picked him up at the Kansas City Southern station at 12: 55 pm, gave him lunch, followed by a nap and at 4 o'clock she had high school students

> Judy Haas, Janice Douglas, Lissa Ballentine and Richard Bush to talk to ON (Ogden Nash)--- ON slept late. DL fixed breakfast...Dinner, chicken and cheese cake, MFL early to bed. ON and DL talk until midnight. Ogden figures he slept 22 hours of the 48 here. DL and ON read papers, then Nash to 12:55 train for Texas and Alabama. (Mary's Diary, April 12 & 13, 1957, Box 8-d, **Daniel Longwell Papers**, Rare Book & Manuscript Library, Columbia University in the City of New York)

A lot of special people visited the Longwells over the years and in 1958, it was T. Tetley Jones of Tetley Tea. One day I gave Mr. Longwell a ride home. It was a spring day and my high school graduation was approaching. I had the top off the T-Bird and we talked about my going to Tulane I suppose. I drove him into their driveway with their tall home looming over the garage door. He got out of the car and said to me after he shut the car door, "There is something called the Big Time, but you may already have missed it." I puzzled over that remark for years. I thought the Flower Box City featured in LIFE magazine, a new high school and rocket engines for space travel was pretty big time. In the years between leaving seventeen and living to seventy, I have learned about the life Mary and Dan Longwell lived. Only now do I understand what he meant by what he said. He was quite reflective at the time, but neither Dan nor Mary ever quit creating a better place for us all to live.

In 1959, another of Neosho's entrepreneurs, Russell Hunt, phoned Dan from Washington to see if he could do anything for him while he was in Washington, DC. Dan took the opportunity to tell him to call on our local Representative and Senator and some men at the Interior Department's Fish and Wildlife Service to see about rehabilitating the local fish hatchery which just happened to be the first National Fish Hatchery established by the US Government on land given by the city of Neosho. Hunt followed up on the suggestion, a $300,000 cash appropriation was passed and by 1961, improvements neared completion. Many tulips were planted at the rehabilitated fish hatchery. Today it is even more impressive with a new visitors' center and projects of bringing endangered species like the prehistoric pallid sturgeon back to strength in Missouri and Mississippi waters. (Box 66, **Daniel Longwell Papers**, Rare Book & Manuscript Library, Columbia University in the City of New York)

I think I can say without contradiction that those of us from Neosho who went to Tulane University in New Orleans had such fun stories about our hometown that other students wanted to visit us. One such young man was Tony Weir of the United Kingdom who was on a Marshall Scholarship to Tulane and later was Fellow at Trinity College, Cambridge, who became known for a distinguished law career. This is just one of the situations where we benefited from being from a town Dan Longwell had touched with his own wit and intelligence.

Therefore it was no surprise to learn that when the Neosho School Superintendent Bob Anderson came up with the dream of a community college for our area that he talked about it to Dan Longwell. The two of them and a leader of MacDonald County contiguous to the south of Newton County, James Tatum, worked with the Missouri state legislature to get a law passed that would allow Newton and MacDonald Counties to form a two-county college district for a two-year college which would be supported by local taxes. The new college was named Crowder College for the former Camp Crowder and would use surplus buildings left behind at its closing.

Promoting the idea to the public was right up Longwell's alley, as we say in the Ozarks. One of the things he did was to get the newspapers to invite people to write letters stating if they would find such a college useful to the advancement of their educations. Would they attend? Many people in this district could not afford to live away from home to attend the state colleges. The outpouring of responses to this request was amazing. I happened to be home on vacation from New

York in 1961 at the time of the voting. Mr. Longwell asked me if I would spend the day reading some of these letters over the radio which I did.

Mr. Longwell's long association with the Air Force, which at this time owned the land and buildings which could be the place for the college location, was helpful in getting what was about to be declared surplus property and could be given for the establishment of Crowder College. The people did vote to tax themselves for the college and these many years later it is a thriving complex with a high degree of community support from both counties and an enrollment that equals what Neosho's population was when Longwells' first moved to Neosho.

Dan Longwell would have been pleased to learn that one of the Presidents of Crowder College would be Dr. Alan Marble. As a youngster Marble and his cousins used to bicycle to the little Ragan School to play. The coal shed was their "hideout". Mr. Longwell would make sure they were safe and then invite them across the field to the house for lemonade and cookies. Mary would serve and Dan would tell them stories such as his meeting Mickey Mantle. Marble said that meeting Mickey Mantle in the Big Apple was about the "most impressive credential a person could carry." Longwell would also listen to the boys' stories and news of the community from a boy's point of view "for as long as it took." Marble adopted that as his own practice later in life as an educator, "Take time to listen to the younger generation." (Marble Interview, 2011)

When the college's Community Center building was built, the Board of Trustees set aside a museum space for the Longwell Museum. It holds a portion of the art Dan and Mary had collected over the years and is now a thriving component of the Crowder College Art Department. The Longwells not only gave some of their art collection, they also made sure the Crowder library got off to a good start with a good selection from Doubleday.

The Longwells believed in having books…and reading them. In a letter Mary had written to Mr. Luce in 1955 she thanked him for giving $100,000 to her alma mater, Wellesley College for the library in honor of his mother. This letter was found in the Time Inc. Archives,

> May I, as one graduate of Wellesley who was introduced to the endless pleasures of English literature in that old library, say Thank You, just on behalf of myself and those other graduates who believe that the library is the heart of the college.

The Longwell's Neosho life was not all farming and community concerns. They continued to enjoy each other's company in a way other couples might envy. They were definitely a behind-the-scenes team. Mary told me that they had a list of books which they could talk about knowingly but had never read. I was therefore delighted to find the list of these books in a letter to Ken McCormick, written July 1958. He was Editor-in-Chief then at Doubleday and wrote back that he "loved the game" they "had invented."

Most of this book is about what the Longwells have done; now here is what they had not done…or read. They each had a separate list:

> *"Books I've Talked about & Never Read"*
> MFL: *Moby Dick, Brothers Karamazov, Swann's Way, Look Homeward Angel, Gone with the Wind, Anatomy of Melancholy, Ulysses, Aeneid, Arabia Desert, Wind in the Willows.*
> DL: *Moby Dick, Tom Jones, Peyton Place, Decline & Fall, Canterbury Tales, Churchill on World War II, Divine Comedy, Arundel, Red Badge of Courage, Poems of Emily Dickinson.* (Box 73, **Daniel Longwell Papers**, Rare Book & Manuscript Library, Columbia University in the City of New York)

Other things I found in Mary's diaries brought my own life back to me because I knew the people they knew but I learned things I had not known. I did not know that our neighbor lady across the street taught Mary how to fry chicken. Mary wrote of their eating at our local cafes downtown which are now all gone.

Mary served on the local library board and volunteered to go over the children's books. On June the 10th, 1957, she worked at the library from 10 to 11:30. She met Dan at the Big Spring Inn for lunch. After lunch she went to the Chamber of Commerce with a letter nominating Neosho for the All American City award ready to be typed. Her diary reads,

C of C too busy to type—MFL very cross about whole deal. Drove out to nursery & ordered more plants."

A week later, June 18th the Diary reads,

"MFL to office to do filing and fell off chair while trying to fix Venetian blind. Very un-nerving. Went home and DL got alcohol for rubbing, etc...DL went to council meeting...MFL and Daisy Mahin to Jones Drug store for a soda. (Box 8, **Daniel Longwell Papers**, Rare Book & Manuscript Library, Columbia University in the City of New York)

Mary had also told me a story about Dan having a cousin called Terry. She said her name was actually "Indian Territory." It seems the child was the baby of the family and was always just called "Baby". When she went to school the teacher said she had to have a name. When she told this to the family at the supper table the father asked what she liked best at school and she replied she liked learning about Indian Territory, so that is what they named her. Imagine my surprise when the Diary read "Sunday, May 26, 1957, 'Late lunch on patio. DL cousin Terry (Indian Territory)...pleasant family gossip.'" (Diaries 1940-1968, Box 8, **Daniel Longwell Papers**, Rare Book & Manuscript Library, Columbia University in the City of New York)

In 1958, I left Neosho for college in New Orleans. I was able to graduate Phi Beta Kappa in three years having done a Junior Year Abroad at Glasgow University. Then I received a Woodrow Wilson Scholarship to Yale to study in the International Relations Department. As soon as the Longwells learned of my acceptance at Yale, I was the recipient of a Western Union Telegrams from them and I unabashedly reveal them here:

> YALE IS TO BE CONGRATULATED. BLESS YOUR HEART YOU WERE ALWAYS HEADED TO THE BIG TIME AND ARE ON YOUR WAY. DAN LONGWELL, WE ARE BOTH SO VERY PROUD OF YOU DAN HAS BUBBLED ALL DAY LOVE, MARY LONGWELL.
> March 14, 1961.

> ORDERED FANFARE OF TRUMPETS, FLOURISH OF CORNETS AND SOME PIPING DOWN THE VALLEY WILD. PHI BETA IN THREE YEARS AND FROM SUCH A GOOD COLLEGE. BLESSINGS AND LOVE FROM DAN AND MARY LONGWELL.
> March 16, 1961.

After one year at Yale, on August 16, 1962, I was able to send them a Western Union telegram

> PRESIDENT KENNEDY HAPPY ONE LESS UNEMPLOYED. BEGIN AUGUST 27 AT LIFE MAGAZINE. MOST PLEASED, JUDY

This was also a banner year for Neosho as the Longwells got the citizens involved in another mammoth project. Unlike the flowerbox project, the city-wide home coming party for "locally born and reared" Thomas Hart Benton only lasted a couple of days. Benton, accompanied by his wife Rita and his daughter Jesse, arrived in Neosho on the Kansas City Southern's Southern Belle on May 12, 1962. He was also accompanied by former President and Mrs. Harry S. Truman and the head of KCS, Mr. Bill Deramus. A crowd of citizens, officials and students greeted them at the KCS train station with all the pomp and circumstance a small town can muster.

A showing of Benton's work hung in the city auditorium and Longwell estimated some 3,000 viewed it taking great care "not to touch." The Bentons had lunch with dignitaries down town and then attended events on the square such as authentic dances by native Americans and meeting old friends and neighbors from childhood and high school days.

Thomas Hart Benton and Harry S Truman, Neosho, 1962

(Box 59, **Daniel Longwell Papers**, Rare Book & Manuscript Library, Columbia University in the City of New York)

Meanwhile the Trumans had lunch and a short nap at the Longwells home. Miss Edna Rich, a lady who helped rear me and my siblings helped Mrs. Longwell serve the

Trumans. She proudly told us that President Truman asked her if he "might have another biscuit."

On June 7th, a Thursday evening, Columbia Broadcasting Co. aired a special show about Benton in their "Accent" series. The opening scenes and a few others featured his Home Coming Day in Neosho. In fact one might guess that the Neosho party day was a good prompt for CBS. (Box 59, **Daniel Longwell Papers**, Rare Book & Manuscript Library, Columbia University in the City of New York)

The Thomas Hart Benton Home Coming Day allowed the Longwells to rest and relax for a change. But in all honesty, they needed to "get out of town" to do that. They decided to do a trip to Scotland and England which turned out to be a very good thing for me. I was to be married in May 16, 1964, and they offered their home for the Groom and my Maid of Honor and the groom's mother. Dan even instructed his secretary, Violet Carrick, what magazines to leave around the house. Having met the groom, Robert Buwalda, at Christmas and knowing my bridesmaid, Sally Scott, also a reporter at LIFE, meant the house guests were reliable. Our wedding present was two engraved prints of the Port of Glasgow.

The Longwells relished their trip visiting friends and reliving histories as tourists do. They did not see Sir Winston Churchill on that trip of 1964 and on January 24, 1965, Churchill died. February 3, 1965, Dan was writing a sympathy note to his son and Dan's first Churchill friend, Randolph Churchill. (Box 61, **Daniel Longwell Papers**,

Rare Book & Manuscript Library, Columbia University in the City of New York)

> I cannot help remembering the many kindnesses to me on the part of so many Churchills in the past. I tried in my small way to pay homage. It was a great privilege and honor to know Sir Winston and to work with him on the publication of his war memoirs. (Box 61, **Daniel Longwell Papers**, Rare Book & Manuscript Library, Columbia University in the City of New York)

In 1965 the Longwells' lives changed drastically. Dan had a stroke on April 15, 1965. Henry Luce immediately sent a bouquet of red roses which caused "a sensation" in the hospital and Mary wrote to thank him. More appreciated than roses would be the letter Luce wrote May 1, which has an almost tearful ring to it:

> Dear Dan:
> More than I could express in a telegram and more than can be expressed in any way, I am distressed by the blow to your health. I hope by the time this reaches you Mary will be able to send us good news of your recovery....My love to Mary –and to you I send the strongest possible order to get well.
>
> Affectionately, s/ Harry

Mary's May 3rd letter was her response to Luce's letter May 1, 1965: "Dan's left side, arm and leg, were paralyzed, but fortunately his mind was not." (Box 73, **Daniel Longwell Papers**, Rare Book & Manuscript Library, Columbia University in the City of New York)

Mary commented on the impact of Dan's stroke in her April 15, 1968 Diary entry (Box 8-d, **Daniel Longwell Papers**, Rare Book & Manuscript Library, Columbia University in the City of New York)

> Three years ago on April 15, DL had his stroke. Rather depressed today – in evening asked about it and he said he had always been so active, so busy with so many things, it was hard to adjust to his "new life."

Edna Ferber died the next day (April 16, 1968) and Mary took the opportunity to engage Dan in speaking about her. For the last nearly four years of Dan's life, Mary took every opportunity to "interview" him. The Time Inc. history by Robert Elson was underway and Mary and Dan were a big part of the source material as it was clear that Dan's memory was intact. They also kept up correspondence with friends with Dan dictating and Mary writing and typing or typing being handled by their office secretary. Dan had some rehab and they employed helpers as needed. Though Dan could hold a book, he could not turn the pages and often Mary read papers, magazine articles and even books to him.

Young friends and protégé's would visit as would Longwell contemporaries. However, these visits were few and far between. Friends from New York would call and that was very welcomed by Mary. Mary was not one to live in isolation. She continued to go to church and occasionally out with her women friends for lunch. She referred to them as "this odd group" which had continued celebrating each other's birthdays since one of them turned 40 years ago.

My mother was in this group and we came to calling them the "Ripsnorters." Mary shortened that to just the "Snorters" who got together for some destination lunch and a visit to an antique store. They had a wonderful time being silly. But for the most part Mary was as homebound as Dan except for trips out to the farm and a morning look in at her office.

Years before the stroke, the Longwells had a little publishing business of their own in a different office off the square on East Main. They published the Neosho Nurseries Catalogue and had also provided the programs for the Thomas Hart Benton Day. When Dan's coming out of the stroke became hopeless, Mary opened an employment business in that office. She had Ms. Carrick as the secretary and Mrs. Mickey (Linda) Poor as the girl to call on employers.

One day Linda confided to Mary that she and her husband would like to adopt a child. Mary knew a woman at the Presbyterian Church who was connected to the social welfare department at that time and soon the Poors had the first of their two adopted daughters. Like Dan, Mary would step in to help wherever she saw an opportunity to be helpful. (Poor Interview, 2010)

There is no telling how many scholarships they helped get for the young people who wanted to further their education but did not have enough money to meet that need. In her Diary, February 23, 1968, Mary records a line from Jessamyn West's *To See the Dream* that she liked.

> "If I had money I think I'd set up a 'Small Pleasures Foundation for the Young'—never more than $100."
> That's what we seem to do now and it is fun for us & for them.
> (Box 8-d, **Daniel Longwell Papers**, Rare Book & Manuscript Library, Columbia University in the City of New York)

Mary had also joined Neosho's New Century Study Club. At one meeting she attended at our house she gave a program on Rachel Carson's book *Silent Spring.* Her diary records her amusement at the mathematical conclusions of how many cookies might be needed for an upcoming ladies' tea: four dozen from each member would be 1,300 cookies. (Diary, Jan 22, 1968, Box 8-d, **Daniel Longwell Papers**, Rare Book & Manuscript Library, Columbia University in the City of New York)

But for the most part Mary began to realistically assess the situation. Henry R. Luce died of a heart attack on February 28, 1967. This brought back many memories and letters between John Shaw Billings and the Longwells recounting their time with Luce at the beginnings of LIFE. Dan was always complimentary of Luce as an "inventor" of departments in LIFE especially "The Lead, The Essay and the Party and even Speaking of Pictures." Longwell named him one of the great editors of all time along with Billings, George Horace Lorimer, Gertrude Lane of *Woman's Home Companion,* Lord Beaverbrook, F. N. Doubleday, Alfred Knopf and Turner Catledge of *The New York Times.* (Letter to Billings, March 8, 1967, Box 60, **Daniel Longwell Papers**, Rare Book & Manuscript Library, Columbia University in the City of New York)

In a letter to Billings March 30, 1967, Longwell comments again on Luce's editorial powers indicating perhaps they were more inventive than managerial.

> Harry could get a simple issue of LIFE in such a twist that he had to send the art director and two layout men to Chicago to close it all. (Box 60, **Daniel Longwell Papers**, Rare Book & Manuscript Library, Columbia University in the City of New York)

A year later (1968) the Time Inc. history was finished and Mary had to get in last notes to Elson as the book was on its way to press. She had read it to Dan for the most part. Her appraisal was this: "This is really the story of Luce & how he built his publishing empire. Ends Dec. 8, 1941." (Sunday, Feb. 11, 1968, Box 8-d, **Daniel Longwell Papers**, Rare Book & Manuscript Library, Columbia University in the City of New York)

In late March 1968, her Diary records that she was tired and blue and "can't see any light in the forest." She was thinking she should sell the Employment Agency due to her lack of enthusiasm. Then the weather warmed up and she was able to take Dan out to the farm and around Crowder College. However on the next day she drove alone down into Oklahoma and sat by a "large body of water—Lake something—smoking a cigarette—just running away, but the rut is getting deeper." (Diary, March 25 & 26, Box 8-d, **Daniel Longwell Papers**, Rare Book & Manuscript Library, Columbia University in the City of New York)

However, the Longwell energy fuelled their resilience and letters with ideas went in all directions and manuscript corrections and suggestions to the Time Inc. history continued. That was pretty much finished in October of 1968.

It was Mary's job to notify the principals that Dan had died mid-afternoon November 20, 1968. He had outlived those projects and many of his close friends: Nelson Doubleday, Theodore Roosevelt Jr., Tom Chrystie, Edna Ferber, Harry Luce and Sir Winston Churchill. Mary saved over 150 condolence letters to be later found in Box 84, **Daniel Longwell Papers**, Rare Book & Manuscript Library, Columbia University in the City of New York.

When Dan Longwell died November 20, 1968, at his home in Neosho up the street from my parents' home, I was only a month from being widowed myself. On December 22, 1968, my husband died at my parents' home where we had come for Christmas. I moved back to Neosho with my two young daughters and lived with my parents. I would walk up the hill and visit Mary and the dachshund, Dinah. As widows, our friendship deepened. Fortunately for me, the age of people never meant much to the

Longwells. In fact, Mary told me once that one reason they liked Neosho was because people of all the ages "ran around together."

When my New York friends would visit, she would take us all for a picnic out to the farm. When her New York friends would visit, she would invite me and my daughters

Picnicking at Longwell Farm, c. 1970 (Author's photo)

up for dinner. She referred to my two and four year old daughters as "cute little parties." It was rather a rough time, but Mary knew what to do for us both.

She organized a trip to New York City and we stayed at her club, the Cosmopolitan Club. It was such an intimate and private place—the tonic of gracious living.

One afternoon, Mary and I had tea in the club's small patio garden. It was truly a place for "ladies", and I was so glad to be there.

This was not the first time I had been treated to a club visit by the Longwells. The summer my mother accompanied me driving to Yale summer school to learn French, Mrs. Longwell had used her AAA membership to give us sequential maps to New York and then New Haven. We drove my 1957 Thunderbird. We stayed at The River Club as guests of the Longwells who were back home in Neosho. Mr. Longwell told us to visit the Metropolitan Museum of Art, which is always a mind-changing experience. In fact, any time spent with the Longwells was a mind-changing experience.

The next trip Mary invited me along was to Dallas, Texas. (This trip deserves to have Texas spelled out.) We were invited to the ranch of Holland McCombs. Mr. McCombs was a character of the first and finest order. He had been in the Dallas Time Inc. office forever and had long taken direction from Dan Longwell with such rewarding assignments as rounding up Tom Lea to paint Sergeant Bieber for the LIFE Defense Issue. Later he did research with Lea for a book on the history of the King Ranch.[45]

In 1938, when Dan and Mary got married, Holland sent them a table cloth guaranteed not to fade and some processed deer. At any rate, the memoir of Daniel and Mary Longwell has to include Holland McCombs.

Shortly after Dan died, Holland journeyed to Neosho to visit Mary. My parents and I were included in some of that visit. The Texas visit had another cast of characters. Mary and I were invited to Wheelock, TX along with Carl and Shelley Mydans, and Tom and Sarah Lea.

Wheelock was a post office stop at an intersection of country roads. Holland called the country store and post

---

[45] Tom Lea's experience during the war was shattering. He experienced Peleliu under constant fire for 32 hours in a scooped out trough and was hit by burning shrapnel on his leg. He sketched and made notes on the beach, but returned to the States to paint. The war ended and he was offered the chance to go back to Japan for post-War painting, but Lea decided against it. Longwell's November 7, 1945 telegram describes his thoughts: "Delighted you're not going back to Japan. Let's forget war and think about cattle." Consequently Lea painted the history of the Longhorn cow. At the request of Stanley Marcus, LIFE gave those paintings to the Dallas Museum of Fine Arts in 1950. (Box 17, **Daniel Longwell Papers**, Rare Book & Manuscript Library, Columbia University in the City of New York)

office their "Federal Building." The ranch house was an antebellum home with three story tall crepe myrtle trees. My parents had those around our patio in Neosho, but we called them bushes and they were only a half story high.

Every meal was served at a harvest table in a sunny room just off the kitchen. At every meal we were welcomed by the African-American ranch foreman with his daily oration about the upcoming events of the day. There was no formality and he spoke in his kitchen apron. It was hearing grace without asking grace.

Visit to McCombs Ranch, 1968

(Photo by Carl Mydans; given by Mydans to Judith Haas Smith)

It was at these mealtime gatherings that history was spread out with the beans and cornbread. It was in this setting that Carl and Shelley Mydans would talk a little about their experience of being interned by the Japanese in Manila, the Philippines. They and 2000 other civilians were crowded into the compound of Santo Thomas University. Carl and Shelley were imprisoned there for eight and a half months before being taken to Shanghai, China, and from there released to sail home of the last trip of the neutral Swedish ship, the *Gripsholm*.

Tom Lea talked about President Johnson turning down the portrait Lea had done of him. In retrospect, could it be the President made a mistake?

At any rate, I loved this time and probably did not grasp the significance of it all until these many years later.

Back home in Neosho I went back to college to get a teacher's certificate and Mary began putting together the eighty-nine archival boxes that would go to Columbia University in 1977.

I was hired to teach at the Neosho Junior High School and began in January of 1971. Mary told me that I could use the old Ragan School house if I could think of something to do with it. I taught 12 ½ years in the Neosho public schools but the summer of 1971 was probably the best work as a teacher I ever did. I had fifteen students who each paid $15 to attend what I called the Ragan School Enrichment Program.

My father nicknamed it Rural Radcliffe and the name stuck. Its purpose was to teach the students about leaving home and conversing with ease in the "Big Time." Mary approved and the students are all grown up but still talk about it with affection. The diplomas read that the "graduate" was now "an authorized conversant on the American fine arts."

Unfortunately we had a strong wind storm and a tree fell on the Ragan school house and Mary's Neosho lawyer advised her to have it taken down.

Mary asked me to serve on the first Board of Directors for the future Longwell Museum at Crowder College. We would meet for tea prior to the Board meetings to try and guide things the way she thought they should go, but it did not always work out as planned.

Mary had begun to visit friends and her only living relatives in California. After getting all the archiving done and her art collection sent to various galleries, she moved to California. We would talk on the phone some. I asked her to come back for a wedding in 1983 and she agreed, but called a few days later to say she did not think she could make the trip.

Mary died in La Jolla, California, August 11, 1984, where she had lived at a Presbyterian retirement place. She and Dan are buried side by side, each with their own stone, on the hill of the Ragan Cemetery, land they added to the community's grave yard. Their stones are engraved in the Roman Gothic which they called Tudor Gothic after the Art Director Dan recruited for LIFE in 1941. The stones were designed by Bernie Quint at Mary's request when Dan died. Bernie Quint was the then Art Director of LIFE magazine. The LIFE magazine the Longwells gave birth to died December 29, 1972.

If I may be allowed to turn the phrase and reapply the wonderful words Ogden Nash said in 1970, so that his words refer to both Dan and Mary,

"Their voices were not as loud as the thunder, but their illumination lasted longer than the lightning." This was their legacy.

Gravestones designed by Bernard
Quint using the "Tudor Gothic"
font (Box 72

Photo by Stephen P. Morrow

BIBLIOGRAPHY

<u>Archives</u>

Rare Books and Manuscript Library, Columbia University, City of New York

Redcliffe Plantation, State Historical Site, Augusta, GA

South Caroliniana Library, University of South Carolina, Columbia, SC

Time Inc. Archives, New York, New York

Tom Lea Institute, El Paso, Texas

<u>Books and Periodicals</u>

Benton, Thomas Hart, *An Artist in America*. Columbia: University of Missouri Press, 1968

Billings, John Shaw, *Diary*, Columbia, SC: South Caroliniana Library, University of South Carolina

Brinkley, Alan, *The Publisher*. New York: Alfred A. Knopf, 2010

Busch, Noel F., *Briton Hadden*. New York: J.J. Little and Ives, 1949

Churchill, Winston S., *Painting as a Pastime*. New York: Cornerstone Library, 1965

Office of Students, "Directory of Offices and Students". New York: Columbia University, 1928

Dobie, J. Frank, *Apache Gold and Yaqui Silver*. New York: Bramhall House, 1972

Doubleday, F. N., *The Memoirs of a Publisher*. Garden City, NJ: Doubleday and Company, 1973

Elson, Robert T., *The World of Time Inc.—The Intimate History of a Publishing Enterprise, 1941-1960*. New York: Atheneum, 1973

Elson, Robert T., *The World of TIME INC. The Intimate History of a Publishing Enterprise, 1923-1941*. New York: Atheneum 1968

Ferber, Edna, *A Peculiar Treasure*. New York: Doubleday, Duran and Company, 1939

Fuchida, Capt. Mitsuo, et al., *Reader's Digest's Illustrated Story of World War II*. Pleasantville, NY: Reader's Digest, 1969

"FYI Time Inc. In-House Newsletter, 1947," New York: Time Inc. Archives

Graebner, Walter, *My Dear Mr. Churchill*. London: Michael Joseph LTD, 1965

Graves, Ralph, *The LIFE I Led*. New York: Tiasquam Press

Greeley, Jr., Brendan M., ed., *The Two Thousand Yard Stare—Tme Lea's World War II*. College Station: Texas A & M Press, 2008

Hamblin, Dora Jan, *That was the LIFE*. New York: W. W. Norton nd Company, Inc., 1977

Hicks, Wilson, *Words and Pictures*. New York: Arno Press, 1973

Jessup, John K., *The Ideas of Henry Luce*. New York: Atheneum, 1969

Kantor, MacKinlay, *Missouri Bittersweet*. Garden City, NJ: Doubleday and Company, Inc. 1969

Kantor, MacKinlay, *The Voice of Bugle Ann*. New York: Coward-McCann, Inc., 1935

LIFE Magazine, Vol. 1, No. 1, November 23, 1936

Lord Moran, *Churchill—Taken from the Diaries*. Boston: Houston Mifflin Company, 1966

Morely, Christopher, "Grub Street Runner," Original Copy in Box 8, **Daniel Longwell Papers**, Rare Book & Manuscript Library, Columbia University in the City of New York. Used with Permission of the Morely Estate

Morely, Christophre, *Briefcase Breviaries*. Garden City, NJ: Henry and Longwell Publishers in Petto, 1926

Mydans, Shelley Smith, *The Open City*. Garden City, NJ: Doubleday, Doran, and Company, 1945

Nash, Ogden, "Reminisces of Dan Longwell," *Columbia Library Columns*, Vol. XIX, May 1970, University of Columbia, New York

Nash, Ogden, *Many Years Ago*. Boston: Little, Brown, and Company, 1931

Nash, Ogden, *The Private Dining Room*. Boston: Little Brown, and Company, 1949

Olson, Lynne, *Citizens of London*. New York: Random House, 2010

"Omaha…150…and Counting," *Omaha-World Herald*, June 13, 2004

Parker, Douglas, Ogden Nash. Chicago: Ivan R. Dee

Ricketts, Harry, *The Unforgiving Minute: A Life of Rudyard Kipling.* London: Chatto and Windus

Rogers, Cameron, *The Magnificent Idler.* Garden City, NJ: Doubleday and Company, 1926

Roosevelt, Jr., Mrs. Theodore, *Day Before Yesterday.* Garden City, NJ: Doubleday and Company, 1959

Rouse, Blair, ed., *Letters of Ellen Glasgow.* New York: Harcourt, Brace, and Company, 1958

Sale, Sara L., *Bess Wallace Truman.* Lawrence, KS: University Press of Kansas, 2010

Schorer, Mark, "The Burdens of Biography," *Michigan Quarterly Review*, Vol. I, No. 4, Ann Arbor, MI, 1962

Schorer, Mark, *Sinclair Lewis.* New York: McGraw-Hill Book Company, 1961 Tomlinson, H. M., *A Brown Owl.* Garden City, NJ: Henry and Longwell, Publishers in Petto, 1928 Wainwright, Loudon, *The Great American Magazine.* New York: Harper Collins, 2006

Ziegler, Philip, *London at War, 1939-1945.* New York: Alfred A. Knopf, 1995

Internet Locations Consulted (Partial List)

Daniel Longwell www.zoominfo.com/p/Daniel-Longwell/177605571

"Once Doubleday Was a King, Now House Gets a New Look" www.nytimes.com/1996/10/06/nyregion

World War II Timeline www.shmooop.com/wwi/timeline

Interviews

Bethea, Anne	2013
Bourgoin, Marisa	Archives of American Art
Clark, Fred	2010-2015
Cope, Anne Bush	2010-2015
Dolence, Glen	2010
Farber, Rudy and Dorothy	2010
Genisio, Susan	2010
Goforth-Steward, Billie Jo	2010
Graves, Ralph	March 2010-August 2011
Graves, Eleanor	March 2010-June 2010
Hastings, Arthur	2011
Hill, Bobbie	2010
Holloway, Rebecca	2010
Hooper, Bill	2010-2015
James, Larry	2010
Kane, Suzy T.	2009-2015
Kelly, Dallas	2010-2015
Lane, Betty McGrane	2013/2015
Lane, Mary Beth	2010
Lentz, Eileen	2010
Ludiker, Sue Lewis	2011
Mace, Carroll	2011-2015
Marble, Ed.D., Alan	2011
McClintock, Shirley Sprague	Jan. 2011-Mar. 2015
Metheny, Bradie	2010
Morris, Betty	2012-2015
Ngoima, Murray Thomas	2013-2014

Oatman, Judy McNamara	2014
Olive, MD, George	2013
Orton, Lyman	2014
Owens, Lillian	2012
Pearl, Tom and Peggy	2010 and following
Poor, Linda	2010
Shaver, Michael B.	2010
Stolley, Richard B.	March 2010
Stratton, Jean	2010
Tatum, Jim	2010
Wilson, Gladys	2010-2014
Wolfe, Skip and Family	2010
Wood, Andrew	2010 and following

Other

Court Report of the Corcoran, et al., v. Time, Inc. Case, Supreme Court, Bronx County, New York, 1941

Barnum, Donnel, Lost Vermont Images Curator, The Vermont Country Store, Manchester Center, Vermont

CPSIA information can be obtained at www.ICGtesting.com
Printed in the USA
LVOW11s0011220715

446930LV00001B/1/P